The Black American in Books for Children:

Readings in Racism

Edited and with an Introduction

by

DONNARAE MacCANN

and

GLORIA WOODARD

The Scarecrow Press, Inc.
Metuchen, N. J.   1972

Library of Congress Cataloging in Publication Data

MacCann, Donnarae, comp.
 The Black American in books for children.

 CONTENTS: Black perspective in books for children,
by J. Thompson & G. Woodard.--Black and white: an
exchange, by G. A. Woods & J. Lester.--Aesthetics,
morality, and the two cultures, by E. Geller. [etc.]
 1. Children's literature, American--Addresses,
essays, lectures. 2. Negroes in literature--Addresses,
essays, lectures. 3. Publishers and publishing--
United States--Addresses, essays, lectures. I. Woodard,
Gloria, joint comp. II. Title.
PN1009.A1M23   810'.9'352   72-4490
ISBN 0-8108-0526-X

CONTENTS

iii

ACKNOWLEDGMENTS

Rae Alexander: WHAT IS A RACIST BOOK? Reprinted from Interracial Books for Children (Vol. III, #1, 1970) by permission of the Council on Interracial Books for Children, 29 West 15th St., New York, N.Y. 10011.

Augusta Baker: GUIDELINES FOR BLACK BOOKS: AN OPEN LETTER TO JUVENILE EDITORS. Reprinted from Publishers' Weekly of July 14, 1969, published by R.R. Bowker Company, a Xerox company. Copyright (c) 1969 by Xerox Corporation.

Jessie M. Birtha: PORTRAYAL OF THE BLACK IN CHILDREN'S LITERATURE. Reprinted with permission of the Pennsylvania Library Association.

Lois Kalb Bouchard: A NEW LOOK AT OLD FAVORITES: "CHARLIE AND THE CHOCOLATE FACTORY." Reprinted from Interracial Books for Children (Vol. III, #2 & 3, 1970) by permission of the Council on Interracial Books for Children, 29 West 15th St., New York, N.Y. 10011.

Bradford Chambers: WHY MINORITY PUBLISHING? NEW VOICES ARE HEARD. Reprinted from the Publishers' Weekly of March 15, 1971, published by R.R. Bowker Company, a Xerox company. Copyright (c) 1971 by Xerox Corporation.

Bradford Chambers: BOOK PUBLISHING: A RACIST CLUB? Reprinted from the Publishers' Weekly of February 1, 1971, published by R.R. Bowker Company, a Xerox company. Copyright (c) 1971 by Xerox Corporation.

Paul C. Deane: THE PERSISTENCE OF UNCLE TOM: AN EXAMINATION OF THE IMAGE OF THE NEGRO IN CHILDREN'S FICTION SERIES. Reprinted from the Journal of Negro Education (Spring, 1968) by permission of the author.

Hoyt Fuller: PRESS CONFERENCE EXCERPT. Reprinted from the Special Supplement of Interracial Books for

Alfred Prettyman: PRESS CONFERENCE EXCERPT. Reprinted from the Special Supplement of Interracial Books for Children (Vol. III, # 2 and 3, 1970) by permission of the Council on Interracial Books for Children, 29 West 15th St., New York, N. Y. 10011.

Albert V. Schwartz: SOUNDER: A BLACK OR A WHITE TALE? Reprinted from Interracial Books for Children (Vol. III, # 1, 1970) by permission of the Council on Interracial Books for Children, 29 West 15th St., New York, N.Y. 10011.

Albert V. Schwartz: "THE CAY": RACISM STILL REWARDED. Reprinted from Interracial Books for Children (Vol. III, # 4, 1971) by permission of the Council on Interracial Books for Children, 29 West 15th St., New York, N.Y. 10011.

Dorothy Sterling: THE SOUL OF LEARNING. Reprinted from the English Journal (February, 1968). Copyright (c) 1968 by the National Council of Teachers of English. Reprinted by permission of the publisher and Dorothy Sterling.

Isabelle Suhl: THE "REAL" DOCTOR DOLITTLE. Reprinted from Interracial Books for Children (Vol. II, # 1 and 2, 1969) by permission of the Council on Interracial Books for Children, 29 West 15th St., New York, N.Y. 10011.

Binnie Tate: IN HOUSE AND OUT HOUSE; AUTHENTICITY AND THE BLACK EXPERIENCE IN CHILDREN'S BOOKS. Reprinted from School Library Journal, October 1970, published by R.R. Bowker (Xerox Company). Copyright (c) 1970, Xerox Corporation.

Judith Thompson: BLACK PERSPECTIVE IN BOOKS FOR CHILDREN. Reprinted by permission from the December 1969 issue of the Wilson Library Bulletin. Copyright (c) 1969 by The H.W. Wilson Company.

George A. Woods: BLACK AND WHITE: AN EXCHANGE BETWEEN GEORGE A. WOODS AND JULIUS LESTER. Reprinted from The New York Times Book Review (May 24, 1970); (c) 1970 by The New York Times Company. Reprinted by permission.

INTRODUCTION

By Donnarae MacCann & Gloria Woodard

The racial crisis has continued unabated into the 1970's--a crisis marked by massive urban riots during the past decade and the brutal assassination of popular civil rights advocates. Black students are cognizant of many of the subtle and conspicuous forms of racism in American society and in the schools in particular. They have made vociferous demands for more balanced textbooks; they have organized boycotts against schools and other establishments in an attempt to alter the prevailing explosive situation. In essence, they have helped bring the racial polarization into focus, though few encouraging signs of change have yet materialized.

One way to alleviate the negative racial attitudes and behavior of white Americans toward black Americans and to nurture the self-esteem and racial pride of black Americans is for schools and libraries to foster an effective program of intergroup education. Both institutions in the past have neglected this and have merely been supportive of traditional systems in racial relations. Together with the other agents of socialization (churches, mass media, peer groups) they have served to initiate and reinforce the dominant cultural values of the society. In this case they have served to reinforce myths and distortions conjured up to justify white supremacy and its corollary, the inferiority of minority groups in general and black Americans in particular. Moreover, schools and libraries have given many black children negative attitudes of themselves, undermined the foundations of racial pride, and thwarted motivation. Concomitantly, agents in the socialization process have developed in white youngsters a conscious and unconscious feeling of white supremacy.

Martha W. Carithers, in a recent review of the literature on school desegregation and racial cleavage, asserted that children have racial attitudes at an early age. She writes,

1

> In examining the literature, it becomes apparent
> that early in his life the child develops an aware-
> ness of racial differences. No matter at what point
> in his school life desegregation takes place--kinder-
> garten through high school--the child does not ap-
> proach integration in vacuo. This early awareness
> of racial difference, along with the values attached
> to such differences, play a part in the formulation
> of the stereotypes which the child carries with him
> through his school years. Such racial evaluations
> are manifest or latent. . . .[1]

Psychologists Mamie and Kenneth Clark have conduct-
ed manifold studies on the racial attitudes of young children
in the United States. Their findings illuminate how the
socialization process has had a deleterious effect on black
youngsters. They found that these children expressed a
marked preference for white dolls over black dolls, and ex-
hibited self-misidentification. Moreover their studies indicated that black youngsters were racially aware at the age of
three.[2]

Kenneth Morland confirmed these findings in the early
1960's. Using pictures instead of dolls, he asked children to
select the picture of the child they preferred to play with. He
found that black children showed a marked preference for
white playmates. This preference, he contends, is developed
early in life.[3] Suzanne Keller found that black youngsters,
in addition to showing misidentification, have a much lower
self-concept than their white counterparts. Lower self-con-
cepts retard motivation and affect academic achievement
adversely.[4]

Research has also shown that white children develop
negative attitudes about black Americans before the kindergarten years. Mary Ellen Goodman documented the fact that
children between the ages of three and four were aware of
racial differences.[5] Trager and Yarrow found that white
youngsters generally in kindergarten and the first and second
grades have negative attitudes and express hostility toward
black Americans.[6] These studies show what the agents in the
socialization process have produced, for racial preference
and cognition are not present at the time of birth.

We believe that one salient reason for the negative
attitudes held by blacks and whites has been the treatment of
American blacks in books for children. Initially, blacks

were omitted from trade books for children in the same sys-
tematic manner as in textbooks in the social sciences and
humanities. Nancy Larrick, former president of the International Reading Association, commented on her conversation
with a black child concerning invisibility of blacks in children's books:

> 'Why are they always <u>white</u> children?'
>
> The question came from a five-year-old Negro girl
> who was looking at a picturebook at the Manhattan-
> ville Nursery School in New York. With a child's
> uncanny wisdom, she singled out one of the most
> critical issues in American education today: the
> almost complete omission of Negroes from books
> for children. Integration may be the law of the
> land, but most of the books children see are all
> white. . . .
>
> Across the country, 6,340,000 nonwhite children
> are learning to read and to understand the American
> way of life in books which either omit them entirely
> or scarcely mention them. There is no need to
> elaborate upon the damage--much of it irreparable--
> to the Negro child's personality.
>
> But the impact of all-white books upon 39,600,000
> white children is probably even worse. Although
> his light skin makes him one of the world's minori-
> ties, the white child learns from his books that he
> is the kingfish. There seems little chance of de-
> veloping the humility so urgently needed for world
> cooperation, instead of world conflict, as long as
> our children are brought up on gentle doses of
> racism through their books.[7]

     The omission problem has, to some degree, gone the
way of the dinosaur. Publishing companies have belatedly
found that it is profitable to print stories with black characters, and many whites have been eager to respond to the call
for more interracial books. But more often than not they
have simply portrayed blacks from the white perspective--
have simply written their values and assumptions into their
works. These values and generalizations are supposed to
describe empirically the real world for blacks, but they do
not.

Barry N. Schwartz and Robert Disch touch on this problem when they write:

> Of the various ways in which white racist fantasies
> and attitudes have found release--from lynching to
> "goodwill" tokenism--perhaps none has had a more
> destructive effect and proved to be more intractable
> than the web of stereotypes, myth, and image spun
> around the lives of nonwhite Americans. . . . The
> nonwhite in America has been consistently degraded
> and dehumanized, through ignorance, malice, or
> both, by publishers, writers, film makers, artists,
> scientists and scholars. . . .[8]

Some black authors are also guilty of writing about
blacks from the white perspective.   Their writings have "in
house" attitudes; they reflect society's dominant racial ideology.
Perhaps, as James Farmer noted, "all of us, white and
black, . . . have been programmed by all of the cultural instruments in our society to think to some extent in a racist
manner"; or perhaps this was the only way black writers could
win the support of the various white-controlled publishing companies.[9]   One author recently reported that "of the 6,000 editorial personnel employed by American book publishers, only
six editors were members of ethnic minorities."[10]   In the
area of children's literature, "not a single major publisher's
book operation is directed by a minority editor."[11]

Aesthetics and Black Perspective

At a time of political and social upheaval, critics of the
arts are understandably concerned that excessive weight may
be given to social themes.   The contemporary British critic
of children's books, Margery Fisher, writes:

> Children's fiction is more often than not reviewed
> and analysed for its content and not for the sum of
> its parts, so that a book of limited literary value,
> perhaps weak in character-drawing or insipid in
> vocabulary, can be recommended because it delivers
> a strong message on an important question.   This
> approach to books for the young must eventually
> dilute their quality as mainstream literature.   As a
> creative artist the writer is more susceptible to
> pressure of this kind from his public than musicians
> or artists are.   We have yet to find a way of

> manipulating a chord so that it directly teaches; we accept that music must make its point more subtly. [12]

Mrs. Fisher's emphasis upon literary standards has long been needed in children's book criticism. But comparisons between music, painting, and literature can be carried only so far. As the late Malcolm Cowley wrote:

> Literature is not a pure art like music, or a relatively pure art like painting and sculpture. Its medium is not abstract like tones and colors, nor inorganic like metal and stone. Instead it uses language, which is a social creation, changing with the society that created it. The study of any author's language carries us straight into history, institutions, moral questions, personal stratagems, and all the other aesthetic impurities or fallacies that many new critics are trying to expunge. [13]

Because language is so indissolubly connected with "history, institutions, moral questions, and personal stratagems," meaning and style can never be neatly separated in works of realistic fiction. A theme discussed throughout this book is the need for black perspective as well as artistry in children's books, a concept referred to as "thinking black," "wearing the shoe of the black American," writing from "inside rather than outside." When a book for children is created from this vantage point, it is likely to be aesthetically effective, as well as socially and psychologically authentic. Whether an author is black or white, if he doesn't have the perspective that places value on black identity, he cannot create a truly individualized characterization of a black person and the whole work suffers. As noted in the first article in this collection, stereotypes are by nature dull; they reduce personality to a formula; they are based on assumptions about all members of a community or ethnic group. The simplistic notions conveyed by stereotypes make inferior art, for they lack depth and the vitality of variation.

Fantasies represent a marginal case in our argument about aesthetics and black perspective because in that one special genre a writer can ignore characterization to some extent and yet produce a consistent, humorous fantasy world. He can use real world settings as they fit into his fanciful scheme, but also get by without writing "from the inside" about human personality. In a book such as The Story of Dr.

Dolittle, the fantasy world is, in a technical sense, well-conceived, but the portrayal of blacks as inherently inferior is pernicious. Therefore the critic is forced to choose between two sets of values. On the one hand he must consider racism and its psychological damage to the child, and on the other the technical competence of the author.

But even aesthetically we can question whether Dr. Dolittle is a great character, knowing now more about what he represents and why he is by no means "great" to the Afro-American. As a character, has he not lost his humor and become repugnant to new generations of whites as well as blacks?

We are left with the conclusion that in all modes of fiction, aesthetic and sociological criteria are not very often in conflict. Literary fantasies marred by racism have lost their original power to please even white audiences. And a writer cannot successfully produce black American realism unless he "thinks black" to a considerable degree. "Thinking black" may come from being black or conceivably it may come from reading so many works by black authors that something fundamental happens to a white writer's whole outlook. There is little evidence however that white writers for children have given themselves even the experience of reading great black literature--the powerful works of the black novelist, dramatist, essayist, and poet.

The Censorship Question

One of the writers represented in this collection, Jessie M. Birtha, recommends that racist classics be placed in historical research collections rather than in children's libraries. The debate revolving around this recommendation is illustrated by a case in 1971 in San Jose, California. The head librarian of the San Jose Public Library (who is also a member of the American Library Association's Intellectual Freedom Committee) stated the typical ALA position in these terms: "to remove the book [Epaminondas and His Auntie by Sara Cone Bryant] would be outright censorship and to place it in the Research collection would be a subtle form of the same thing."[14] He criticized the NAACP as follows:

> It is ironic . . . that the NAACP, which has fought so valiantly against the suppression of ideas regarding the contributions of black citizens to American

> History is now cast in the role of suppressor of
> ideas with which [that] organization disagrees. [15]

This comparison involves things so vastly dispropor-
tionate that the whole fallacious character of the librarian's
argument should have become apparent. The exclusions and
distortions in the teaching of American history about blacks
have been well-documented and are now widely admitted. Yet
this fact is, in the view of the San Jose librarian, equivalent
to what would be taking place if a racist children's book were
transferred to a research collection. Such superficial comparisons have often been used as a means of evading social
change. But beyond the invalid comparison, there is a
noticeable deficiency in perspective when someone refers to
racism as merely an idea "with which [that] organization
disagrees." This view is out of line with the findings of psychologists, who maintain that racism is something destructive
to the human personality--destructive to both the perpetrator
and the target.

What harm would come to children if books like Little
Black Sambo, Epaminondas, or The Story of Dr. Dolittle--
artifacts from a benighted and regrettable age--were treated
simply as documents in the study of social history? They are
not books for children if: 1) racism is an evil, based upon
falsehood; and 2) racism often becomes embedded in children
by the time they are three or four years old. The fact that
the black characters in the Sambo and Dolittle books are not
actually Americans is beside the point, since these books
have been widely available in America and have been used in
such a way as to become associated with Afro-Americans.

In the long struggle to eradicate racism in children's
rooms in public and school libraries, the NAACP's chief op-
ponent has been and remains today the American Library
Association. The Fifth Article in the Library Bill of Rights
reads: "The rights of an individual to the use of a library
should not be denied or abridged because of his age, race,
religion, national origins or social or political views." The
position of ALA's Intellectual Freedom Committee is that the
age of the borrower must never be allowed to interfere with
the circulation of books--that parents, not librarians, are the
sole legitimate arbiters. This position is the very opposite
of the position taken in a Supreme Court opinion in 1963 which
urges the separation of children from adult audiences in the
viewing of certain films.

Courts have provided no legal precedent for separating
children and adults with regard to racism in books. But the
precedent for treating children and adults differently when
"harmful" material is disseminated, does exist. And although the only content deemed harmful at this time is that
which is lewd or obscene, racism has often been justifiably
referred to as the greatest "obscenity" ever invented. Anyone placing racism in that category sees the censorship of
racist children's books as a logical extension of the opinion
of Supreme Court Justice Brennan when he said for the court's
majority (Jacobellis vs. Ohio):

> We recognize the legitimate and indeed exigent
> interest of States and localities throughout the
> Nation in preventing the dissemination of material
> deemed harmful to children.

Justice Brennan refers also to the opinion of Judge
Frost in State vs. Settle (Rhode Island Supreme Court, 1959).
Whereas the Jacobellis case had to do specifically with films,
the Rhode Island case was about the regulation of pictures,
books, pamphlets and magazines. "The purpose of the
statute," said Judge Frost, "is clear. It is for the protection of youth. . . . It is designed to prevent such publications [those which are lewd, obscene, indecent, etc.] from
passing into the hands of boys and girls of an impressionable
age. . . ."

Mortimer Adler takes this position philosophically
when he says: "It is proper for the prudent man to super-
vise the ways in which works of art reach their audience,
to say, not what shall be made, but what shall be received
and by whom and under what conditions."[16] We would argue
that the writer will write what he must, for only in this way
can we have real children's literature or literature of any
kind; but society will accept and reject what it must in the
education of children, in order to develop progressively a
less prejudiced, polarized and sick nation.

Social commentators, as well as librarians, sometimes
try to toss off this whole issue with a few sarcastic remarks.
Columnist Russell Kirk wrote in 1964: "These 'human relations council' busybodies--generally a humorless breed--ap-
parently think that Little Black Sambo is not representative
of American colored children."[17] He then discusses the
tigers in the story and the East Indian setting; but he fails
to show that this non-African setting had no bearing whatever

upon the history of the book's usage in America--a racist
usage connected with the ridicule of blacks.

Controlling racist reading material for children cannot be compared in any way with the provision of materials
for either adult or young adult readers.   By the time a student reaches high school, he should be able to study the
racism in a book with sufficient depth to understand it.
Donald Gibson, referring to college age readers, notes in
his article in this collection:

> . . . opponents of the book [The Adventures of
> Huckleberry Finn] have seen something in it which
> is really there and needs to be dealt with. . . .
> It should be presented as the work of a man whose
> intentions were in large measure good, but who was
> not entirely able to overcome the limitations im-
> posed upon his sensibilities by a bigoted early en-
> vironment.   It should be shown to be a novel whose
> author was not always capable of resisting the
> temptation to create laughter though compromising
> his morality and his art.   In short the problem of
> whether to teach the novel will not exist if it is
> taught in all its complexity of thought and feeling,
> and if critics and teachers avoid making the same
> kinds of compromises Mark Twain made.[18]

Censorship of any type or degree in the adult sphere
is illegitimate, for one can never decide which adults might
be qualified to choose for other adults.   But children are not
allowed to choose for themselves in any case.   In the field
of children's literature, adults alone make the decisions about
books--about what to write, publish, purchase, award a
prize, and make accessible.   There is no question of who shall
decide for whom, except to determine which group of adults
it will be.   ALA says it must be a child's parents.   But why
should it not be black Americans when a book deals principal-
ly with black characters?   Does anyone doubt that most white
Americans are poorly qualified to make judgments about black
literature, about models which correspond to the black American's reality?   As James T. Stewart says of black artists:
"our models must be consistent with a black style, our
natural aesthetic styles, and our moral and spiritual styles."[19]
Dr. J. Deotis Roberts of Howard University speaks of the
American treatment of the black man as having produced "a
unique type of spiritual experience both personal and collective."[20]

The fear that giving special treatment to racist children's books will produce a flood of censors is understandable. Yet it is the role of librarians and other educators to explain the differences in things. There is a difference between a racist book and one containing, for example, violence. Violent action (a frequent target of censors) is not an evil per se in literature. If used in the right way, in a mythical context for example as in the folk tale, it provides a needed contrast with the forces of good; it has a dramatic function which results in accentuating the desirability of non-violence. This is not the case with racism as usually found in children's books, where dramatic treatment of the topic has provided no adequate compensation for the racist treatment of characters.

Librarians should urge the active involvement of Afro-Americans at every juncture in book publishing, criticism, and distribution. They should be aware of black responses to racist books and withdraw their support from such books-- classics or prize winners or not. Those librarians who are white should try to recognize that there are aspects of the black experience they are unqualified to judge. When tax-supported children's rooms stop giving financial support to racist writers and publishers, regardless of their good intentions, then the time may come when racism will not be supported in children's books.

Notes

1.   "School Desegregation and Racial Cleavage, 1954-1970: A Review of the Literature" in Journal of Social Issues, Vol. 26, Autumn, 1970, p. 26.

2.   Clark, Kenneth B. and Mamie P. "Emotional Factors in Racial Identification and Preference in Negro Children" in Journal of Negro Education, Vol. 19, 1950, pp. 341-350.

3.   Morland, J. Kenneth. "Racial Acceptance and Preference of Nursery School Children in a Southern City" in Merrill-Palmer Quarterly of Behavior and Development, Vol. 8, 1962, p. 279.

4.   Keller, Suzanne. "The Social World of the Slum Child: Some Early Findings" in American Journal of Orthopsychiatry, Vol. 33, 1963, pp. 823-831.

5. Goodman, Mary Ellen. Race Awareness in Young Children. Addison Wesley, 1952, pp. 2-25.

6. Trager, Helen G. and Martin R. Yarrow. They Learn What They Live. Harper and Row, 1952, pp. 140-155.

7. Larrick, Nancy. "The All-White World of Children's Books" in The Saturday Review, Vol. 48, September 11, 1965, p. 63.

8. Schwartz, Barry N. and Robert Disch. White Racism: Its History, Pathology and Practice. Dell Publishing Co., 1970, p. 383.

9. Farmer, James. "Develop Group Pride and Then Cultural Pluralism" in Black Protest Thought in the Twentieth Century, 2nd ed. edited by August Meier, Elliott Rudwick and Francis L. Broderick. Bobbs-Merrill, 1971, p. 571.

10. Chambers, Bradford. "Book Publishing: A Racist Club" in Publishers' Weekly, Vol. 199, February 1, 1971, p. 94.

11. Ibid.

12. Fisher, Margery. "Rights and Wrongs" in Top of the News, Vol. 26, June 1970, pp. 376-377.

13. Cowley, Malcolm. "Criticism: A Many-Windowed House" in The Saturday Review, Vol. 44, August 12, 1961, p. 11.

14. "NAACP vs. Epaminondas" in The Wilson Library Bulletin, Vol. 45, April, 1971, p. 718.

15. Ibid.

16. Adler, Mortimer. Art and Prudence. Longmans, Green, 1937, pp. 449-450.

17. Kirk, Russell. "Why Punish Little Black Sambo?" in The Omaha World Herald, November 8, 1964.

18. Gibson, Donald B. "Mark Twain's Jim in the Classroom" in The English Journal, Vol. 57, February, 1968, pp. 196, 202.

19. Stewart, James T. "The Development of the Black
    Artist" in Black Fire: An Anthology of Afro-Amer-
    ican Writing, edited by Leroi Jones and Larry Neal.
    Morrow, 1968, p. 3.

20. Robert, J. Deotis Sr. "Black Consciousness in Theo-
    logical Perspective" in Quest for a Black Theology,
    edited by James J. Gardiner, SA and J. Deotis
    Roberts, Sr. Pilgrim Press Book, 1971, p. 62.

PART I

BLACK PERSPECTIVE:
THE BASIC CRITERION

1. BLACK PERSPECTIVE IN BOOKS FOR CHILDREN

Judith Thompson and Gloria Woodard

> I, too, sing America. I am the darker brother. [1]
> (America never was America to me) [2]

These lines from two poems by Langston Hughes indicate the dichotomy of American life for black Americans. They suggest what "blackness" should mean in the context of American life, and what it does mean. Neither message is new. Every leading spokesman of every generation of black Americans has revealed the depths of bitterness engendered by the frustration of being the darker brother in a white America. Only recently, however, have we begun to face the difficult fact that "whiteness" is still the major criterion for full participation in American life. W. E. B. DuBois emphasized the extent of this condition when he depicted the black American as born into

> . . . a world which yields him no true self-consciousness, but only lets him see himself through the revelation of the other world. It is a peculiar sensation, this double-consciousness, this sense of looking at one's self through the eyes of others, of measuring one's soul by the tape of a world that looks on in amused contempt and pity. [3]

Our increased awareness of these facts puts a new responsibility on all of us concerned with children's literature. It points to the necessity to re-examine children's books about black Americans, and to begin from a fresh standpoint. We can be glad that the days of direct caricature are behind us, but a less obvious misrepresentation is widespread in children's books today. We must ask to what extent and by what means have narrow ethnic attitudes pervaded books about black Americans, even those books specifically written "to further interracial harmony"? We must ask whether these books are providing meaningful identifica-

14

tion for black children, as well as real insight for white
children into the historical, ethnic, and cultural characteristics of black Americans. Finally, we must frankly ask whether the image of the white American has been made to
seem more desirable than that of the black American in
these books.

The popularized slogans "Black Pride," "Black Power," and "Black Is Beautiful" are based on the most universal concern of man: identity.   They deal with the eternal
questions--who am I, where did I come from, where am I
going?   Of the two literary genres, fact and fiction, it is
the fiction which is too often irrelevent and inadequate as a
guide to answering these questions for black children.   The
histories and biographies are illuminating black experience;
the fiction is not.   The histories are providing identification
and inspiring pride, in self, in ethnic group, in African
heritage; the fiction is not.

The research required of a writer of non-fiction
partially explains this.   It must be granted that to have been,
and to be, a black in America is a unique and perhaps un-
precedented human and historical experience.   As an ex-
slave advised Julius Lester in his introduction to To Be A Slave,
"If you want Negro history, you will have to get it from somebody who wore the shoe and by and by . . . you will get a
book."[4]   Whether a writer is white   or black, if he immerses
himself in the history of a period or in the life of a man, he
must to some degree "wear the shoe" to report the experience accurately.

Fiction demands a similar kind of "self-conscious-
ness."   As James Baldwin puts it,   "One writes out of one
thing only--one's own experience."[5]   The credentials of the
writer who undertakes a book about blacks must include a
black perspective based on an appreciation of black experience. "Good intentions" are not enough.   The writer of
books about black children must understand the importance of
ethnic consciousness before writing about the goal of ethnic
irrelevancy.   Conscious of the inequities suffered even after
many blacks became "just plain Americans," blacks today
refuse to erase the "black" from black American.   They
refuse to make invisible that one attribute which connotes
their unity, culture, and heritage.   Certainly, integration
and assimilation are not possible until the recognition of and
respect for these differences are fully realized.

Hopefully, we can all learn to "wear the shoe,"

actually or vicariously, but we are not all qualified to write
about what we learn. It is this combination of black consciousness and creative ability which will finally result in
good books about black children. When a writer lacks these
credentials, the result is too often a kind of verbal minstrel
show--whites in blackface--rather than the expression of a
real or imagined experience derived from wearing the shoe.

Too many of the integrated books or books for "interracial harmony" tend to reinforce the very attitudes they are
trying to dispel. In too many of these books the white child
dominates the story. He is the controlling factor, the active character. The focus of the story is on his character
development. The black child is then necessarily placed in
a subservient role. He is the passive character. He is the
problem which causes the white child to act. He literally
and figuratively waits for the white child to invite him in,
to figure things out, to be enlightened. In short, the black
child is the problem: the white child has the problem.

In Fun For Chris, by Blossom Randall, Chris the
white boy is shown in a fully depicted environment complete
with understanding mother, doting grandmother, lovely home,
fenced-in backyard with all the childhood toys: swing, sand-
pile, ladder, etc. Toby, the Negro boy, is a shadow in
comparison. We are told he is older than Chris; he refers
to a mother for whom he runs errands; he teaches Chris to
build sandcastles, and he is, as Chris discovers, "brown
all over." Other than these few references to a life, family,
and environment of his own, Toby has no identity except as
Chris' playmate, as the beneficiary of Chris' largesse, for
which he waits every day, sitting outside the gate.

It is not what is said about Toby that raises objections to this book, it is what is omitted. The story gives a
white child no insight into the real life of a black child, and
it gives a black child no real reflection of himself. The
perspective is that of a white world, a world in which the
black child is an outsider who endures while the world decides his fate. Told from such a perspective, all the explicit explanations of human equality or racial irrelevancy
cannot rise above the implicit inferences of white "superiority."

In the many books for older readers dealing with
racial conflicts--in schools, the ghetto, "white" neighborhoods, at the swimming pool, etc.--the implications of

white superiority take several forms.   In these books, rarely are blacks depicted as effecting the changes that affect
them.   In fact, the blacks in these stories are represented
as ineffective, whether as individuals, American citizens, or
an ethnic group.   They neither protest, demand, or even
suggest that changes be made.   Moreover, they are often
made to blame themselves rather than society for the various conditions of extreme poverty, segregation, or social
ostracism.   Nor do these books present a coalition of black
and white working to effect changes--a cooperative endeavor
based on mutual respect.   Instead, the happy ending or successful endeavor is usually due to the intervention of a white
benefactor.

In Call Me Charley, by Jesse Jackson, the moral is
clear.   The success of black endeavor is dependent upon the
magnanimity of white people.   In order to receive the be-
stowal of this magnanimity, black children must meet certain
standards set by a white-middle-class society.   The index
of acceptability is often marked by superficial criteria which
are set even higher for blacks, whether they be manners,
standards of dress, or speech patterns.   It is Charley's
mother who instructs her son in the ways of the white world
and the role of the black boy in it.   These instructions con-
sist of platitudes that are demeaning and repressive:

> You'll have to keep out of trouble.   It ain't like
> you were one of the other boys. . . And watch
> your manners, boy.   Good manners go a long way
> to help a colored boy get along in this world. You
> got to keep trying.   You got to work harder than
> anybody else.

By the end of the story, all these platitudes are
realized by Charley (with the help of his friend's white
liberal parents), and one more "exceptional" Negro has been
accepted by the white world.

The perverse relationships that racial discrimination
engenders have not been misrepresented in this book or in
others with a similar theme.   In a climate of prejudice,
blacks do have to try harder and be better in order to be
accepted into schools, jobs, or neighborhoods.   However, by
revealing the situation and only obscuring both the real solutions and the real feelings of blacks about these conditions,
the various systems of institutionalized discrimination are
made to appear inevitable.

In the novel Tessie, written by the same author and published last year, a slightly greater sense of "black consciousness" is evinced by the younger generation--Tessie and her friends--while the idea of integration through the acceptance of individual exemplary Negroes is shown as an older-generation viewpoint.

Another facet of the white perspective is seen in the social significance attached to skin pigmentation. The hierarchy, of course, is that white is best and extreme darkness most undesirable.

In The Empty Schoolhouse, by Natalie Carlson, the narrator, Emma Royall, makes these remarks about the difference between herself and her sister:

> Lullah is the spittin' image of Mama and her kin. Her skin is like coffee and cream mixed together and she has wavy hair to her shoulders. Me, I'm dark as Daddy Jobe and my hair never grew out much longer than he wears his.

That the comparison of these physical differences is not simply an objective appraisal is revealed within a few lines, wherein the emphasis is clearly on self-depreciation (italics my own): "Little Jobe looks like me and Daddy Jobe, but he's a handsome little boy all the same,"--or in spite of the fact that he is dark and has short hair.

The objections are to the subtle and probably unconscious perspective which presents a young black girl in terms of self-hatred and a feeling that white is preferable to dark. On page one, fourteen-year-old Emma introduces herself to us in terms of self-worthlessness: "I always tell myself, since you quit school in the 6th grade, you'll never be anything but a scrub girl at the Magnolia Motel." Her sense of identity is sharply circumscribed by her employment throughout the book: "You'll just have to try to be the best scrub girl there is," she reminds herself repeatedly and in various ways. When the priest conducts the annual blessing of the sugar cane harvest, Emma comments: "It made me feel like I was made special by God and real important to Him even if I was just a scrub girl." Finally, she is overcome by a feeling of nostalgia when her father relates the "good old days" of picking sugarcane: "I wish I'd lived then. . . I'd be a field hand instead of a scrub girl." Not only is it unrealistic for a young girl to identify

herself entirely and on all occasions in terms of her occupation, it is an exaggeration which turns the admirable traits
of endurance and perseverance into a mere caricature.

The glorification of poverty has been a familiar theme
in children's books throughout the ages.   One immediately
thinks of Louisa May Alcott's Little Women or Dickens'
Christmas Carol as two examples.   Both books provide
children with a dramatization of how, with courage and high
optimism, people can overcome or cope with the indignities
and deprivations that poverty can engender.   The writer
who undertakes the description of such a situation, however,
walks a thin line between developing characters who cour-
ageously make the best of a bad situation, and characters
who, by their reaction to this situation, glamorize abject
poverty.

Evan's Corner, by Elizabeth Starr Hill, a book for
younger readers, succeeds in walking this line, and the result is an intimate story about a black boy whose yearning
to find a corner of his own in the midst of a large family in
small quarters is immediately recognized as a universal one.
The focus of the story, however, is not on the family's im-
poverished condition, but on the personal problem of the
child and his solution to it.   The book reveals a sensitive
understanding of children and their need for both a corner
and companionship.   It also reveals an understanding of the
ghetto situation, in which some ingenuity is demanded for
one to find a corner of his own.

A book for older readers, Roosevelt Grady, by Louisa
Shotwell, involves an entire family's search for a corner of
its own, a "Promised Land . . . a place where everybody
has a chance--a place where everybody can be somebody."
It is the story of a black migrant worker's family and its
search for security and stability--a job, a home, a school.
Admirable qualities such as patience, courage, endurance,
and optimism are presented as characteristics of the Grady
family.   But, despite its good intentions, this book rein-
forces stereotyped beliefs about Negroes as a race, rather
than individualized solutions to universal problems.   The
idea on which the story is based suggests that blacks do
not have very high expectations, ambitions, or ideals.   Furthermore, the situations the family encounters are always
appalling; the response of the characters is inappropriately
cheerful.   In short, the story depicts people striving for,
settling for, and reacting with enthusiasm to subhuman

conditions.

At one point in the story, the family finds itself oc-
cupying the attic floor of a house "with a roof so low and
sloping that most places ... even a nine year old could easily bump his head" and with windows filled with dust and cob-
webs, and with drawers and cots to sleep on that "smell of
dirty clothes and dust." Stock responses come from each
member of the family. From Mama: "Those dormer windows give our attic a real glory." From six year old Mat-
thew, "as he wrinkled up his nose and sniffed at the smell
of dirty clothes and fish": "It's a satisfactory smell. I like
it."

It is this vast discrepancy between situation and response, between event and reaction, that results in characterization wholly unrealistic. The nine-year-old hero, Roosevelt, responds similarly to an authoritarian, brow-beating
teacher: "Maybe she ... wasn't such a bad teacher after
all ... even if she did teach with a stick ... Maybe the Opportunity Class was a good place for bean-pickers. A place
where they could find out things. If they asked." These
words of apology, justification, and self-recrimination are
spoken by a black character, but the words are white. If a
black child were to identify with this boy, he would have to
incorporate in his perception of life that 1) being beaten or
abused by a teacher is an acceptable practice; 2) there is a
caste system in our democracy, which, if you are of a mi-
nority--bean-picker or black--means there are specially designated, circumscribed facilities for you; and 3) if you don't
get an education under these conditions, it's your own fault.
You didn't ask the right questions.

At the end of the story, Mama's dream of a Promised
Land is supposedly fulfilled in the attainment of a remodeled
bus with cold running water and a little potbellied iron stove
to keep them through winters known to be so harsh that their
white benefactor cautions them: "Nobody has stayed in one
of these buses all through to spring, but that's no reason
you shouldn't try." The mother's response is not mild relief, but tearful joy: "I like it fine, Roosevelt ... All I
don't like is thinking about when ... we have to leave all
this behind."

In a land of opportunity and a multi-million dollar
economy, is it realistic to depict a family finding happiness
and fulfillment in the attainment of less than substandard

housing? The mother's high optimism should be inspiring;
but if the final outcome for this family is considered fortunate, the optimism here borders on simple-mindedness, and
the final conclusion the reader makes about these people is
the racist platitude: "It sure don't take much to make them
happy. "

A Fair Judgment?

The question sometimes arises as to the legitimacy of
any kind of literary judgment which takes sociological or historical factors into account. The British author John Rowe
Townsend states that:

> to assess books on their racial attitude rather than
> their literary value, and still more to look on
> books as ammunition in the battle, is to take a fur-
> ther and still more dangerous step from literature-
> as-morality to literature-as-propaganda--a move
> toward conditions in which, hitherto, literary art
> has signally failed to thrive. [6]

In part, one must agree with Mr. Townsend's thesis.
Books should not be evaluated only in terms of the racial
attitudes presented in them. In fact, it would be better if
books were not written for the sole purpose of presenting
certain racial attitudes. When the principal concern of literature becomes polemics and manifestos, idea replaces
characterization, and the reader leaves the book with a slogan rather than an experience. And whether that slogan be
"Black Power" or "Brotherhood," the reader will be cheated
of sharing the conflicts, dilemmas, and personal solutions
which result from individualized characterization.

On the other hand, it is precisely because we have
failed to examine our own racial attitudes fully enough that
the sociologically determined stereotype continues to pre-
dominate in books about black children. Such stereotypes are
created when the traits assigned to a character do not derive
from the story, but from assumptions about all members of
the community or ethnic group. They produce not only an
inferior literature; they encourage simplistic notions about
human nature and reduce the complexity of personality to a
formula.

The very appearance of blacks in American literature

has been historically and culturally determined. The abnormal invisibility of blacks in American literature corresponds to the invisibility foisted on them by American society.
When blacks were finally represented in literature, they were presented in terms of the conceptions white society had of blacks, rather than perceptions of them as individuals. Thus, blackness is depicted as a stigma, poverty as an inevitable condition to be endured with cheerful optimism, and the solution to racial discrimination as the independent effort of individual blacks who are strong enough to pull themselves up by their own bootstraps.

The inferiority complex of an Emma Royall, the limited horizons of the Gradys, the obsession of Charley's mother with conventions of acceptability, are realistic in the sense that such distortions of the healthy personality do in life exist. However, it has not been emphasized that these traits are not inherent; they are not ethnically derived; they are not natural. The characters in these books fail to show that it is one's environment which engenders such perverse self-images. It has not been made clear that the environment itself is unnatural, man-made.

Unless conscious efforts are made by those who read, review, and publish children's books, blacks will continue to be left out, shaded in, or given a token place outside the mainstream of children's literature. To readjust the balance, black writers, artists, and consultants must become involved in replacing the sociological images with the many and varied self-images of black Americans. The range of individuals within the black culture is as great as that within any other ethnic group. It is those books which give us intimate experience with this great range of characters, all of whom are black, all of whom are different, that will finally further interracial harmony.

To judge literature in terms of the racial attitudes presented in them is actually to judge whether the writer has gone beyond and behind sterotypes, myths, and ideas about blacks, to develop characters whose ethnic, social, cultural, and personal experiences mesh in all the complex ways they do in real life. The literature that will truly give black children a sense of identity will not be literature-as-morality nor literature-as-propaganda, but literature as human experience. To black children, blackness is an intrinsic and desirable component of that human experience.

The better books depict black children as individuals whose identity includes name, home life, family, friends, toys, hobbies, etc. In addition, they are black, American, and first-class citizens. These books lead children natural- ly to the conclusion that differences--in personality, abilities, background--are desirable among people. Books of this sort which have already been published include the "interracial" Gabrielle and Selena, by Peter Desbarats, and Hooray for Jasper, by Betty Horvath. Charming and individualized black children are the central characters in the Ezra Jack Keats books, The Snowy Day, Whistle for Willie, Peter's Chair, and A Letter to Amy, as well as in the books Sam and Big Cowboy Western, by Ann Herbert Scott, and What Mary Jo Wanted and What Mary Jo Shared, by Janice May Udry. Books like these, on this level, should be so numer- ous that children will not be able to browse through a library shelf without finding one there.

One limitation to most of these books, however, is their emphasis on, identification with, and relevance only to middle-class children. For too many black children, they depict an environment removed from their immediate experi- ence. Stevie, a recently published book by a young black writer, John Steptoe, provides black ghetto children with identification. The writer simply presents a problem famil- iar to all children--the intrusion of a younger child on a small boy's time, friends, and family and his ambivalent feelings about the situation. To this extent, the book reflects no peculiarly black perspective. Identification for the young black reader rests in the central character's intimate knowl- edge of the black subculture--his use of informal grammar and idiom, his loosely structured family life, his sophistica- tion and independence in worldly matters, and his brief sketches of the kinds of good times city children make for themselves--from the familiar game of cowboys and Indians to the less usual experience remembered nostalgically by Robert: "And that time we was playin' in the park under the bushes and we found these two dead rats and one was brown and one was black. "

The value of such a book is that it assures the ghetto child that he, too, is visible--that he is important enough to be reflected in that literature which has always been made to seem too cultured to admit him.

Behind the Magic Line, by Betty K. Erwin, and Soul Brothers and Sister Lou, by Kristin Hunter, are among those

few books for older readers (9-16) which reveal, in fictional
terms, some degree of black consciousness. Neither one is
entirely successful, but they can be considered a step from
the white perspective of the black condition, to a black perspective of reality--a view from inside the individual person-
alities of the characters.

Behind the Magic Line is a humanistic story about a
young black girl, "her dreams and determinations." Throughout the book, there is an emphasis on black pride and human dignity. Flaws in the book include underdeveloped characters and Hollywood touches of fortunate coincidences, as
well as these overworked ingredients: the fatherless family,
the matriarch, the son who is in trouble with the law. However, this book does attempt to give motivation for each of
these phenomena, motivation which puts the blame not on the
individuals, but on an employment system which perpetuates
the fatherless family, on the traditional tendency to place un-
due suspicion on members of the black community and on
racist individuals who still think black means slave. As in
Roosevelt Grady, the final situation the family finds itself in
is hardly cause for rejoicing, but members of the family
seem to realize this and their reactions are ambivalent.

In Soul Brothers and Sister Lou, the ghetto culture is
graphically depicted and the main character and her search
for self-identity are realistic. The drawbacks lie in the one-
dimensional treatment of the minor characters, an unrelent-
ing series of melodramatic situations, a hastily compiled
ending, and a kind of immediacy of response to pleasure and
pain that cheats the reader of the experience of real tragedy.
These flaws weigh more heavily for some readers than for
others, but many readers can use this story as a bridge
from pure pulp fiction to the excellent black fiction written
for adults.

The timeliness of these books compensates in part for
their weaknesses. The relief these books provide from white
paternalism, white perspective, and white domination is an
important compensation for many black children.

The bulk of that literature which provides identification for black children has so far been confined to the histories, biographies, and autobiographies. To date, informational, biographical, historical, and scientific books are far
superior to the fictional works. Documentary materials are
now being collected and edited with the young reader in mind.

Skillful organization, careful research, and clarity of style
may be found in such excellent books as Julius Lester's To
Be A Slave, Dorothy Sterling's Tear Down the Walls, and
William L. Katz's Eyewitness: The Negro in American History. These books clearly answer the question of black identity, not only for young black readers, but for young readers
of every ethnic background, and for us, their older counter-
parts--uninformed or misinformed as we have been.

In addition to these general histories, many of the
recently published biographies of individual black Americans
can be highly recommended. These range from the brief
biographical sketches designed for middle and upper elementary grades (e.g. Lift Every Voice, by Dorothy Sterling and
Benjamin Quarles) to such fully developed biographies as
Langston Hughes, by Milton Meltzer, Journey Toward Freedom: The Story of Sojourner Truth, by Jacqueline Bernard,
and Captain of The Planter by Dorothy Sterling. Fictionalized
histories and biographies include Emma Gelder Sterne's The
Long Black Schooner; The Voyage of The Amistad, Ann
Petry's Tituba of Salem Village, and Harriet Tubman: Conductor on the Underground Railroad. Four anthologies designed for the young adult reader which span history, diction,
and poetry are Chronicles of Negro Protest, by Bradford
Chambers; Black on Black: Commentaries by Negro Americans, edited by Arnold Adoff; Black Voices: An Anthology of
Afro-American Literature, edited by Abraham Chapman; and
I Am the Darker Brother, poems by black Americans, edited
by Arnold Adoff.

Although the criteria for heroism are indeed variable,
in re-evaluating biographies for children, it can readily be
seen that the blacks recognized in children's literature in the
past were usually those who attained some success by adher-
ing to white values. Today it is important for children to
know about Denmark Vesey and W. E. B. DuBois as well as
Ralph Bunche, and George Washington Carver. These biographies give children historical perspective relating to recent
human rights movements, and a link to the autobiographical
revelations of modern heroes: Malcolm X, Eldridge Cleaver,
and Martin Luther King. These books, as well as autobiographies such as Anne Moody's Coming of Age in Mississippi
(which traces the experiences of a young black girl from her
childhood in the South to her activities as a young student in
the civil rights movement), show that militancy is not a fad.

The significance of these histories and biographies cannot be stressed enough.   The contributions of Afro-Americans to American history have heretofore been distorted or excluded; and can we ever fully realize the loss of identity that generations of blacks have experienced by being deprived first of their original culture and then of any recognition of their contributions to the culture that was thrust upon them? Excellent books such as these recapture to some degree that consciousness of heritage for the present generation of children.

The details of black history cannot be skipped over by any of us concerned with children's literature.   The evaluation of children's books implies judgment, and a valid or educated judgment is made from experience.   The more profound the experience, the better the judgment.   Until now, we have all learned only a portion of our nation's history, but in order to be good book critics as well as whole Americans, we must learn the rest.

Only a detailed knowledge can provide us with the perspective necessary for building totally new understandings and relationships.   To quote James Baldwin:

> For history ... is not merely something to be read.   And it does not refer merely, or even principally, to the past.   On the contrary, the great force of history comes from the fact that we carry it within us, are unconsciously controlled by it in many ways, and history is literally present in all that we do.   It could scarcely be otherwise, since it is to history that we owe our frames of reference, our identities, and our aspirations. [7]

Notes

1.   Langston Hughes.   "I, Too, Sing America," in The Weary Blues, Knopf, 1926.

2.   Langston Hughes.   "Let America Be America Again," Esquire, July 1936.

3.   W. E. B. DuBois.   "Souls of Black Folk," in Black Voices, edited by Abraham Chapman, Mentor, 1968.

4.   Julius Lester.   To Be A Slave.   Dial Press, 1968.

5. James Baldwin. "Autobiographical Notes," in Black
    Voices, op. cit.

6. John Rowe Townsend. "Didacticism in Modern Dress,"
    The Horn Book, April 1967.

7. James Baldwin. "Unnameable Objects, Unspeakable
    Crimes," in Black on Black; Commentaries by Negro
    Americans, ed. by Arnold Adoff, Macmillan, 1968.

2. BLACK AND WHITE: AN EXCHANGE

Julius Lester and George Woods

An article in the Book Review last season prompted the following letters between Julius Lester, author, and George Woods, The Times' children's book editor.

April 10, 1970

Dear George:

One of the more pleasant ways I've found of surviving is to read the newspaper several months after it has come out; thus I have just read The New York Times Book Review of December 7 and your article on the best books for young readers. I must say that I found some of the things you said about black books rather disturbing and rather than keep my comments to myself, I feel warmly enough toward you to write.

First, to quote you: "... I don't like the so-called books for blacks ... They have merit; they're an attempt to right a long-standing injustice, but it's a stampede that has produced words and pictures without heart, without soul." You go on to mention the Black Champions of the Gridiron as one book of this sort, and, no matter what you may think of football, the fact remains, that as a black parent, I'm happy that such a book is available. No, it's not great literature or anything else, but if my son or daughter becomes interested in football, at least I'll be able to hand them a book that talks of their people in the sport, instead of a book that pretends that a black man never set a cleated shoe on the gridiron.

You go on to say that "The best books in this area are about blacks and for whites. The whites are the ones who need to know the condition of their fellow humans. The Negro knows his condition. It's the white who must be brought to sympathy and understanding." There is one erroneous assumption here which is a rather serious one--"The

28

Negro knows his condition. " If "the Negro" (and we do prefer
to be called blacks) knew his condition, then there would be
no mass sentiment saying that "black is beautiful," or a desire for black studies. Yes, blacks know their condition on
a gut level, but to have that articulated, to read about it in
a book is to become conscious where before one was unconscious. It is the black writer's job to tell black people about
themselves. Too much of black writing has been blacks writing to whites.

A book written by a black for blacks is not, however,
closed to whites. And until whites learn to read and understand these kinds of books, there is no possibility of any
kind of understanding of blacks by whites. We no longer (and
never did) need whites to interpret our lives or our culture.
Whites can only give a white interpretation of blacks, which
tells us a lot about whites, but nothing about blacks. But,
the way it generally turns out is that the white perception of
blacks becomes accepted as the thing itself, as black reality.
Thus, when the black expression of the black reality begins
to get through to whites, whites are angered and uncompre-
hending, because they have been fed this white fantasy which
never had anything to do with us. Whites will never understand the black view of the world until they get it straight
from blacks, respect it, and accept it. Could you take se-
riously a history of Jews written by an Arab? The idea is
so ridiculous as to be insulting. No one would bother to buy
the book, even if it got published. Yet, whites think nothing
of buying a book about blacks written by a white. Indeed,
they almost prefer it. After all, blacks are bound to be
prejudiced toward their own, aren't they? Sometimes, I'm
tempted to write a history of Judaism for children just to
get the point across.

I'm not sure I'm being too clear. Basically I'm not
sure if you realize that when it comes to books by and about
blacks, you need new standards with which to evaluate them.
When I review a book about blacks (no matter the race of
the author), I ask two questions: "Does it accurately present the black perspective?" "Will it be relevant to black
children?" The possibility of a book by a white answering
these questions affirmatively is almost nil.

I have been very amused to note the different recep-
tions accorded my own books for young readers, To Be A
Slave and Black Folktales. The former received a fantastic
reception. The latter, while being well-reviewed, has not

been reviewed nearly as extensively and will definitely not be getting any prizes. And the reason to me is clear. The latter is directed totally toward black children. Perhaps it is even one of those books, which in your words, comes "calculatingly from the head." That's what one editor told me. If so, so be it. But To Be A Slave was no different. It's just that one is more easily accessible to whites than the other. Whites have to open themselves a little more to dig Black Folktales. They have to make an effort. In other words, they have to meet me on my ground, and that is what whites have always been loath to do where blacks are concerned. I'm making the rules now and changing the game a little. So, they want to pick up their marbles and go home.

Both of us find ourselves in a position of being able to influence the thinking of thousands of people. That is an enormous responsibility, as I know you are painfully aware. To discharge such a responsibility requires in each of us the ability to grow, to change, to understand. And that is an ongoing task.

I fear that the two paragraphs you wrote about black books in the 12-7-69 Book Review did not reflect the kind of understanding that will eventually get us to that point in history where whites will be able to accept blackness as a good that has value in and of itself and is not the least bit threatening to them, that is, if they are willing to meet the challenge and undergo the changes necessary for them to accept blackness.

                                        Sincerely,
                                        Julius Lester

                                             April 20, 1970

Dear Julius--

I'm glad you feel sufficiently warm towards me to write when something I've said disturbs you. Being able to talk to one another is the important thing; just don't become so outraged with me that you stop talking.

Let me explain my feelings in greater depth: I've got a prejudice--I try not to look at kids as white or black. Sounds very noble of me, but I mean it. I don't want to break kids down into all different kinds. I want kids in gen-

eral to have good books, something to make them laugh or
cry, something they can live inside of for a little while and
take some part of its message away with them. I want books
to move them for good, make them heroes some day in the
future.

In the same article you criticize me for, I said
Sounder was an outstanding book. Some people tell me it's
a book for blacks and black librarians tell me they wonder
how they can give such a book to their students when the
protagonist is silent and suffers and endures. Those librarians tell me that their kids are activists today and likely to
be contemptuous of the book. Just the same it's a great
book because somewhere up North, maybe there's a kid
brother to one of those snarling white young hoods in Chicago
I saw in the paper four or five years ago protesting housing
or Civil Rights, who doesn't really know what's going on,
but will stick with his older brother because that's his identification. Maybe he'll come across Sounder and say "Is that
what we did to those people? Humiliate, degrade, cripple
and kill, mangle a kid's fingers, put them in jail because
they stole to feed a hungry family?" Maybe he won't be in
the next mob, shouting epitaphs, throwing rocks.

It's the same with Jazz Man for me. The book is
filled with the small significant details of real life that are
not found in other books, for whites or blacks. It has a woman who walks up five flights of stairs, fast at first, then
slower because it's a tough climb for a woman who has
worked all day, and there's the thud of a bag of groceries
on the kitchen table. There's a world out there that Mr.
Middle Class White America doesn't know anything about.
And his kids are in danger of growing up to be just like him.
Maybe a Jazz Man will let him know that there's a hell of a
lot going on in the world that's pretty lousy and maybe sometime he'll be able to do something about it.

But let's go a little farther together. I've been talking about fiction mainly. I have no objection to "Black
Pride," "Black History," etc. I've seen a hundred titles
like them in the past several years. Of course a lot of
them are written by whites, but I'm very apprehensive about
knowing the color of the author, just as I would be to know
about his religion or politics. I judge a book by what it
says, by what kind of an effect I think it will have on chil-
dren--for the better, I hope, always for the better.

If we are arguing specifically about books for the black child to read, to make him aware of his heritage, give him pride, a sense of identification, etc., well, then you are right; we do need those books.   But we're being over-sold on them.

There's a reluctance on the part of most reviewers to criticize books for and about blacks.   I didn't read of anyone knocking <u>Black Is Beautiful</u>.   I didn't think it was an adequate book in spite of its laudable purpose.   Maybe you'll say it makes the black child proud of himself and not damn his color.   I don't think it's color that makes a person beautiful or ugly--it's his heart and his soul and his humanity.

As for <u>Black Folktales</u>, well, I like it.   I didn't think it was as compelling as <u>To Be A Slave</u>, but I recognized a strong, masculine voice behind it and that's what I liked about it.

As for <u>Black Champions of the Gridiron</u>.   Brings me full circle.   It's a book that separates us.   How would you like to see "White Champions of the Gridiron?"   I don't mind anthologies in which four or five of the six players are black just so long as they play a good hardnosed brand of football, but at present it seems we are trading on their blackness.

If it comes to a showdown in this matter between us, you'll probably win.   By birth, upbringing, present existence, I'm the product of an all-white world I suppose.   But I'm trying to understand and be reasonable.   On the other hand, you've had the bad experiences and you know what you're talking about.   You've seen the hate and arrogance, suffered the lash and you know what your soul cries for.

Yes, you're right in wanting more books for blacks. I don't want them shut off.   I wish they were better and when they're bad I hope we won't be afraid to say so.   But more than anything I still want books that talk about both of us, all of us, as plain people.

I appreciate your having taken the time to call me down.   I hope I've said nothing here to make you tune me out.

Best wishes,
George A. Woods

May 1, 1970

Dear George:

Please don't think that my personal feelings toward you have changed because of our different views on books for black children, etc. I wouldn't have written my previous letter if I hadn't felt that you are one of the few honest people in this business we find ourselves a part of and that you would respond honestly, without any personal animosity toward me.

I guess our basic difference comes around your "prejudice." "I try not to look at kids as white or black ... I don't want to break kids down into all different kinds." But the fact remains, whether we like it or not, that kids are black or white, that we live in a world where race has meaning, conferring superiority to white and inferiority to black, and what blacks are now trying to do is to destroy that value system, because that value system destroys them. Because race has been used as a weapon against blacks, blacks must use it as a weapon to free themselves. It is the factor which has oppressed them as people. Thus, there will be books aimed at black children, because, heretofore, the books have all been aimed at white children.

It's strange that whites fear that anything addressed to blacks is an automatic rejection and condemnation of them. That is not necessarily so, unless whites make it so. But whites do not want to acknowledge the fact that if they want to know blacks they will have to immerse themselves in what blacks have to say, and that there is no white Dante who can take them gently by their lily-white hands and lead them on a guided tour of blackness and keep them from getting a little singed by the fires. When I want to know more about the Jewish experience, I read I. B. Singer. There is as yet no black writer who has done for the black experience what Singer has done for the Jewish experience, but he has the advantage of being able to look back, of not having to be involved in a day-to-day battle. The black writer is intimately involved in the process his people are going through--trying to recreate themselves. In this process, there are going to be books by blacks which are bad. There are also going to be some new and exciting ones.

You are right when you say that "color does not make a person beautiful or ugly." In an absolute sense, that is

correct.   Down here on earth, however, color determines
standards of beauty.   I don't know if blondes have more fun,
but enough people seem to feel that they do so that Clairol
isn't about to go out of business.   Color has determined not
only my standards of beauty, but where I lived, worked, ate
and slept, not to mention what neighborhoods I was in after
dark.   No, color does not have any relation to the inner
reality of a person, but, in this society, color has come to
be synonymous with the inner reality, whether we like it or
not.   When I was a kid, I didn't know why white people hated
me.   They didn't know me, didn't even know my name, but
knew that they had something against me.   I couldn't ignore
that.   I couldn't close my eyes and say that it didn't matter.
It mattered, because whites made it matter.

   Ultimately, it is to no one's benefit to be colorblind.
Even in the best of all possible worlds I want to be looked
upon as a black.   Race consciousness does not have to mean
conflict and hatred.   And, in the battle to see that it doesn't,
I must address myself to blacks, to write books that hopefully will give black children the strength and pride that have
been deliberately kept from them.   It will be a long time before the mass of whites look upon black children as blacks
and as individuals.   I do not exist in this country as an individual.   I am a black.   White America has so decreed it,
and it could be fatal to ignore the fact.   I want black children to have that black sense of self on which to build.
When you come right down to it, they have nothing else.

   White writers are so dishonest.   Seldom have they
written what they could have and should have, which is, the
white side of racism.   I'd like to see a children's novel
about a little white boy who goes with his father to a lynch-
ing.   Or about a little white kid who goes with his mother
to scream at black children on the first day of integration at
some southern school.   White writers think they can write
sympathetic, cloying little books about blacks.   Who needs
white pity?   Whites are not guiltless.   Americans love to
write about guilt in Germany after Hitler.   What about white
guilt in America since 1619?   After all, I wouldn't be in
this predicament if white people had left my great-great-
grandparents where they were.   There wouldn't be any race
problem if whites hadn't created it.   Where are the books
for children that deal with whites and their racism?   They
don't exist, because it is easier to be paternalistic than honest.

You shouldn't apologize for being who you are.   As
long as you and I, as individuals, can talk to each other and
know that the other will listen with respect and think about
what is being said, things aren't all bad.   We're both, in
our own ways, trying to deal with the challenge of the sixties
and the seventies.   There are some, in fact many whites
whom I would (and do) "tune out."   As this letter should indicate, you are not one of them.

Sincerely,
Julius Lester

3. AESTHETICS, MORALITY,
    AND THE TWO CULTURES

    Evelyn Geller

    The painful rift in perception between our black and
white cultures ... is exemplified in two children's books of
widely varying perspective that were published last year.
They are the Newbery winning Sounder, by white William
Armstrong, and Julius Lester's Black Folktales.

    Criticisms of the former range from charges of in-
authenticity and irrelevance to an activist youth, to outright
racism. Black Folktales, though well received, has been
criticized for "reverse racism," by some black librarians
among others, and been excluded from several children's
collections. Both works raise the question of who can speak
for the black experience, but more, how one is to weigh
quality in the light of moral content.

    In the spring 1970 Newsletter of the Council on Inter-
racial Books for Children, Tom Feelings argued that Armstrong's old black storyteller could not have been honest, his
relationship being conditioned by the need for survival rather
than honest communication. The point is not implausible--
Joel Chandler Harris made a similar observation in his 1881
introduction to the Uncle Remus stories. Extending his criticism, Feelings said that whites would rather see whites write
about the black experience, and willingly perpetuate old stereotypes.

    A fascinating elaboration appeared in an interchange be-
tween Julius Lester and George Woods, the New York Times
children's book editor, in the Times' spring children's book
issue. Lester felt the modest reception of Black Folktales
as compared with To Be a Slave was due to the fact that he
had written the former expressly for black children and that
whites must open themselves more to understand it. "In
other words, they have to meet me on my ground, and that
is what whites have always been loath to do." But he also
argued the importance of this experience. "Whites do not
want to acknowledge the fact that if they want to know blacks

they will have to immerse themselves in what blacks have to
say. ... There is no white Dante who can ... lead them on
a guided tour of blackness and keep them from getting a little
singed...."

On theoretical grounds, one wants to argue the notion
of separateness or the idea that no white can project himself
into the feelings of another race.   Paula Fox, white, writes
with true artistry about blacks; Virginia Hamilton, eschewing
pseudo-integrated stories, is married to a white; mediocrity
also exists among black authors.   And in quite another context, Kathleen Cleaver has severely challenged Lester's contention that no white should speak on a black issue.

But the broad empirical record negates these exceptions.   The stamp of aesthetic approval has ranged from the
racism in Dr. Dolittle and other Newbery winners to recent
books that are still being fed to our children.   The few passages of hostility in Black Folktales are small in comparison,
and are a price worth the insight gained into black culture
(though that, granted, is a benefit to whites rather than
blacks).   A book does not make a curriculum.

At the same time, one may question whether a superb
book like Sounder is not also aesthetically flawed by its moral limitations--its nostalgic evocation of endurance with all
hostility (except in one fantasy passage) repressed; an insensitivity which puts a man to jail for stealing food yet neglects
to describe the economic impact of his imprisonment on his
family; and its final tone of specious optimism which denies
the irrevocable psychic damage to the child of the experiences so vivdly evoked.

In accepting the National Book Award for The Fixer
in 1967, Bernard Malamud asked whether aesthetics could
divorce itself from the moral issues of the age.   He reviewed the grisly history of his lifetime: a depression that
corroded America, the Moscow trials, Nazism, Hiroshima,
Joe McCarthy, a "young American president who had the back
of his head shot off into the hands of his wife," and Vietnam,
where "a small, gentle-faced people, caught between two
armies, have become living torches."

And he asked: "How can one think of diminishing,
underplaying, or giving up content in fiction if he has been
moved by these events and attempts to understand them?...
Art must interpret or it is mindless.   Content cannot be dis-

invented.   If the world, as some say, is an aesthetic, so too, in a way, is humanity....   Art is, moreover, the invention of the human artist, not an act of God or nature.   To preserve itself it must, in a variety of subtle ways, conserve the artist through sanctifying life and human freedom. "

4. IN HOUSE AND OUT HOUSE:
   AUTHENTICITY AND THE BLACK
   EXPERIENCE IN CHILDREN'S BOOKS

   Binnie Tate, with comments from a committee
   of Los Angeles children's librarians

History records accounts of the "house" servant during the period of American slavery, who was supposedly
treated better than the field hand. Legend also implies that
the house servant was loyal to his master and often felt superior to his black brothers and sisters in the field.

This typically white analysis sees slaves as most people see blacks today, ignoring the implications of the ways
in which domestic slaves really acted (Nat Turner was one),
and making no attempt to translate the common "in-group"
attitudes they shared with the field slaves. For overriding
all differences in treatment was the fact that all slaves were
oppressed as members of the black race. House servants
and other blacks were part of the system established to rele-
gate a group of human beings to servitude by law. Being
part of a group aware of its separateness promotes separate
attitudinal and cultural development. Thus all blacks must
have had "in house" feelings and attitudes beyond the understanding of whites.

Today we find expression of this commonality as
blacks affirm their own foods, their own jokes, their own
way of handling particular situations, et cetera. Whites are
often surprised to find that even with the many variations in
class and in levels of consciousness, blacks share a core of
attitudes which breeds an unconscious unity.

It is this difference in perspective that writers Julius
Lester and Tom Feelings recognize when they charge that
blacks should be writing about blacks.... Even in the area
of evaluation, the subtle cultural biases were confirmed as
our joint committee of children's librarians--two white, two
black--sat down to evaluate children's books about the black
experience.

The Slave Experience

To Be a Slave (Dial, 1968) by Julius Lester is indica-
tive of writing based on a special kind of social cognizance.
When this black man steps into the shoes of a slave, an eloquent and gripping account results. Although this book has
been highly praised, emotions rise at Lester's more recent
Black Folktales (Baron, 1969). In the latter, the author rejects perpetuation of the slave syndrome on all levels including religion.

> TATE: Writers like Lester make clear a state-
> ment that one way to build positive values is to
> destroy negative ones through literary works for
> children.

> WHITE: When librarians choose not to purchase a
> book because its black consciousness becomes of-
> fensive to white attitudes, then we are denying full
> representation of 'unpopular' points of view in our
> collections. Arbuthnot's middle class attitude of
> building white values through children's books is
> questionable at this point in our evolution.

Two fiction books were discussed in contrast to Julius
Lester's works: Venture for Freedom by Ruby Zagoren
(World, 1969) and Sophia Scrooby Preserved by Martha Bacon
(Little, 1968). These two accounts of slave life reflect the
"white viewpoint." One white committee member initially
saw Venture as "an honest account based on historical documents," but further discussion exposed several distortions.

After being brought to this country, Venture seldom
had thoughts of his origin, his tribe, his parents, et cetera.
The characteristic Christian illusion of the "heathen" accepting the "better life" without question is apparent here. The
common, perverted concept of loyalty to the master remains
intact throughout the book. One black member of the committee also argued that Venture, who eventually gained freedom, was again reduced to slavery through the implications
at the end of the book.

> TATE: Why should his white oppressors, from
> whom he bought his freedom, feel they showed re-
> spect for Venture by preceding his black brothers
> and family in the procession to his grave? The
> author was apparently unaware of the patronizing

implications of this passage.

Sophia Scrooby Preserved maintains some stereotypes
of the acquiescent, happy, and grateful slave.   Yet this book
moves somewhat more toward serving the needs of the black
child.   The reader is attracted to the book with the image of
a beautiful black girl on the cover, and within the story Sophia never loses her pride in and awareness of her heritage.
The positive image is continued in her companionship with
the Scrooby child, to whom she is clearly superior in character and intelligence.   Books that portray the black child as
equal or superior to whites are too few, though the reverse
can readily be found.   Young girls respond favorably to the
Victorian style and format of this book.

The Cay by Theodore Taylor (Doubleday, 1969), highly
praised as a book about interracial understanding, appears on
many "Black Experience" lists.   One committee member accepted this book as an "excellent survival story. "   Mr. Taylor fully depicts Philip's revulsion toward Timothy, describing him as old and ugly.

> His face couldn't have been blacker, or his teeth
> whiter.   They made an alabaster trench in his
> mouth, and his pink-purple lips peeled back over
> them like the meat of a conch shell.   He had a
> big welt, like a scar, on his left cheek.   I knew
> he was West Indian.   I had seen many of them in
> Willemstad, but he was the biggest one I'd ever
> seen.

This very real white reaction on Philip's part remains
throughout the story as truth.   Thus the author fails in his
attempt to show Philip's growth in human understanding.
Philip's image of Timothy remains unchanged, though he supposedly grieves for the man who gave his life for him.

> WHITE: Timothy's dignity is apparent throughout,
> but nowhere is there an articulation that his back-
> ground and culture were germane to his humaneness.

The author's point of view posits complete acceptance of
Timothy's servitude and Philip's condescension.   Upon re-
turning to his community and regaining his eyesight, Philip
spends a lot of time talking to the black people.   Philip
states:

I liked the sound of their voices. Some of them
had known old Timothy of Amalie, I felt close to
them.

This is the extent of his racial appreciation. This is
typical of the books which supposedly show racial understanding.

The black people Philip talked with still had full lips
and flat noses. If judged by the aesthetic standards the boy
Philip had applied to Timothy, they apparently remained ugly
and inferior.

TATE: How can this book be acclaimed as an outstanding novel of interracial understanding? Can
racial understanding really be so separate from
racial appreciation?

Implicit racism becomes apparent in many ways. Reflecting society in general, children's stories symbolize black
and white as evil and good respectively, one example being
a folk tale titled The White Bride, The Black Bride. In
stories like these racism is not explicit but fraught with negative connotations for any young child.

The question of validity and integrity in the writing of
books about blacks arose constantly in the discussions. Generally it was felt that this question applied both to black and
white authors. It was agreed that on a subject as critical
as race, authors must follow one of the first rules of writing,
"Write what you know about." White authors have permeated
the field of black literature with books born of guilt and wish
fulfillment. Good intentions are not enough, for inbred racism coupled with "out house" attitudes continue to negate and
denigrate the black image and experience.

How much racism and patronage is retained in a white
author's best and sincerest efforts to write about blacks?
The 1970 Newbery winner, Sounder by William Armstrong
(Harper, 1969), was much discussed. Again, white committee members were confronted by the "in house" attitudes of
blacks. The black librarians accepted Tom Feelings' comment that this book is synthetic as a representation of the
black experience. How much truth would a black man expose
even to his closest white friend in the South? The pain resulting from inhuman treatment is hard for even blacks to
express. Could Armstrong then possibly portray the gripping

trauma felt by this black family?

> GODDARD: In the story, these feelings are exemplified through mild anger and pathos. Yet today's urban child has little understanding of the black silent submission born of necessity for the preservation of life, particularly in the South.

This book, then, should not appear on lists called "the black experience," but rather should be realistically considered as a white interpretation of that experience. Some may consider Armstrong's version important for the white child, and there is impact both in his visual description of the oppressive Southern atmosphere, and his fine literary style. Many black children will bring to the book the "in house" feelings which are sublimated in this story, and anger may be the result.

Another "out house" attempt to depict the rural Southern black experience for younger children is Oh Lord, I Wish I Was a Buzzard (Macmillan, 1968), supposedly the depiction of a black girl's wishful thinking as she works in the cotton fields. Many blacks are immediately repulsed by the title, with all its negative implications, coupled with a picture of a black child. The father and children are so neatly dressed for working in the fields. They remain clean spotless and smiling throughout. Even if there is any validity in portraying a girl wishing to be a buzzard, the agony of slaving in hot dusty cotton fields should have been visible in the art work. A white romanticized presentation of farm life, this book represents the society's commercialized attempt to define a problem and solve it strictly in its own terms.

> GODDARD: Black authors also must be challenged to recognize their white attitude as they effect writing for children. Several have already been challenged on this account by black youth.

Lorenz Graham is one black author with integrity who still writes largely from an outdated point of view. Although in I, Momolu (Crowell, 1966) the African perspective is evident, Graham's perception of the "white hope" continues in Whose Town (Crowell, 1969).

> GODDARD: Mr. Graham is a product of the times when "in house" black attitudes could not be expressed openly.

His writing reflects his inability to see beyond the protective
vision of an integrated or assimilated society.   Today's minority tastes are changing.

By contrast, Virginia Hamilton has written several
superb pieces of literature about blacks with no attempt to
present pseudointegrated circumstances.   Her books are
straightforward and literary, and present positive black imagery important for the "in house" appreciation by the white
child.   Zeely (Macmillan, 1967) is an excellent example of
positive symbolism.   Time-Ago Tales of Jahdu (Macmillan,
1969), her most recent title, depicts blackness without reference or apology to whiteness; it is right in every emotional
and literary sense.   In turn, House of Dies Drear (Macmillan, 1968) introduces the richness of 19th century black
American history.

Validity and integrity both were questioned in Not Like
Niggers (St. Martins, 1969), by the black author Williams.
As a retrospective dissection of a poor Southern Negro family in the early 30's, the author's adult perception fails to
authenticate the feelings of a five-year-old child.

> GOLDNER: His observations are painfully valid,
> but the problems of society which caused the de-
> velopment of such attitudes are not stated or im-
> plied.

As a book for children it falls short, probably because of
the editor's lack of insight.   Accepting this book with its in-
ternal flaws was probably easier than helping the author realize the full potential of his book.   How are children to understand that consciously negative attitudes within the black family are directly imposed by the values translated from the
mainstream of society?   For young white audiences, too, the
attempt to arrive at some racial understanding can become
confused.   Why does the author expose only the negative connotations of "nigger"?   This book is based on "in house" experiences which adult blacks can appreciate, even though
they may not be entirely aware of the broader implications.
But by failing to provide a rationale or basis for these feelings, the book makes a very negative statement for black
children.

Harriet and the Promised Land (S&S, 1968), by the
black artist Jacob Lawrence, has been questioned by many in
the black community.   It is a strong, stylized depiction of the

dehumanizing process of slavery.   The best uses of this book
are not with children, format notwithstanding.   Though Lawrence makes a magnificent statement, a sophisticated appreciation is required to explain the significance of the artist's
style.   Some librarians, recognizing the artistic value of the
book, have nevertheless emasculated it by classifying it as a
picture book.   Books like Harriet presuppose a certain level
of maturity and perception on the child's part, as does Not
Like Niggers, without which it can harm the child.   In working with children one must realize that they usually don't see
beyond face value to symbolic levels.

Realism

Realism can be portrayed effectively in books for
younger children.   Evan's Corner (Holt, 1966) by Hill briefly
and adequately tells the need for a child to discover "self. "
The crowded city environment is reproduced without apology
and false idealism.   John Steptoe, in Stevie (Harper, 1969),
presents a relevant portrayal of the black ethos for the very
young.   Mild dialect, urban environment, and realistic characterizations emerge to authenticate a black child's experience
with a young visitor.   While actualizing city life, the univer-
sality of Stevie's experience makes this book appealing to all
children.

General appeal, along with black characterization, is
achieved in Paula Fox's How Many Miles to Babylon? (David
White, 1967).   Bored with school, the black boy who lives
with three aunts leaves school and walks into the hands of
thugs who kidnap him and use him as a decoy.   Knowledge
of the inner city is evident as the author interprets the spirit
of boys as well as troubled adolescents.

In Gunilla Norris' The Good Morrow (Atheneum, 1969),
a young black city girl with feelings of great uneasiness, fear,
and shyness goes to camp.   Some of her apprehension is natural, but a great deal of it stems from her awareness that
her black skin makes her different from the rest of the children in the camp.   The theme of adjustment to a new experience and facing up to inner and overt confrontation is well
handled.   Any child, black or white, will recognize the truth
of this little girl's struggle.   For black children in particular, this story acknowledges some facts of their lives.

The recently published Lillie of Watts (Ritchie, 1969)

by a Los Angeles area author, Mildred Walter, is an honest
attempt, though not as well written as the two books mentioned above. Realism and empathy out of authentic black
experience are evident.

Cognizance of the historical presence of white racism
is more evident in nonfiction books like Bradford Chambers'
Chronicles of Negro Protest (Parents, 1968); Robert Goldston's Negro Revolution (Macmillan, 1968); Dorothy Sterling's
Tear Down the Walls (Doubleday, 1968); Janet Harris' Black
Pride (McGraw, 1969); and Milton Meltzer's In Their Own
Words (Crowell, 3 vols. , 1964-1967). Yet even in nonfic-
tional documentation, the need for commitment is inescapable.
In these books, too, one becomes aware of insidious statements and condescending tones which mar the strength of a
promising title.

We suggest that every librarian and teacher, in as-
suming the responsibility of presenting books about blacks to
children, read adult titles to understand some of the complex
and varied levels of racial consciousness existing among
blacks. It may then be possible to weed the denigrating titles
from the mass of "out house" literature and find those which
really come closest to:

--Providing authentic situations and palatable illustrations which realistically reflect black images and experience;

--Filling the void of positive materials with which
black children may identify;

--Giving black children a new cultural and historical
awareness in an African heritage of which they can be proud;

--Bridging the cultural and social gaps between black
and white children which society has imposed through racial
stereotypes and blatant lies;

--Contributing to the call for a new humanism which
can be heard throughout the world.

COMMENTS

Rosalind Goddard, Children's Librarian, Ascot Branch Library:

As a black librarian working with black children, I

have been offended countless times by books which negate and
"innocently" disparage the image of the black man in text and
illustrations. Most of these books are dated in their depiction of blacks physically, mentally, and socially. I call for
the removal from significant compiled booklists of irrelevant
and dated books for use with children, especially black children.

Ignorant, well-meaning writers fail to capture and relate the truth of the black experience. Even in recent treat-
ments of slaves, stereotyped images are created of the infinitely happy black acquiescent to the white, incapable of accepting his own personal and physical blackness.

Valid books for the black child must capture truth and
the sense of a definite culture through authentic settings and
character portrayals. White authors have often used stilted
stereotypic duplication of supposed "colored folks talk,"
while recreating the black image in unreal illustrations, thus
failing to develop a black human who comes across to the
reader in terms of his blackness.

Let us remove the old and deal with gut reality, not
with placid idyllics.

Jane Goldner, Children's Librarian, Panorama City Branch
Library:

Black is beautiful--why not? As long as slogans are
defined by what I, white and making-it, know to be true.   I
know, because my heart is in the right place.   So everything
published that fits my definition is acceptable and good for
black kids, because I understand it.   The Cay, Venture for
Freedom, Sounder, Nitty Gritty (Dutton, 1965), are real experiences, say I.

But when my assumptions are challenged, when Julius
Lester says accept me on my own terms, which are not and
never have been yours, can I? Mostly no.   I would then
root out all the deep prejudices I couldn't admit.   It's easier
to dismiss Julius Lester and Tom Feelings by calling them
too sensitive or reverse racists, when they protest the depiction of the black experience by whites.

The dominant society has controlled every aspect of
life so that it can mold the images needed to keep it cohe-

sive.   When its control is threatened, especially politically
and socially, society denies the validity of the challenge and
then suppresses it.   This phenomenon operates in the micro-
cosm of books.

Thus publishers, editors, librarians, and teachers
can produce books and lists that are worthless for anything
but bolstering their own egos.   The use of lists by Effie Lee
Morris, Augusta Baker, and hundreds who have thrown together compilations is worthless in contributing to black identity or black consciousness.   The irony is that these individuals have a religious "high" over their good hearts and works.

We have hopped onto the band wagon of a cause: the
Black Kid's Identity.   We are going to give it to him, come
hell or high water, because cultural identity is good, important, nice, and gets federal money.   We take the idea, suck
out its meaning, cling to the empty form, and despise the
substance.   Lester's Black Folktales becomes black racism
because we don't want to read about black rage.   Anything
that really tells us of feelings and lives we don't want to
recognize frightens us.   But no one can tell you what it
means to have your finger in the fire unless his has been as
badly burned.

Dead End School (Little, 1968) and Sophia Scrooby Preserved, books by whites, give a sense of struggle and humanity in writing about blacks, but not for blacks.   Bonham
senses social brutalization in Nitty Gritty, but not for blacks.
These books help white kids begin to move out of their neighborhoods, but won't get them into a black man's soul.

Lester, Steptoe, Walter, and Hamilton know.   Black
kids sense it ... and so do the shocked and frightened white
adults.

What hit me painfully and demoralizingly in my discussions with black librarians was to face the extent of my
dogmatism.   If an item met my definition of what was necessary for the downtrodden, it had to be good for them, god-
damn it.   Without the face-on meeting with blacks themselves, a white really can't know what a fool he is.   Books
by Lester are like knives, laying bare flesh.   Writing of
this caliber and integrity must be the direction.   More blacks
as editors and reviewers, more interchange between black
and white librarians, are needed.

Read Autobiography of Malcolm X (Grove, 1965; pa. Grove), Soul on Ice (McGraw, 1968; pa. Dell), Manchild in the Promised Land (Macmillan, 1965; pa. NAL), To Be a Slave (Dial, 1968; pa. Dell), and Huey Newton to start getting an idea of what black is. Then when something honest and fine in a kid's book appears, you won't toss it on the reject pile because you can't handle it.

Edith White, Senior Children's Librarian, Western Region:

Through our sensitizing process of our conversations, I have become increasingly aware of how subtle and complex racial attitudes are. Unthinking, earnest, liberal whites are just as susceptible to implicit racial biases as the boldest bigot. Well-meaning attempts at "interracial understanding" are often based on assumptions that are really condescending in nature. Our ethnic attitudes are built in deeply. Society in general is loaded with cultural characteristics, attributes of smell, voice, food, and looks are judged as "good" or "repugnant," depending on associations built up over many years. Each of us must be aware and appreciate that our own preferences are not necessarily correct or the best.

I, too, have been party to the unconscious sin of racism by lack of appreciation. Sympathy falsely equated with understanding is complacent indulgence of people who think they are different from the unfeeling majority and who are fighting a subliminal guilt. Thus, we find librarians praising books which seem to exemplify what they consider positive attributes: humanity; acceptance of one's burdens in life; faith that God will sustain and provide.

No longer can the oppressed be expected to accept adversities. No longer can we say that literary merit is or should be our sole criterion in book selection. Our responsibility to humanity takes precedence.

5. GUIDELINES FOR BLACK BOOKS:
   AN OPEN LETTER TO JUVENILE EDITORS

Augusta Baker

One of my pet irritations today is the whole idea that
the great interest and upsurge in books about black life has
just come along. 1937 and 1938 were the years when the interest in this whole subject was born. We realized then
there was a great need for this kind of material. I worked
in Harlem just opposite a public school, and I hadn't worked
there very long before I realized that the boys and girls, all
Negro boys and girls, knew three people--Frederick Douglass,
Booker T. Washington and George Washington Carver. And
that was it. When we gave book talks about Phyllis Wheatley, Robert Smalls and others, these children had no idea
who these people were. We thought that they certainly
should have books which would introduce them to the important people in their own heritage. It goes without saying
that if the Negro boys and girls didn't know about these people, white children did not know either. Some of them had
not even heard of Frederick Douglass, George Washington
Carver and Booker T. Washington. So the need was recognized as early as the 30's.

At that time, at Countee Cullen Regional Branch, which
was then 135th Street Branch, we set up a model collection.
In order to do this we had to think about criteria. We
couldn't just pick up one book after another and say, "Well,
I like this book, so this book should go in. I don't like this
book so out it goes. " We had to work with some kind of
guidelines. Since then, we've added a few more. We can
afford, now, to add "quality. " We absolutely couldn't consider "quality" in 1939, 1940, 1941, because we really had
very few books to meet our general criteria. However, we
still use the same guidelines today.

We selected illustrations as the first one, because as
we watched our boys and girls in the library, we realized
that they went to the shelves, took down a book and looked
at it carefully. They looked at the illustrations, before they
did any reading. Children, today, approach books the same

50

way.   We do want the illustrations to be attractive.   We do
not want these Negro boys and girls to look like white children with brown wash or black wash spread over them.   We
want them to have the features, to have the distinction, to
have the attraction that one finds among Negro boys and girls.
Let the characters be natural.

Our next criterion is a matter of language.   We discarded the books that were so full of dialect that you couldn't
understand them.   Rarely do we find a book today where the
dialect is author-created, but imagine what we ran across in
those days!   There were plantation stories then, with all
these little children playing together, born and raised on the
same plantation.   A great deal was made in the beginning of
the book of the fact that both the black children and the white
children were born on and never left the plantation, and were
raised together by "Mammy."   Then you'd come to the dialog.
The white children would speak as if they had Ph. D.'s from
Oxford, but you couldn't understand one word the little black
children were trying to say because you were bogged down in
the "deses" and "doses."   We don't come across too much
of this today.   When we do we're naturally upset about it.
We watch more for this kind of dialect when we read the
stories where the locale is West Indian.   Some of the editors
are having problems with the West Indian speech, which is a
very distinct pattern of speech.   Regional vernacular is fine,
but if you use it, then all of the characters should speak the
same way.   If they all came from the same place, with
roughly the same economic standing and the same general
education, they're going to speak pretty much the same way.
So we still look for this--consistency in speech patterns.

There is no place for the hero of a story to use derogatory terms.   One of the last disagreements we had with
some people was about what constituted a derogatory term.
I think the last word we really gave up was "pick-a-ninny"
because this, for so long, was "a term of great affection."
Other terms, such as "darkie" and "nigger" were dropped
without too great a problem, but it took a little doing to give
up some of those other "affectionate" terms.   Gradually, we
got this point across.   There is never an excuse for such
words to appear editorially or for the author himself to think
this way.   If a book is historical in background, however, it
must be true to the times.   In Hildegarde Swift's Railroad to
Freedom, she explains to the boys and girls that she uses
certain words because they are historically accurate.   When
the patroller, who has been chasing the escaped slave, catches

Harriet Tubman, he does not say, "And now, Miss Tubman,
will you please return to the plantation with me?" He is apt
to use more "colorful" language. So that when we're looking
at the books, we recognize this. It's just the same with the
realistic stories of today. You have the pattern of speech
that one finds in the streets, and this is part of the atmosphere of the story. We try very hard, though, to make sure
that the hero doesn't use this kind of language indiscrimi-
nately. There still is this criterion to be applied. There
still is a feeling about the use of this kind of language and
its indiscriminate use.

Themes and Attitudes

Another general criterion is theme. In the late 1930's
and in the 1940's, when we reached theme, we really had
reached a barrier. If we had applied the criteria of today,
where we now expect a full picture of Negro life, we wouldn't
have had any books. We did have about 40 books in the
James Weldon Johnson Memorial Collection, but in all of
those books, the Negro was portrayed in some kind of servile
position, and it was unheard-of to portray a black man as
anything other than a servant. This just wasn't done. Since
that time, of course, children's editors have taken care of
that problem, but we never have had as wide a range of social life portrayed in children's books as there should be.

I'm sure that juvenile editors must be absolutely del-
uged with manuscripts on the current scene. This always
happens when the public says, "we need something." But
perhaps editors will keep in mind some guidelines when they
are wading through all those manuscripts--good, bad and in-
different. I think, first of all, the characters should be just
people and circumstances should be normal circumstances.
In stories about city life I am pleased to see children of all
sizes, shapes and colors. I would hope that situations would
be normal situations. I would hope that we would not take a
manuscript and go through every third page and paint one
child and every fourth family black to integrate the book.
Where it is a normal situation or there is a normal reason
for there to be a black family with the white families, fine.
Sometimes, however, we lose track of this, and the upper
most thing in our minds is to get that book integrated. We
still do not have to be afraid to publish a few stories that
aren't integrated, especially if the integration is artificial.
If it's a normal part of life for the families and children in

the book to be all kinds of families and all kinds of children, fine. This is as it should be.

Older editors will remember that there was a time when realistic fiction was one of the hardest subjects to get published. Back in the old days the nonfiction was strong, the fiction had to be very pleasant. Follett had the courage to publish Lorenz Graham's South Town, but there were many who thought that the children weren't quite ready for this kind of story. Now, we have a number of good, realistic stories but we still need more realistic books. I have a feeling that we have not quite moved into the area of what I call "an unhappy ending." I believe some of the ghetto stories, some of the very realistic stories, are very good--until we come to the end. Something happens, and perhaps it's that we do not really carry that realism to the end. The thing which impressed me with Edgar Allan was that the author made no attempt to give it a they-lived-happily-ever-after ending. Edgar Allan is based on the truth and the author had the courage not to twist that truth. I would hope, too, for books about a Negro family that does not necessarily find itself in the slums. There's still room for stories on all levels, all facets, of black life; all black people are not in the ghettos and slums.

It is interesting how stories come along in waves. It seems that right now we're on a "foster home kick." This is fine, if the author really knows about what he is writing. The person who writes realistic fiction must be inside, writing about life, rather than outside, looking in on it. Then he has written a book which youngsters will say really has soul, as opposed to a book which just doesn't quite make it. This requires fine writing, along with the other criteria.

A guideline for imports: these are the books which we must examine very carefully and which we must read and reread. Many of the books which are published first abroad reflect certain attitudes that we would hope to eliminate. These attitudes sometimes are so subtle that, in a very quick, cursory reading, you may miss them--the books on Africa, for instance. Illustrations are an important matter. A book came across my desk a few days ago and from a quick glance, the text seems to be all right. The illustrations, however, leave something to be desired. I feel that, if we apply certain criteria to the work of our own illustrators, we have no right to accept less than that when the illustrations have been made by someone abroad. Several

books have now come across my desk with illustrations that,
had the book originated in America with an American artist,
would be considered bordering on the stereotyped. If the illustrations border on the stereotype for an American artist,
they border on the stereotyped for all artists, even very
famous and well-known ones.

        Guidelines for reissues and reprints of our own old
titles: these should be read very, very carefully, in the
light of today's thinking.   Editors should not be over-influ-
enced by the importance of the author.   After all, there are
many authors whose whole outlook on life has changed in the
last 20 or so years.   These people have grown, they have
changed their attitudes, they are influenced by social life
around them just as we are; so, it might even be doing a
disservice to them to reissue some of those books.

        The books on the history of the black man, the books
on civil rights and nonfiction in general are good.   They are
so numerous that we now apply literary standards to them.
This is something that we did not do a number of years ago.
If the attitude was right, if the book said what we really
wanted it to say, that was sufficient.   Now we ask that the
nonfiction book meet the same literary standards as all our
other books.   It should be lively and entertaining rather than
encyclopedic.

Authors and Illustrators

        About black authors and illustrators: like white au-
thors and illustrators, they are not all good.   I had an agent
call my office recently.   She had called several children's librarians and they had referred her to me.   She identified
herself and said, "It is very, very necessary for me to get
two things.   I need some manuscripts on black life and black
children; and, more than that, I very badly need some books
where the authors are black.   I could sell them overnight!"
She hesitated and then she said, "Mrs. Baker, I wonder if
you would consider writing a book. " Well, we had a little
session about respecting the rights of children to have good
books and not to have quite so many of these contrived books.
Children don't care whether the author is green, lavender or
what.   They won't read badly written, contrived books.   Of
course, talented black authors and illustrators should be encouraged.   I believe they will come to the fore, that they
will be encouraged to produce good books because there is

great talent there.   It simply needs to be found, and nurtured.
Many editors have taken black illustrators and turned them
loose and said, "Create.   You can create any way you want,
you don't have to create black." We know Alvin Smith and
others like him who are marvelous illustrators working with
general themes.   I'm very, very excited right now to have
seen the jacket of Countee Cullen's Lost Zoo, a beautiful,
sensitive book written by a black poet who wasn't even thinking about race when he created this book.

Another area is one I call "books dealing with the
black child's own feelings and emotions." We are getting a
number of these books.   Sometimes, I don't know whether
these are books for children or about children, but we have
received some very interesting ones.   It's Wings That Make
Birds Fly (Pantheon) is a very, very sensitive book in which
the author records the words of a black child.   The Way It
Is (Harcourt) is also very interesting.   It is composed of
photographs taken by a group of teenagers with their own descriptions of the photographs as text.   I think each one of
these books really has to be dealt with individually.   They
are so different.   Some are very good and some simply
aren't.   I take a good hard look at the concept books, such
as Color Me Brown and Black Is Beautiful, that attempt, I
suppose, to make the very small child aware of this kind of
thing.   These must be written very well.   Editors must be
very critical when they get this kind of manuscript.   They
must make sure that it is well done and that it is going to
reach the age group for which it is intended--and that it is
for children and not about them.

I think the books must be worth reading.   I think that
is the very first criterion of all.   A book has to be about
people who are individuals with character and who really
come alive.   I keep Anne Carroll Moore's books on my desk,
and when I need a little sustenance, I very often go back and
reread them.   In one of her books she tells about a young
author who came to see her because she was disturbed about
whether she was writing the right kind of books for children.
I think Miss Moore's answer holds for all of us today.   She
told this young woman: "I think you have the biggest chance
in the world, if you keep straight on working and appraising
everything you do on the basis of sound criticism.   Writing
for children, like daily living with them, requires a constant
sharpening of all one's faculties, a fresh discovery of new
heights and depths in one's own emotions.   The saving conviction is that children have as many and as varied tastes in

reading as grown-ups. In the matter of their reading, I
think that they have more sense since they are entirely un-
concerned with other people's opinions of books. When they
are bored, they stop reading the book. 'I didn't like that
book' is reason enough and it admits of no argument." If
we think about the child who is going to decide whether this
book is read or not read, we will come out on the right
track whether we are writing about whites or blacks.

6.   WHAT IS A RACIST BOOK?

Rae Alexander

To what extent has the resurgence of Black pride and self-awareness been communicated to Black children?

In 1939, Kenneth B. Clark and Mamie P. Clark found that Black children evaluated Blacks negatively and evaluated whites positively.   In their monumental study, Black children between the ages of three and seven were presented with a black and a white doll and asked which was "nice," which "looked bad," which they would "like to play with," and which was "the nice color." The Black children invariably preferred the white doll.

Thirty years later, Steven R. Asher and Vernon L. Allen of the University of Wisconsin, substituted puppets for black and white dolls and asked both Black and white children which they preferred. Again, the white puppet was most often preferred and the black puppet most often rejected.

If the studies cited here are valid, Black may be beautiful for contemporary Black youth involved in a new appreciation of Black ethnicity, but apparently the Black Revolution is too new and too tentative for its values to have filtered down to Black children, who are still emotionally and otherwise conditioned by the prevailing white culture.

Books Still Insidious

Based on the books I read in the course of compiling a revision of the N. A. A. C. P. 's recommended book list (Books for Children: Black and White--A Selected Bibliography), I feel I am in a position to draw this conclusion: Despite the growing number of books depicting the Black experience, the image they give of the Black American is still one of the more insidious influences that hinder the Black child from finding true self-awareness.

In evaluating Black and biracial books for pre-school through sixth-grade levels, a major criterion was that no

57

book would be listed if it was considered likely to communicate to either a Black or a white child a racist concept or
cliché about Blacks; or failed to provide some strong characters to serve as role models.   Even one such stereotype
would be enough to eliminate an otherwise good book.   Underlying this criterion was my own experience with many teachers who are insensitive to the racist content of books or who
are not equipped to handle such material adequately in their
classes.   The tragedy is that so many teachers fail to expose racist material for what it is, and they fail to make
use of it as a basis for discussing prejudice.

    One might say that the basic consideration in my not
including a given book in the N. A. A. C. P. list was the pain
it might give to even one Black child.   Naturally, there were
additional criteria.   The book must be appropriate for use in
(1) an all-Black classroom, (2) an all-white classroom, and
(3) an integrated classroom.   If a book did not completely
satisfy each of these criteria, I excluded it from the bibliography.   To illustrate how these standards were applied, I
will mention first several books that I did not include in the
list and the reasons why.

Marred by Racial Slurs

    A number of poignant and stirring stories I did not
list because they were marred by racial slurs.   Even such
an imaginative and exciting story as L. M. Boston's Treasure of Green Knowe (Harcourt, Brace & World) I excluded
because of a derogatory description of a Black boy's hair.
("Think of Jacob's crinkly hair, hardly the length of a needle.
The most she could do with it [in her embroidery] was tedi-
ously to make knots. ")   In contrast, the author writes elsewhere of a white person's "tresses. "   ("... he was a vain
man with hair he was proud of ... There was enough of Cax-
ton's hair to do the whole chimney. ")

    Not Over Ten Inches High, by Harry Levy (McGraw-
Hill Book Co.), is a delightful and charming story.   On the
first page, one reads, "only a small tuft of kinky hair
showed from one end.... "   In A Sundae with Judy, by Frieda
Friedman (Scholastic Book Services), the author writes,
"She hadn't noticed how dark Barbara and Bob Williams were,
or how much Mayling's eyes were slanted.... "   I do not
know whether passages such as those quoted express prejudice
on the authors' part, but I do know that in white America this

is the language of racism, and it is what children hear.   I
freely admit that in winnowing books, I was primarily concerned with what the child would be receiving.   I was on the
child's side, all the way.   The Black child reading passages
like those mentioned here surely senses that his appearance
is being unfavorably described, which is hardly conducive to
strengthening self-esteem.   One has only to imagine how the
child must feel when such slights are read aloud in the presence of white classmates.   Equally important, how must they
condition the white child's concept of Blacks?

A problem of another kind arose in connection with
books that reflect the recent and entirely well-intentioned emphasis on offering children material about American life as
it really is.   One must consider the effect of this realism
on the positive self-image we want Black children to develop.
Blacks in the ghetto struggle with life from the day they are
born.   It is true that ghetto youngsters often find pallid fare
those books that are favored in the suburbs.   However, in
assessing the "realistic" books, the portrayal of ghetto life
is often overwhelmingly negative.   There are hurtful parents,
broken homes, and emotionally nonsupportive friends and
teachers.   These are facts of life, and the children who face
them must cope as best they can.   On the other hand, I believe that the constant exposure of ghetto society in this light
is destructive--both of the Black child's view of himself and
of the white child's understanding.

For essentially this reason, I excluded the much admired books of Frank Bonham.   Two, in particular--The Nitty Gritty and The Mystery of the Fat Cat (E. P. Dutton)--
emphasize a demoralizing, decadent side of Black life, which
in these books is always, alas, overcome only by the direct
or indirect intervention of The Man.

For much the same reason, I did not include the autobiography It's Wings That Make Birds Fly, edited by Sandra
Weiner (Pantheon Books).   Ten-year-old Otis tells his story
in his own words, which Miss Weiner recorded.   It is a
story of a broken home, punitive adults, over-crowded housing, inadequate play facilities, harassment of younger by older children, and the eternal benevolence of whites toward
Blacks.   A paragraph at the end of the book states that Otis
was killed in an accident while playing in the street.

Portrayals Too Bleak

I do not doubt the human truth of this autobiography, nor, in more general terms, do I question its social accuracy. But in the unrelievedly bleak and dismal portrayal of lower-class Black life, this book takes no notice of the fact that many poor Blacks do possess personal values, that they have the will and strength to help their children strive to master their environment--qualities that, as it happens, are unnoticed and unsupported by many teachers and administrators. For the young white reader, this book supports rampant stereotypes, but it offers no insight at all into the "hows" and "whys" of ghetto life. For the young Black reader, the book too strongly affirms that all the Otises of today are doomed from birth.

Of the books that do foster a healthy self-image in the young Black reader, I should like to mention three. Bimby, by Peter Burchard (Coward-McCann), is an historical novel set in the Sea Islands, off Georgia, just before the Civil War. Although young Bimby has not experienced slavery directly, it is through the mature wisdom of the old slave Jesse that he comes to understand what it means to be a man, and that he must himself find his own freedom. The author's illustrations enhance the story's underlying wistfulness and sadness. Black youth will find Bimby a strong image with which to identify.

Canalboat to Freedom, by Thomas Fall (Dial Press), vividly portrays the life of an ex-slave, Lundius, who risks death to help his Black brothers escape to freedom via the underground railroad. He meets and befriends a white indentured servant named Benja, who is young and inexperienced in the ways of the world. Lundius helps Benja and others in practical, protective ways, but he is also for them a symbol of strength; it is his qualities as a man that so powerfully affect others and that enable Benja to carry on the work of Lundius after he has been killed.

Bimby and Canalboat to Freedom stand apart from the general fare of children's books on slavery in three important respects. Bimby and Lundius are luminous, three-dimensional characters, very real and very much alive. Both possess an inner strength that enables them to strike out at the system in a positive way. Both are figures drawn from historical experience, and they will foster respect and pride in Black children today.

Member of the Gang, by Barbara Rinkoff (Crown Publishers), is a story of today. The young Black hero, Woodie
Jackson, feels he amounts to little at home, in school, and
at the settlement house where he spends his afternoons. His
father is hardworking, gruff and stern; his mother is gentle
and on the overprotective side. Woodie jumps at the chance
to join the Scorpions, because he thinks membership in the
gang will make him important to himself and others. Following the inevitable street clash, arrest, and appearance in
Family Court, Woodie is assigned a Black probation officer
who gives Woodie the kind of encouragement and support that
parents and teachers have failed to provide. Together they
build a new perspective on life for Woodie, and for the boy
the world takes on a very different meaning. The black and
white illustrations by Harold James dramatically interpret
Woodie's shifting moods and feelings. The merits of this
book are several: there are many Woodie Jacksons in our
world, and the author has captured their reality in her central character. While Woodie's parents have negative qualities, the reader is allowed to see that their attitudes are
oblique expressions of their concern and love for their son.
The Black probation officer projects a strong Black image.

In considering the constructive potential of biracial
books for children, one does not ask that they be antiseptic
in portraying harsh realities; one hopes that increasingly, authors, Black and white, will foster awareness and sensitivity
in their young readers; and, specifically, in the case of
Black children, one hopes they will be helped to know better
their own strength and power to bring about change.

Postscript

When I prepared the N. A. A. C. P. list, the Newbery
Award-winning Sounder by William H. Armstrong was un-
available for review. If I were to consider Sounder for the
list, I would reject it as a racist book. I found Sounder offensive and demeaning to Black people....

What the white author of Sounder has done to the
Black characters is to diminish their role as instruments in
effecting change. More important, the author has denied
Black youth the privilege of having role models with which
they can identify and find fulfillment, and on that ground
alone the book fails to meet a basic criterion used in selecting the N. A. A. C. P. book list.

The white author of <u>Sounder</u> renders the father and
boy impotent, much as William Styron portrayed the character of Nat Turner.   The mother's character pales against
the strong Black women history tells us about--Harriet Tubman, Sojourner Truth.   When you study the Black actors in
<u>Sounder</u>, you wonder how Black people could have survived
social genocide since 1619.

7. PORTRAYAL OF THE BLACK
   IN CHILDREN'S LITERATURE (Excerpt)

Jessie M. Birtha

> I am only one, But still I am one.   I cannot do
> everything, But still I can do something; And be-
> cause I cannot do everything I will not refuse to
> do the something that I can do.

It was with this quotation from Edward Everett Hale
in mind that I accepted the responsibility of addressing librarians on the currently important subject of the "Portrayal
of the Black in Children's Literature." Qualifications?   I
am a children's book selection specialist in The Free Library
of Philadelphia, but I have an even more important qualifica-
tion.   I am black.

I would like to share with you, from the viewpoint of
a black librarian, some of the background of thought which
goes into the selection of children's books relating to black
Americans.   I shall attempt to help you form some criteria
for determining which books are good, which are mediocre,
and which, for one reason or another, are not acceptable,
and may even be objectionable to the very persons to whom
the author may have felt they would have appeal. . . .

Thinking Black

There is a certain corner in North Philadelphia which
I pass whenever I travel by bus from my home to the Central Library.   There is a brick wall of a store whose front
faces the side street.   Like almost all surfaces which afford
a writing area these days, the wall is covered with graffiti.
Standing out among all of the scribbling is stenciled in bold,
black letters impossible to overlook: "BLACK IS BEAUTI-
FUL.   BLACK IS A STRUGGLE.   JOIN THE STRUGGLE."
A few feet farther on the wall one reads: "ARE YOU
THINKING BLACK TODAY?"   I am going to ask you to
"think black" with me.

You may have seen the Warren Schloat filmstrip
"Growing Up Black" in which several black adolescents express their reactions to the experience of growing up black
in America.   Although it was not especially emphasized,
there was one thing which the youngsters had in common.
All had grown up black looking at white faces in their school-
books and--if they had access to a library--in their picture
books and storybooks.   They looked at white faces in magazines and newspaper advertisements and in television com-
mercials.   They played with blonde, curly-haired white dolls
and paperdolls, or white soldier and sailor toys; they went
shopping and bought clothes displayed on white mannequin
children.   Whenever anything black was shown, it was something either to be laughed at, ridiculed, or had otherwise unfavorable connotations.   It was the poet Robert Burns who
said, "Oh wad some power the giftie gie us To see oursels
as others see us!"   For generations the black person has
been given the opportunity to see himself as the other race
saw him.   Needless to say, it has not done too much for the
"good neighbor" policy within America.

Twenty years ago, the job of listing the best in children's books would have been comparatively simple.   Even
during the period called the Negro Renaissance in the 1920s
there were few children's books.   I recall the joy with which
I discovered Jessie Redmond Fausset and the Langston
Hughes novels at a time when, had there been children's
books, I would have been devouring them.   Langston Hughes,
Countee Cullen, Claude McKay all held--and will always
hold--a special place in my heart.   They were about people
like me.   I could identify with their sentiments and emotions.
Yet, I was still hoping that somewhere I would come across
some stories about Negro children or Negro teenagers.   Of
course, I still read the stories of white girls going happily
off to camp and riding horses and sailing boats.   I must
have been about twelve when I became fed up with reading
about Campfire Girls and Girl Scouts when we did not even
have a black Girl Scout troop in town.

Publishers as well as writers have been latecomers
to the realization of the need (and market) for books by and
about the Negro as well as inter-racial books.   They have
been unaware or unwilling to include the black segment of
the United States population in history or fiction.   If America is the melting pot which social studies teachers present
to their children, it is a melting pot in which one of the basic ingredients has been left out of the soup.

As recently as 1967, John Killens, novelist and writ-
er-in-residence at Fisk University, wrote:

> The American Negro remains a cultural nonentity
> as far as books, television, movies and Broadway
> are concerned. It is as if twenty million Ameri-
> cans do not exist; twenty million people are com-
> mitted to oblivion. . . . A Negro child can go to
> school and look into his school books and children's
> books and come home and watch television and go
> to an occasional movie, and follow this routine
> from day to day, month to month, and year to
> year, and hardly if ever see a reflection of him-
> self. . . .

Since the Kerner Report in 1968 pointed out the facts
of racism and prejudice in America, there has been a conscious effort among publishers, authors, illustrators, and librarians to improve the situation. (There have also been op-
portunists who jump on the bandwagon because writing a
black book is the current thing. It will sell.) In just two
years, the words of John Killens are no longer true. In the
fall of 1968 from the sidewalks of New York to the wide
spaces of the West, the world of television suddenly became
an integrated world. Books with Negro characters and Negro themes became more prevalent.

Book Selection Problems

With the wealth of material available today in trade
and library editions and the now popular paperbacks in chil-
cren's titles, with the increased amount of Federal funds
many libraries are receiving to expand their collections, with
the expanded racial integration in education and housing bringing different groups of people closer together, it is easy for
a librarian to have the best of intentions and still be confused about book selection. Even black people do not always
agree on a name acceptable in referring to themselves: Negro, colored, Afro-American, Afram, or black. Some librarians tend to buy any book that appears to be integrated.
Others cautiously delay buying until they have seen two or
three favorable reviews in outstanding periodicals. I believe
that the two most difficult situations for quality book selection about or by the blacks are: (1) a white librarian in an
all white area; and (2) a white librarian in an all black area.
The integrated areas in between are not always easy. Some-

times there are repercussions when one least expects a com-
plaint--such as the adult reader who complained about the
mother in The Snowy Day because she was fat....

Guidelines

There are two questions which a librarian might ask
herself when selecting books.   First, "How would I feel upon
reading this book if I were a black child?   Particularly an
inner city black child?" Second, "If I were to borrow this
book from the library, would I return to get another book
like it?"   These two questions can help to answer whether
this is a suitable book for either a white or a black child.
If it contains material inappropriate for a black child, it is
also unsuitable for a white child, for the white child would
derive from this book a distorted picture of a black child,
his emotion, his behavior, his background.

Any book, adult or children's, must first of all meet
the essentials of good literature along the lines of plot, content, theme, characterization, style, and format.   The Selection Policies for Children's Books of The Free Library of
Philadelphia includes the following statement under "Factors
to Be Considered in the Selection or Rejection of Books."

> In judging books, several factors blended with com-
> mon sense and experience in book selection must
> be kept in mind: (1) the literary quality of the
> particular title; (2) suitability in content and vocab-
> ulary for children through the eighth grade; (3) need
> for the subject matter.

Among factors which determine the exclusion of certain books for children are: (1) lack of good taste or sufficient literary merit; (2) an inaccurate, unfair, unhealthy picture of the subject....

Quoting again from The Free Library's book selection
policy concerning selection of books according to subject, under "Human Relations" the policy states:

> The library considers the removal of prejudice and
> ignorance regarding racial, ethnic or religious
> groups of peoples one of its major responsibilities
> and to this end makes a continuous effort to include
> in its book collection for children titles which will

foster healthy attitudes along these lines.   Books
on other countries, races, nationalities, and religious groups are carefully selected; and, in general those bearing serious discriminatory remarks or
attitudes are not purchased.   If possible, books on
these subjects are reviewed for accuracy by a member of the particular national, religious, or racial
group involved.

Points for Evaluation

I would like to draw from my own experience to cite
a few specific points of concern in selecting books with a
racial or integrated theme.

1. Approach

Does the author know black people well enough to
write about them?   Is he, himself, unbiased enough to interpret the content of his book with clarity and meaning?   Many
white authors fail in this matter without realizing why.   An
old Indian saying is "Never attempt to judge another man until you have walked in his moccasins."   Some of the least
successful books about Negroes written by white people have
been due to an attempt to write the story from the black
point of view.   (Some writers have succeeded tremendously:
Dorothy Sterling, Frank Bonham, Marguerite De Angeli, all
have possessed the necessary understanding of human nature,
perceptiveness for locale and relationships, and love of people of all kinds.)

Is the author so involved in conveying his message
that the plot is subjugated to his ideas?   Is the presentation
honest and unsentimental or is it overwritten to prove a
point?   Does the author realize the true feeling of his subject
or is the story the same old story he would have written of
a white child, but written with a "color-them-black" slant?
Does the book address itself to the white reader, leaving
the black reader with a left-out feeling?

2. Style of Writing

Is it dated as far as descriptions, attitudes, or incidents are concerned?   This does not refer to a book like
Margaret Strachan's Where Were You That Year?, about the
civil rights voting campaign in Mississippi, but to books

which may arouse resentment in the manner in which things
are told. A good book may be ruined for a child when he
reads accurate descriptions of all characters until he reaches
the black child and reads of his "flashing white teeth" or
hears him referred to as "the bug-eyed boy," or if the author assumes that black children feel that the darker they
are, the dumber they are, or if the author speaks of black
people as "darkies."

3. Characterization

Are characters offensively portrayed in any way or
are they shown in a realistic way? Not all Negro characters
must of necessity be good, or exemplary in behavior, but if
they are bad or cowardly, is there reason other than that
they are black? Is the hero in the story the Negro who most
nearly resembles white in appearance? Do the characterizations in the book misrepresent the Negro as a person in a
derogatory way which will insult him or give the child who
has never known a black person a mistaken impression of
the race? A minor character represented in an unkind or
degrading manner may seem inconsequential to a white reader, but may cause a black child to reject any other book by
that author. Do the characters act consistently and normally
or do we find a black boy sadly leaning on a fence while his
antagonistic white neighbor paints it black?

4. Language

Dialogue is very close to characterization. How do
the characters speak? Is the language natural and convinc-
ing? What about colloquialism and dialect?

Some mention of the Joel Chandler Harris Uncle Remus stories is appropriate, as they have been victim of condemnation in many library areas. Few children are capable
of reading the written dialect of the Brer Rabbit tales. Distinction must be made between Harris's sincere attempt to
preserve consciously the essence and language of the folk
tales of the southern Negro for posterity, and a book which
frames the dialogue of minority groups in dialect, colloquialism, and broken English as a display of the character's
ignorance or intellectual inferiority.

5. Illustrations

In books for children, illustrations supplement the

text in a way that is not as necessary in most adult books.
Many children judge a book by its illustrations. If these
portray abnormally proportioned, repulsive characters following the old stereotypes of books of past decades, children
are certain to reject the book.   Fortunately, most illustrators of today try hard to present a realistic image.   Children do not expect every character to be beautiful.   In fact,
they identify more readily if characters look more like people they are likely to meet in everyday life.   Sometimes,
illustration errs in subtle ways.   A recent picture book tends
to perpetuate the feeling of inferiority in children by the fact
that all persons in charge, all authority figures, are white.

6. Bias

This refers to bias or prejudice of the author rather
than of his characters, unless he is obviously using them to
express his own feelings.   "Happy plantation books" which
picture the Negro as happily accepting his lot in the South
fall into this category.   The librarian should ask himself if
the book is presented in an objectionable manner or whether
it instead respects the intelligence of the reader, and allows
him to make his own evaluation of the theme, the plot, the
characters and their actions, without false or forced morali-
zation on the part of the author.   Books selected for purchase should be those which broaden the child's horizons
rather than those which direct his viewpoints into narrow
channels.

These are some of the points I consider in evaluation
of books on blacks and integrated books.   I have not touched
on non-fiction in a specific way.   A great deal could be said
concerning selection of non-fiction, but inaccuracies in non-
fiction, condescensions and degrading statements, are more
readily recognized than in fiction.   The sin has been as
much one of omission as of improper coloring of facts--and
people.   Generations of black youngsters grew to adulthood
believing that the only part their race played in American
history was as slaves, lacking even the initiative to strike a
blow on behalf of their own freedom.   When the fact recently
was established that in the existing histories the black American's participation and contribution had been ignored, a major hurdle was overcome.   Hopefully, we will no longer discover books with such questions as "What jobs other than
porters can you think of that a Negro in your community can
hold?"   A sincere effort is now being made to include the
black American in his place in history in a way that will

foster pride in his own heritage and respect in the eyes of his white classmates.

I could talk with you about awareness and about sensitivity to change in the composition of your library public, in the reading abilities and interests of your library children, but these things, as librarians, you already know. The public library is one segment of the establishment which cannot reject change and remain static, or it signs its own death warrant. Book selection, too, is a changing thing; we are constantly modifying our book selection policy at The Free Library. Our replacement lists are yearly evaluated and changed. We get an increasing demand for books on blacks from our branches in both black and white areas. They ask for histories, black biographies, poetry, integrated picture books, specific people, and events. There is a demand for Ebony magazine, even among our youngsters. We find seventh and eighth graders of both races reaching ahead into young adult material for such meaningful titles as To Sir with Love (Braithwaite), Manchild in the Promised Land (Brown), A Raisin in the Sun (Hansberry)....

Children's Book Selection "Affects Eternity"

The selection of books for children is one of the most important responsibilities of the librarian, for children's minds are impressionable--ideas, attitudes, and ideals are being formed. The author, the publisher, and the librarian, in their key positions, must join together to help prevent old, time-worn prejudices from being carried forward into new generations. Children neither need books to foster antagonism, hatred, and militancy in the blacks nor to promote guilt feelings or distrust in the whites. This is a NOW generation. They are not responsible for the evils of the past. Children need books through which both blacks and whites can be educated to real life situations through accurate portrayal of life; histories and historical fiction which show the total picture, not a partial picture; and biographies that present people to whom children of all races can look for inspiration to live better lives.

Let us realize that the world is changing at a faster rate than it has at any time since the Great Flood. We can no longer hold fast to our old ideas of right and wrong, or of what is needed or not needed in our field of book selection. The violence, new ideas, unpredictable behavior, and restless-

ness of black people are all a part of the turbulence of
change.   The portrayal of the black in children's literature
is an important factor in shaping the end result of this change,
for everything that a child reads plays its part in forming the
adult which he will become.   It may be that our real and
only hope of survival as an undivided nation lies in our children.

So let us have books chosen by perceptive, understanding librarians, books which can help the black child to realize his identity, his individuality, his proud heritage, and his
great potential, books which can help the white child to recognize, understand, and appreciate the tremendous cultural
and historical contribution of his fellow Americans.   These
books should be read by black and white children--not as special books, but because they are good books, meeting the
basic criteria of children's literature and the rigid demands
of children themselves, and should be presented to children
as a part of their normal, everyday reading.

Only when America no longer feels the need of considering the black community as a separate and different part
of this country will Americans achieve their true potential as
citizens of a great and unified nation.

8. WHY MINORITY PUBLISHING?
    NEW VOICES ARE HEARD (Excerpts)

    Bradford Chambers, in collaboration with
    the Minority Publishing Committee of the
    Council on Interracial Books for Children

1) By Oswald White

The publishing industry reflects the attitudes, mores, and stereotypes of our society. Publishers are no more racist than the rest of society. They simply have the forum to project and protect endemic attitudes. I know too many fine people in the publishing industry to make any blanket indictment of the industry. The major problem seems to be a dereliction of the role of a publisher. The role of book publisher is different from that of a newspaper publisher. A newspaper publisher's primary duty is to report on the attitudes and behavior, a book publisher's primary duty is to shape attitudes and influence behavior.

For the three and one-half centuries of Black America's history [in the new world] black and white Americans have been forced to view history from the perspective of white America. We think it is about time that black America got a chance to tell its own story. It is not that we do not trust our white friends to tell the story for us. It is simply that we know he has problems in doing this, and anyway, we'd rather do it ourselves. It's a matter of perspective. I was taught American history from the English perspective and naturally had a different interpretation of the role of Benedict Arnold (a loyal collaborator) from that of Paul Revere (infamous rabble rouser).

Now, no one would accuse Great Britain of racism toward Americans. But one could well understand from reading "Expansion History of the British Empire," why Americans in the 1770's were not yet ready for the full exercise of such citizen rights as the ballot, community control or even more importantly self-government.

From an objective (English) perspective, George Wash-

ington comes across as the leader of a successful revolt
against constitutional authority--sort of a successful Nat Turner.   The Declaration of Independence is given as much respectability as the Black Panther Party Manifesto.   (As a
matter of fact, that Manifesto quotes the preamble to the
Declaration of Independence verbatim.)   The whole American
self-determination movement is French-inspired (the British
had their "communists" too), French-infiltrated and French-
supported.   Of course, the political, economic and social
problems which succeeded the British-granted Civil Rights
(sic Voting Rights cum Housing Rights, etc.) Bill of 1783
proved what the English had been saying for a long time.
Americans just were not yet ready for self-determination.
That's why English liberals were willing to do it for them.

A Liberal Perspective

Having seen history, literature and, in fact, everything else from an objective, liberal British perspective for
the first 21 years of my life, it was quite difficult to see
anything from any other.   It took a conscious effort not to
view George Washington as a successful Nat Turner.   Having
been immersed in this culture for the past 12 years, I can
now see things from the perspective of the American colonists.

No matter how liberal, sympathetic or committed the
Englishman, I do not think he could have made the impassioned speech of Patrick Henry or written the eloquent indictment of the Declaration of Independence.   Try as he would,
his frame of reference and the WASP British ruling class
would keep getting in the way.   Likewise, no white American
could articulate with the impassioned eloquence of Martin Luther King, Jr. and Malcolm X, the anguished heart-cries of
Black Americans.   To understand and to interpret the black
experience, one has to be black--permanently.   Six months,
a year, two years is not enough.   That's just like being a
prisoner of war when you know your side is winning.   Or
like a peace-corps volunteer.

Black publishers are in the unique position of being
part of both the larger white society and the subculture that
is Black America.   Being educated in the predominantly white
universities, living and working among members of the dominant white culture, we are molded and conditioned by that
culture to a degree.   But our frame of reference remains the

rich, pulsating, vibrant and exotic, part American, part Jewish, part Indian, part German, part English, mostly African
Black culture. We are, thus, doubly gifted and peculiarly
suited to fulfill our role as molders of attitudes and opinions,
like referees between two contenders.

As a youngster, I was taught to look upon the Black
leaders of slave rebellions as villainous cut-throats. I was
taught to identify with the wrong side. Of course, nobody
could call Jamaican slaves docile and happy (they had qualified too many white men for tridents and asbestos aprons for
that) so they made them always the villains of the piece.
Having been taught to revere cardinal Christian virtues, you
can guess with whom we identified.

Now that I am the father of three children, born in
this culture, I have a special stake in books that reflect
more accurately, the role that our people have played and
continue to play in the development and enrichment of life
and culture on this planetary playground, and being a publisher, I'd rather do it myself.

2) By Joseph Okpaku

A public may discuss an issue only if the issue is
given expression in the media. That thought which one keeps
only in one's mind is practically a non-existent thought. Giv-
en the dynamics of modern communication, that thought which
can only be presented by word-of-mouth is no more than a
private chit-chat. So that freedom of thought is not defined
by the ability to have a thought--something everyone has
anywhere anyway--but by the existence of a system which
permits the public (i.e., mass media) expressions of opinions
and perspectives identical, or at least reasonably similar, to
ours. Public information and education are not defined by
the freedom to buy the New York Times or PW, but by the
system's provision of such a variety of distinctly different
perspectives that the public cannot confuse interpretation for
truth, and bias for fact. Now, you and I cannot have a dialog if all we both have access to is your opinion--even if it
is your opinion of yourself, and your opinion of me (the hard-
hat); we still cannot have a dialog if you brought material to
include your opinion of my opinion of you, and your opinion
of my opinion of me (the white liberal). After all is said
and done, it is still all your opinion.

This is all we have today.   A Black book through a
white publisher is no different from the <u>New York Times</u> final
version of a dispatch from a Black reporter.   Now you will
rush to say, "Are you suggesting that white should publish
white and Black should publish Black?"   No.

When you talk of social intolerance and social frustration, you are talking about what ails the mass media, including publishing.   Think of a party at which one man does all
the talking, including his telling of your stories on your behalf with you standing right there.   If you can imagine it,
you will begin to understand minority frustration.   Better
still, if you can imagine it, you will begin to get an insight
into minority anger at white liberals.   A liberal is not a
white man who is not a racist beyond the point of possible
salvaging.   To a media-oriented minority person, a liberal
is a man who likes to do all the talking.   In this light, American publishing is <u>ipso facto</u> "liberal."   And that is why articulate minority people dislike it.

You ask me, what do I think?   Well, think of a situation in which we want a dialog.   Let us say we and the general public have access to your opinions, my opinions, your
opinions of me, my opinions of you, your opinions of my
opinions, and my opinions of your opinions.   Now, don't you
think we can begin to talk?   And if these sets of opinions
are brought to you and me as we both step out of the subway
at Times Square, instead of one set (your opinion) being
brought to you and me wherever we are, while on the other
hand we both have to go out of our ways to find the other
set (my opinions), don't you think we can begin to talk of
public understanding and public education?

So if you want to know why we all (Black authors,
white authors, Black readers, white readers, Black publishers, white publishers), if you want to know why we all need
many Black publishers, this is your answer.   A given society is as stable as it is informed.   And with publishing, as
it is today, we cannot say the American public is informed.
And if the American public is not informed, how can we expect it to be tolerant?   This is the position of what I am
tempted to call the "Black liberal."

PART II

RACISM IN NEWBERY PRIZE BOOKS

9. THE "REAL" DOCTOR DOLITTLE

Isabelle Suhl

This is the Year of Doctor Dolittle. Movie producers,
book publishers, manufacturers, promoters and publicists,
headed by Christopher Lofting, second son and sole literary
heir of Hugh Lofting, are trying to turn the little Doctor into
a new Davy Crockett. Many adults, writing reviews of the
film or of the many new versions and adaptations of the stories, deplore these efforts, worry that success may spoil Doctor Dolittle and take comfort from the fact that children can
still discover the "real Doctor Dolittle" in the original books
with Hugh Lofting's own illustrations.

Who is the "real" Doctor Dolittle? And what manner
of man is his creator, Hugh Lofting, who for more than
forty years has been hailed as a genius and his books as
"classics" by teachers, librarians and children's book reviewers? Rarely has a word of criticism of him or his
books been heard. As a result of careful examination of
four of the most popular of these books, I charge that the
"real" Doctor Dolittle is in essence the personification of the
Great White Father Nobly Bearing the White Man's Burden
and that his creator was a white racist and chauvinist, guilty
of almost every prejudice known to modern white Western
man, especially to an Englishman growing up in the last
years of the Victorian age, when the British Empire was at
its zenith. These attitudes permeate the books I read and
are reflected in the plots and actions of the stories, in the
characterizations of both animals and people as well as in
the language that the characters use. Editing out a few racial epithets will not, in my view, make the books less chauvinistic.

Consider the situation in The Voyages of Doctor Dolittle, the second of the books published (1922) and winner of
the 1923 Newbery Medal as "the most distinguished contribution to children's literature" in that year. In this story Doctor Dolittle, accompanied by Prince Bumpo, ten-year-old
Tommy Stubbins, Polynesia the parrot, Chee-Chee the mon-

key and Jip the dog, arrives on Spidermonkey Island off the
coast of Brazil in search of the "Red Indian" Long Arrow,
the world's greatest naturalist.   On his first day on the island, Doctor Dolittle rescues Long Arrow and a group of Indians entombed in a cave and brings fire to the heretofore
fireless Indians of Popsipetel.   This makes him so popular
that he is constantly followed about by crowds of admirers.
After his fire-making feat, this childlike people expected him
to be continually doing magic."   He continues to solve problem after problem for the Indians.   In consequence of his
good deeds they ask the "Mighty One" to become "not merely
the Chief of the Popsipetels ... but to be ... the King of the
whole of Spidermonkey Island."   Reluctantly he accepts, and
with elaborate and fitting ceremony he is crowned King Jong.

Brings White Man's Blessings

He becomes, of course, the hardest-working, most
democratic king in all history and brings his new subjects
many of the blessings of white civilization--proper sewerage,
garbage collection, a pure water-supply system, etc.   He
locates iron and copper mines and shows the Indians how to
use metal.   He holds court in the morning to settle all kinds
of disputes, teaches to thousands in the afternoon and visits
sick patients in the evening.   The Doctor would like to go
home, but the tradition of noblesse oblige hinders him.   He
realizes that "these people have come to rely on me for a
great number of things.   We found them ignorant of much
that white people enjoy.   And we have, one might say,
changed the current of their lives considerably.... I cannot
close my eyes to what might happen if I should leave these
people and run away.   They would probably go back to their
old habits and customs: wars, superstitions, devil-worship
and what not; and many of the new things we have taught
them might be put to improper use and make their condition,
then, worse by far than that in which we found them....
They are, as it were, my children.... I've got to stay."

His animal friends have different ideas.   Polynesia
the parrot "had grown very tired of the Indians and she made
no secret of it.   'The very idea,' she said ... 'the idea of
the famous John Dolittle spending his valuable life waiting on
these greasy natives!--Why, it's preposterous!"   When Polynesia gets an idea, she acts on it.   In a matter of a few
days she works out all the details of their departure, comes
up with all the answers to the Doctor's objections and even

succeeds in getting Long Arrow to urge the Doctor to leave.
With that the Doctor gives in.   Laying his crown on the
beach where his "poor children" will find it and know he has
gone, he heads back for England to carry on his "proper
work" of taking care of the animals of the world.

Kingdom of Fantippo

This adventure with the Indians was not the Doctor's
first experience at playing the Great White Father to ignorant
natives.   In Doctor Dolittle's Post Office, he served a somewhat similar function for the West African kingdom of Fantippo.   This book was the third to be published (1923), but in
time it takes place between the events in The Story of Doctor
Dolittle and the events in The Voyages.   In this story, he
does not become a king, but he does more for that country
while he is there than had ever been accomplished by the
reigning African king.   The Doctor's contribution is neatly
summed up at the end of the book:

> People who have written the history of the Kingdom
> of Fantippo all devote several chapters to a mys-
> terious white man who in a very short space of
> time made enormous improvements in the mail, the
> communications, the shipping, the commerce, the
> education and the general prosperity of the country.
> Indeed it was through John Dolittle's quiet influence
> that King Koko's reign came to be looked upon as
> the Golden Age in Fantippan history.   A wooden
> statue still stands in the market-place to his mem-
> ory.

The pre-Dolittle years of King Koko's reign were not
so "golden. "   In those days he occasionally made war on
other African tribes and took many prisoners.   Some he sold
as slaves to white traders if they offered him especially high
prices; others he kept for himself "because he liked to have
strong men at his court. "   He greatly admired the ways of
the "civilized world" and tried to copy and compete with it.
That was how he had come to set up a post office in the
first place, a most unusual thing to find "in a savage African kingdom. "   There were many false starts before he got
it functioning.   Then one day a "white man explained to him
a new craze for stamp collecting that was sweeping over the
civilized world, " and that was his undoing.   He immediately
shifted from selling stamps for mailing purposes to selling

stamps for stamp collections.   It was a profitable business
for his kingdom, but "the Fantippo mail service was neglected
and became very bad. "   That is why he had to invite Doctor
Dolittle to come to Fantippo and "arrange the post office for
him and put it in order so it would work properly. "

African King Ludicrous

The King is depicted, both in text and drawings, as a
ludicrous figure.   A very vain man, he always insisted--
before, during and after the Doctor's sojourn in Fantippo--
that the stamps for the post office "must all have my beautiful face upon them, and no other. "   He was usually found
"sitting at the palace door, sucking a lollipop--for he, like
all Fantippos, was very fond of sweetmeats. "   When he
wasn't sucking one, he used it as a "quizzing glass" to peer
through in the "elegant manner" of white men.   "But constant lollipops had ruined his figure and made him dreadfully
stout.   However, as fatness was considered a sign of great-
ness in Fantippo, he didn't mind that. "   When Doctor Dolittle
was ready to inaugurate his foreign mail service, it was
King Koko who brought the first letter to be sent off by the
Swallow Mail.   And to whom did he send it?   A friend of
his "who runs a shoe-shine parlor in Alabama"!   Even after
Doctor Dolittle's departure from Fantippo, "the excellent
postal service continued.... The stamps with Koko's face on
them were as various and as beautiful as ever, " including
one special one that showed "His Majesty inspecting his new
ships through a lollipop-quizzing glass. "

Characters All Childlike

The other African characters in this book fare no better than Koko from the pen of Mr. Lofting.   They emerge
as quaint, comic, childlike figures with simple minds and
ridiculous customs and funny-sounding names such as Chief
Nyam-Nyam, King Kakaboochi or the Emir of Ellebubu.
"Now the peoples of West Africa, " says Lofting, "have curi-
ous tastes in dress.   They love bright things. "   On the other
hand, because the weather is hot in Fantippo, the "black
men" there wear only a string of beads.   That is why the
Fantippo postman's uniform ends up being "a smart cap, a
string of beads and a mail bag. "   The Postmaster-General
was "a very grand man, who wore two strings of beads, a
postman's cap and no mail bag. "   To make the post office

operate properly, Doctor Dolittle has to get to it by nine
o'clock every morning, because if he didn't, "the postmen
didn't start working. "

        The animals, too, feel superior to the African people.
The Pushmi-Pullyu tells a story about a tribe of ostrich
hunters, the Badamoshis, who, "like most savage peoples,
are very superstitious.   And they are terribly afraid ... of
anything they can't understand.   Nearly everything they can't
understand they think is a devil. " He also complained of the
mean, "underhanded and deceitful" methods that "black peoples" used in hunting wild animals.   Cheapside the Cockney
sparrow is downright insulting.   He calls the Fantippans
"these bloomin' 'eathens" and derides their town because it
isn't like London.   He refers to King Koko variously as King
Cocoanut or Cocoabutter and to the town as Fantipsy.   He
preferred the company of two Cockney lighthouse keepers to
the Fantippans.   He said that "the faces of those two Cockney seamen were the best scenery he had looked on since
he had come to Africa. "

Most Outrageous Character

        In The Voyages, Chee-Chee the monkey returns from
Africa and recounts how he escaped from Africa by disguis-
ing himself as a girl dressed in clothes he had stolen from
"a fashionable black lady. "   The idea had come to him when
he saw "a lot of people, black and white, getting on a ship
that was coming to England. "   One of the children of a "big
family of funny people" reminded him of a cousin of his.
"'That girl, ' he said to himself, 'looks just as much like a
monkey as I look like a girl. '"

        The most famous of all Lofting's African characters
is Prince Bumpo.   He is at the same time his most outrageous creation, but apparently he was dear to the author's
heart because he is one of the few human characters to appear in several books.   He first appeared in The Story of
Doctor Dolittle and reappears as a major character in The
Voyages and as a minor one in Doctor Dolittle's Zoo.

Color Change Episode

        It is in The Story of Doctor Dolittle that the objection-
able episode about turning Prince Bumpo white occurs.   Brief-

ly, for anyone who is not familiar with it, the story is this.
Doctor Dolittle and his animal friends are on their way home
after curing the sick monkeys of Africa when they are captured for the second time by the King of the Jolliginki,
Prince Bumpo's father.   Polynesia the parrot slips out of
prison, sees Bumpo in the garden reading fairy tales and
overhears him say, "If I were only a white prince!" She
tells Bumpo that a famous wizard, John Dolittle, is in his
father's prison.   "Go to him, brave Bumpo, secretly ... and
behold, thou shalt be made the whitest prince that ever won
fair lady!" Then she rushes back to the Doctor and con-
vinces him that if they are to succeed in escaping prison he
must fulfill her promise, no matter what tricks are necessary to do it.   Bumpo arrives as planned and begs the Doctor to turn him white so that he can return to The Sleeping
Beauty who spurned him because he was black.   The Doctor
concocts a mixture of liquids which turns the Prince's face
white.   In gratitude, Prince Bumpo lets them out of prison
and gives them a ship in which to sail away.

   This summary merely suggests the objectionable nature of the episode.   It must be read in full to understand
the depths of Lofting's racism.   Every line is replete with
insults and ridicule.   Of course, this is not the only racist
incident in the book.   There are many others.   The treatment of Bumpo's parents, the king and queen, is as bad as
any described earlier.   It is impossible for Lofting to depict
Africans, be they kings, princes or ordinary people, with
dignity and genuine human qualities.   The thought obviously
never crossed his mind.   To him they are only vehicles for
so-called humor.

   I asked a Negro friend, who is very much concerned
about the portrayal of black characters in children's books,
to read The Story of Doctor Dolittle and give me her reaction to it.   Her response was so revealing and thought-pro-
voking that I am including a portion of it here in her own
words.

        In this book, black people are projected as being
    extremely gullible, naive, basically ignorant and
    certainly inferior.   This is, of course, personified
    in Prince Bumpo's desire to 'become white.' He
    is willing to sell out everything--even his father's
    authority--to 'become white.' For only if he be-
    comes white will he be able to achieve true and
    lasting happiness.   There is no happiness to be

found in his blackness--in his natural state.

Doctor Dolittle does indeed turn Bumpo white, but
does Bumpo ask how--and for how long?   What of
the effects on his skin?   We are given the answer
--of course Bumpo cannot ever be turned white
permanently.   Is this not a symbolic way of saying
that the black man can never be turned 'white';
that is, he can never be expected to acquire the
virtues, the acculturation, the degree of intelligence,
refinement of feelings, etc., that are the white
man's 'natural endowment.'   Is not Bumpo's a futile
search?   Is not the black man's quest of today also equally futile in light of the attitudes expressed
in Doctor Dolittle about Bumpo and the king and
queen?   Is not the book's ... great success a very
subtle reaffirmation of the basic concept of white
superiority?

Bumpo Appears Again

If the characterization of Bumpo is bad in The Story
of Doctor Dolittle, I maintain that it is worse in The Voyages.   Even defenders of Hugh Lofting have had to denounce
the racism of the white prince episode, but I have yet to see
or hear any serious criticism of The Voyages.   This book is,
apparently, sacrosanct because it is a Newbery Award winner.
I would like, therefore, to turn now to the treatment of Bumpo in this book.

Early in the story, Polynesia the parrot returns to
Doctor Dolittle's household after an absence of five years in
Africa.   One of the first questions the Doctor asks her is
about Bumpo.   Polynesia informs him that Bumpo is now in
England, studying at Oxford University.   The Doctor is naturally surprised.   Polynesia adds, "He was scared to death
to come .... He thought he was going to be eaten by white
cannibals or something.   You know what those niggers are--
that ignorant!"   [This quotation is taken from page 36 of the
official Lippincott edition.   The copy I used was the 35th impression, bought in 1965 for a branch of the New York Public
Library.   In the paperback edition published by Dell in November, 1967, the word "nigger" has been changed to "native."]   Polynesia continues her insulting explanation of why
Bumpo came to England.   Then the Doctor asks, "And The
Sleeping Beauty?--did he ever find her?"

'Well, he brought back something which he said
was The Sleeping Beauty.   Myself, I think it was
an albino nigeress. . . . '

'And tell me, did he remain white?'

'Only for about three months, ' said the parrot.
'. . . It was just as well.   He was so conspicuous
in his bathing-suit the way he was, with his face
white and the rest of him black. '

Insults Not Reproved

I must interject one comment here.   Polynesia speaks
in this insulting way about Bumpo and also directly to his
face on many occasions in all the books in which they are
together, and never does the "good, kind" Doctor object or
reprove her for even her bad manners, to say nothing of her
degrading attitude.

Shortly after this conversation, the Doctor decides to
go on the voyage to Spidermonkey Island, described earlier.
He is looking for just the right person to be the third man
of his crew.   One day when he is on the ship preparing for
the journey, a visitor appears on the gangplank.   He "was a
most extraordinary-looking black man. "   He "was dressed in
a fashionable frock coat with an enormous bright red cravat.
On his head was a straw hat with a gay band; and over this
he held a large green umbrella.   He was very smart in
every respect except his feet.   He wore no shoes or socks. "
Who is this apparition of sartorial splendor?   Why, of course,
none other than "Bumpo Kahbooboo, Crown Prince of Jolliginki"!   (In both name and attire, does he not call to mind
that other Lippincott "classic" Little Black Sambo?)   He has
come to offer himself as the much needed third crewman.
When the Doctor asks what will happen to his studies and
his university career, he replies that he had intended to take
a three-month "absconsion" anyway and that by going with
the Doctor he will not be neglecting his "edification" since
the Doctor is a man of "great studiosity. "   So the Doctor
agrees to take him along.

Prince Turned Cook

From this point on, both in The Voyages and Doctor

Dolittle's Zoo, Bumpo speaks only in malapropisms--once
more, the ridiculous African trying to be white, this time by
unsuccessfully imitating the speech pattern of a cultured, educated Englishman.

On first glance the interracial nature of the crew
might be construed as a positive contribution to race relations, but the opposite is true. Once the voyage is underway,
Bumpo, African prince and Oxford scholar, is consigned to
the stereotyped role of cook for the rest of the crew. Despite his age and college training, he is, at best, only on a
par with ten-year-old Stubbins, the other crewman. On
Spidermonkey Island, both of them help with the teaching of
the Indians, but just "simple arithmetic and easy things like
that. " Only the Doctor can teach the advanced subjects.

In his characterization of Bumpo, Lofting has missed
few of the colonial Englishman's views of the "savage" nature of Africans. In tense, dangerous situations Bumpo is
seen as a man of great brawn, little brain and brute violence.
He is ready to resort to murder to save his friends. When
an obstreperous able seaman turns up as a stowaway who
has been eating up the ship's store of salt beef, Bumpo suggests to Polynesia that while the seaman is asleep, they
"strike him on the head with some heavy object and push him
through a port-hole into the sea.... " Polynesia vetoes the
idea, saying, 'No. We'd get into trouble. We're not in
Jolliginki now, you know--worse luck!" In Doctor Dolittle's
Zoo, the Doctor is just about to be kicked by a man named
Throgmorton. Bumpo rushes to the rescue and lifts the man
up "like a doll. " Fortunately, the Doctor intervenes just in
time. "For the Crown Prince of the Jolliginki was apparently just on the point of knocking Mr. Throgmorton's brains
out on his own doorstep. " Bumpo begs to be allowed to
eliminate this "useless" man, but the Doctor refuses.
"You're not in Africa, now, Bumpo. Put him down.... "
On another occasion in The Voyages he threatens to "choke
the life out of" a Spanish taximan if he refuses to obey certain orders. There is even one suggestion of cannibalism
as a solution to a problem. Polynesia worries that they
have no money with which to replace the salt beef the stowaway ate. "'Would it not be good political economy,' Bumpo
whispered back, 'if we salted the able seaman and ate him
instead?'" Polynesia again reminds him that they are not in
Jolliginki, and besides, "those things are not done on white
men's ships. "

Extravagant praise has been heaped on Lofting's illustrations. Many are, indeed, delightful, but in my estimation,
all the drawings of Africans are as insulting and offensive as
the text. They are nothing more than grotesque caricatures.
In combination with the text, they serve no other purpose
than to make children laugh at those silly, funny-looking
black people.

The Dolittle books have already had a long life and a
wide circulation which is rapidly growing wider. Several
million have been sold in English alone. The Story of Doctor Dolittle was published in 1920, went into twenty-three
printings in ten years and has been translated into twelve
languages. It is now in its 52nd printing in the official Lippincott edition. Only recently Dell-Mayflower published it in
its "complete and original text," but without any Lofting illustrations. Lippincott keeps all twelve titles in print, and
Dell has so far reprinted the first five books in paperback
in a boxed set and as separate books to sell at the very accessible price of 60 cents per book. All twelve titles have
appeared on numerous lists of recommended books for children, including one published by A Special Committee of the
National Congress of Parents and Teachers and the Children's
Service Division of the American Library Association, Let's
Read Together: Books for Family Enjoyment (2nd edition,
1964). At least two prominent list makers have excluded all
the titles from their lists. Nancy Larrick does not include
them in either her Parent's Guide to Children's Reading (Revised edition, 1964) or A Teacher's Guide to Children's
Books (1960). Josette Frank of the Child Study Association
has dropped them from her latest edition (1968) of Your
Child's Reading Today.

Lippincott's Treasury

Of all the many new Dolittle books issued by several
publishers to tie in with the release of the movie last December, I wish to comment on only one, Lippincott's Doctor
Dolittle: A Treasury. The publisher's foreword describes
at great length their pride in being the publisher of the Dolittle books and their responsibility to make sure these books
are "always readily available to all children everywhere" and
"to preserve the heritage of Hugh Lofting as he left it."
They claim the purpose of the Treasury is to "bring more
children ... to Doctor Dolittle than could the twelve separate
books" and "to serve as an invitation to the later ... reading

of the twelve original volumes. " They further assert that
the material in the Treasury is "just as Hugh Lofting wrote
it. " This is not exactly truthful. The book contains excerpts from eight of the twelve Dolittle titles and was very
carefully edited by Miss Olga Fricker, sister of the late
Mrs. Hugh Lofting. Nowhere in any of the selections does
Bumpo appear, although the distorted portrait of Bumpo still
appears on the reproduction of the original title page of The
Story of Doctor Dolittle, which is included. That whole book
has been reduced to fifteen pages. The largest excerpt is of
The Voyages (104 pages), but no longer is there a "third
man" in the crew. Where the excerpt chosen makes it necessary, Bumpo's original role is assigned to one of the
other characters, animal or human. Miss Fricker seems to
understand better than her publisher that it is no longer possible to publish a Lofting story "just as he wrote it. "

All adults who have any connection with the world of
books for any age level are dedicated to the idea that good
books, especially great creative literature, can have a profound and positive influence on the lives of their readers.
Many of us are especially dedicated to providing books for
children that are literary and imaginative in form and that in
content promote and foster better understanding among peoples. If good books can help combat racial prejudice, as
many of us believe they can, then is it not also true that
some books can and do promote and foster racial prejudice?
Must we not then be as willing to combat such books as we
are to promote the others, even if those books have been
called "classics"?

This well may be the Year of Doctor Dolittle, but it
is also the Year of the Riot Commission's report to the
President, in which white racism was clearly and sharply
charged with being the main cause of last summer's race
riots. In the light of that report and of the earlier Supreme
Court decision on desegregation of schools, which pointed out
that making white children feel superior to black children
was as damaging to white children as the reverse was true
for black children, what justification can be found by anyone
--and I ask this particularly of those adults who still defend
Lofting--to perpetuate the racist Dolittle books? How many
more generations of black children must be insulted by them
and how many more white children allowed to be infected
with their message of white superiority?

When will we ever learn?

10. SOUNDER: A BLACK OR A WHITE TALE?

Albert V. Schwartz

In a recent exchange of letters with George Woods,
the New York Times children's book editor, Julius Lester
wrote: "When I review a book about blacks (no matter the
race of the author), I ask two questions: "Does it accurately present the black perspective?" "Will it be relevant to
black children?"

Since the book Sounder by William H. Armstrong
(Harper and Row) has achieved prominence as the 1970 re-
cipient of the coveted John Newbery Medal award for the
year's most distinguished book for children published in the
United States, it merits literary analysis from many points
of view. Lester's two questions represent an ideological approach, and it is from this approach that I wish to analyze
Sounder.

Shelton L. Root, Jr., reviewing the book for Elementary English (May 1970), states: "As important literary social commentary, Sounder cannot be faulted." Root feels
that the injustices of the story will leave the reader "both
indignant and guilty." This commentary is typical of the reviews that have appeared by white critics for white audiences.
Surely this response by white people played a paramount role
in the book's selection for the Newbery medal.

Whose Story Is It?

Mr. Armstrong states in his Author's Note that the
actual story was told to him by a teacher, "a gray-haired
black man." The note continues: "It is the black man's
story, not mine ... It was history--his history." Thus the
author claims authentic Black history originating in the perception and intelligence and "soul" of the Black teacher,
casting the white author in an entirely passive role as the
tale is written. This claim, while undoubtedly made in good
faith, does not bear up under examination.

89

Tom Feelings, in the Spring 1970 issue of Interracial Books for Children, questioned whether a Black man could freely talk to a member of his oppressors at the time the story was first told.   Mr. Feelings stated that a story of the Black Experience must come directly from one who has lived it.   Authenticity or syntheticness would hinge upon that life experience.

Style--White and Black

The style of Sounder is white fundamentalist; the words, imagery, and philosophy are simple, direct, and interwoven into the story are occasional religious tales offering hope of a "heavenly sanctuary. " By contrast, the Negro Spirituals-- "Swing Low, Sweet Chariot" and "Steal Away to Jesus"--embody a struggle for freedom and a hope for a better life here on earth.   The music of Sounder's family is more the "white spiritual" than "blues. "   Black language, a vital and historic means of communication for the creation of a story of Black people, is totally absent.

Whose fault is this?   Did the Black teacher talk the language he thought the white man understood?   Would it be that the white man who listened failed to hear the subtle tones that were spoken to him?   Or is it possible that Sounder is a highly commercial package at this time in synthetic garb?

No Name, Except for the Dog

Why is no one in the sharecropper's family identified by a name, except the dog, Sounder?   The mother is simply "mother, " the father, "father, " and the youth, "boy. "

This would be an acceptable literary device in the hands of a Black author.   For a white author to resort to it immediately raises the issue of white supremacy.   Within the white world, deep-seated prejudice has long denied human individualization to the Black person.   At the time of the story's historical setting, white people avoided calling Black people by their names; usually they substituted such terms as uncle, auntie, boy, Sambo; or they called every Black person by the same name.   The absence of name helped to avoid the use of the polite salutation.

In Sounder, did the Black storyteller really narrate
the story without names?   Or was the unconscious racism of
the white transcriber of the tale actively at work?

Suffering, but Silent

Within the institution of white supremacy, Black people are supposed to express no resentment and suffer in silence.   Black militancy today is forcing whites to consider
Blacks as human beings, but at the time the story took place,
white people assumed that Blacks were incapable of such a
human emotion as suffering.   In the literature of the Southern Tradition, Black people suffered, if at all, in silence.

In Sounder, only the dog expresses reaction and bitterness.   The author actually calls the dog a "human animal."
When the father is taken away by the sheriff, the dog angrily
rushes in pursuit, and by that expressive act risks its life
and is shot.   The mother, the boy, and the other children
say and do nothing.   They are impotent, or at least made
so, by the teller of the story.   What if the boy had reacted
and expressed anger, as he probably did in actual life?
Then the writer might have had to deal with Black "activism"
--perhaps even a Black Panther.   While this might have in-
trigued the literary creative taste of a Black writer, one can
see why a white author would hesitate to construct a forceful
anti-white image.

Compare the forceful reaction of the children when
their dog is taken away!   The innuendo here seems to be
that Black children care more about their animals than their
parents.   Or is it that the institution of white supremacy
permits Black children to show human response to animals
only?

W. E. B. Du Bois wrote The Souls of Black Folk in
the same historical setting as Sounder.   Here is how Du
Bois presented the Black sharecropper: "I see now that rag-
ged black man sitting on a log, aimlessly whittling a stock.
He muttered to me with the murmur of many ages, when he
said: "White man sit down whole year; Nigger work day and
night and make crop; Nigger hardly gits bread and meat;
white man sitting down gits it all.   It's wrong."

Never once in Sounder do you meet the white owner
of the land.   The oppression results from the poverty of the

land and the cruelty of the penal institution.   Yet the father
is crushed, not by the mean prison guard, but by a chance
"act of God."

True to the white Southern fundamentalism of the author, the "boy" meets up with no activist.   His hope lies in
getting an education.   Suddenly, after his father is taken
from him, the boy manages to go to school, where he studies
the words of Montaigne.   "Only the unwise think that what
has changed is dead," says that author.

These words the boy is to contemplate "years later,
walking the earth as a man."   The message for the Black
youth in the story is from Montaigne!   What irrelevance!

Sounder's family is isolated; there is no relationship
with other Black people, except an occasional preacher.
The Bible stories the Black mother tells are exclusively
white Baptist fundamentalism--and very racist.   Her Bible
stories have none of the qualities of Black Biblical interpretation, and so we hear the mother telling her son: "Some
people is born to keep.   Some is born to lose.   We was
born to lose, I reckon."   (Italics added)

The mother in the story is the Black stereotype of the
Southern Tradition.   Toward her children she shows no true
feeling, no true compassion--strictly a Southern interpretation of Black motherhood.   After her son makes great sacrifices to go to school, she even discourages him from going.
After he has searched for his dog for hours, she admonishes
him coldly: "You're hungry, child.   Feed yourself."   This
mother is divested of "soul," a quality a Black writer today
would assuredly have given her.

When Lerone Bennett, Jr. wrote a criticism of William Styron's The Confessions of Nat Turner, he made this
statement about white writers emasculating Black families:
"First of all, and most important of all, there is a pattern
of emasculation, which mirrors America's ancient and manic
pattern of de-balling black men.   There is a second pattern,
which again mirrors the white man's praxis, a pattern of
destructuring the black family ..."   Bennett's statement ap-
plies equally to Sounder.

In the light of an analysis of Sounder, I, for one, respond negatively to the two questions posed by Lester:
"Does it accurately present the black perspective?" and

"Will it be relevant to black children?" I wholeheartedly affirm Lester's next contention: "The possibility of a book by
a white answering these questions affirmatively is nil. "

11. RACISM IN PRIZE-WINNING BIOGRAPHICAL WORKS

Donnarae MacCann

The Newbery prize in children's literature was awarded in 1951 to the fictionalized biography, Amos Fortune,
Free Man (1950) by Elizabeth Yates. Reviewers stressed the
book's "deep religious feeling" and "deep, serene faith," but
their criticism would have been more valid had it stressed
the book's deep-seated racism. This element can be found
in one form or another on nearly every page, and it is ironi-
cal that racist passages are often linked with religious references.

The book tells the life story of Amos Fortune, a
slave in New England during the 1700's who late in life buys
his own freedom. Beginning with the chapter on Amos' capture in Africa we find the author claiming a divine intervention on behalf of the slavers. Amos' docility is described
as if it were a demand of God: he prayed and "the voice of
the land gave answer...." This "voice of the land" told him
as he rode down a river in chains that "this was the time
of birth, the time of renewal." Its inspiration made him go
to sleep rather than make the rescue attempt that Miss
Yates says would have had a fair chance of success.

Describing this capture later on, Amos makes the divine intervention even more explicit: "My hand was re-
strained [from resisting and killing the slaver] and I'm glad
that it was, for the years between have shown me that it
does a man no good to be free until he knows how to live,
how to walk in step with God."

Throughout the biography Africa is depicted as a pa-
gan country, as a place where one could not possibly "walk
in step with God." Amos is even described as feeling somewhat elated by the opportunity to leave his homeland. The
author tells how he suffers from the hunger and wounds in-
flicted on him, and then how another sensation takes over:

> But more than all that he felt something expanding
> within him: a strange feeling that rose to meet

94

> the new world his eyes were absorbing.   It was as
> far from elation as it was from fear, yet it was a
> compound of each.   He who had known nothing but
> jungle now found wonder stirring in him that there
> was a world beyond.

This confused idea, that slavery was beneficial because it led
Africans to Christianity and a "new world," runs through the
entire narrative.   (It's hard to see how Amos' experiences
in American churches provided any illustration of genuine
Christianity.   He was forced to sit in special segregated sec-
tions of the church all his life; and when, at the age of 78,
he was permitted to join a local church, a church elder commented: "What a pity he isn't white.... He could do much
for the church. ")

The author's descriptions are condescending, but beyond that they make the African appear almost sub-human.
For example, after the captives have been waiting for just
three weeks in dug-out pits, receiving rations once a day,
the author says "they had turned into merchandise ... and stood
in a long patient row, like animals trained at last to obey
commands. " In a few more weeks they are said to have
lost their power of speech as well as memory.   After Amos
is shown attempting to communicate with his tribesmen, the
author explains their failure to respond:

> They had been made to forget--not only that they
> were At-mun-shi but that they were men.   They
> made sounds to each other in the darkness of the
> hold, but they were only sounds, they had no
> meaning.

In a very short time the captives supposedly lost even their
ability to recognize Amos, their chief.

Nowhere is there shown any typical human behavior--
conversation, memory, speculations about the future, worry
about family members left behind, plans for escape.   Nor is
the reader given any of the factual, well-documented information about slave resistance involving such tactics as mu-
tiny and suicide.

When information about Amos' tribe is given, it is on
a superficial level and in conformity with stereotypes.   For
example, the author explains that it was the tradition in this
tribe to look up to "someone older and wiser as a protector."

At the time of capture they "ran across the clearing trying
to reach their chief who stood above them in strength and
power, symbolizing protection.... They knew that he would
care for them. "

There is no context provided in which the reader can
understand this tradition in relation to other complex traditions, religious beliefs, economic necessities, historical evo-
lution and so on.   Dependency on a leader is a characteristic seen in total isolation, and in this way given an exaggerated importance that supports the stereotype of alleged African childishness and immaturity.

Descriptions of Amos after his arrival in America
make him appear animal-like or sub-human also.   His owner's wife "bade the boy come and like an obedient dog he followed her out of the room. "   He "squatted on the floor and
grinned up at her. "   His owner discusses with his wife the
possibility of giving Amos his freedom, but remarks:
"...in his untamed state it would not be well to give it to
him too soon.... He is part animal now.   What would he do
but run wild?"

Later in the story Amos is shown to behave in a childish manner.   For example, when he recognizes the financial
need of a white customer, he offers him money asking only
for his customer's "go-to-Meeting-hat in exchange. "   The
customer was "glad to have his [clothes] press cleared of
useless clutter. "   Then Amos prays "Thank you kindly,
Lord,... for all my fine clothes.   Violet's going to be mighty
proud when she sees me in them.... "   The original owner
of the clothes describes Amos in these terms: "[The clothes]
caught his fancy like a child's.   But that's what they are,
those black people, nothing but children.   It's a good thing
for them the whites took them over. "   The author never re-
futes nor discusses this statement nor treats it with irony.
It is left as if it were part of the author's own impression
of Amos.

George M. Fredrickson's recent book, The Black Image in the White Mind, shows the 19th century stereotype of
the black American to have included these traits: docility,
submissiveness, loyalty, cheerfulness, childishness.   In addition, blacks were supposedly musical and "peculiarly susceptible to religious experience. "[1]   Strangely enough, a contradictory set of traits was attributed to them at the same
time.   Professor Fredrickson notes that the attitude toward

the free Negro in the North also resembled the attitude held
toward drunkards and infidels. One colonial journalist was
referring to blacks when he wrote: "There is a point beyond
which the peace of society cannot permit the increase of the
elements of commotion. "[2]

In Miss Yates' characterization of Amos, he manifests
an exaggerated degree of submissiveness long after he is
free. At one point, when attempting to buy the freedom of
his second wife, Amos plays no part in the bargaining at all;
rather he thinks: "nor was it for him to question Mr. Bow-
ers' decision. " This submission earned Amos the prefix
"Mr. , " which by the end of his life often "dignified his
name. " "He had won his way to equality by work well done
and a life well lived. " The idea that some people must win
equality, that only their docility and hard labor will achieve
for them the right to the title "Mr. , " is one of the most
fundamental racist concepts in the book.

The stereotype of perpetual cheerfulness is created by
repeated references to singing, dancing and smiling.   Perhaps the most absurd example is when Amos stands upon the
auction block; according to the author, "It amused him to
hear himself described and he grinned broadly as he listened
to the auctioneer's words. "

Attitudes ascribed to Amos about freedom and slavery
seem contradictory.   The At-mun-shi tribe was said to cher-
ish freedom, and yet we are told that the Quaker family that
first owned Amos periodically offered him his freedom over
a fifteen-year period and he always turned the offer down.
This is hard to comprehend since Amos at the same time advised his fellow Africans to "wait for the free day" rather
than plot to achieve their freedom.   What "free day" did he
have in mind?

As an explanation, the author tells us that Amos' attitude was different from the attitude of other blacks, a contrast which may have seemed commendable to white readers
at the time this biography was written.   "It [the white man's
attitude toward Amos' skin color] did not trouble or vex him
the way it did some of the other slaves with whom he met
and talked.   It puzzled him.   But then, there were many
things to puzzle a man. " Amos seems to classify racism
alongside the "puzzles" of nature, as if it were just an oddity
and not a moral and social evil.

A similar false estimate of slavery is presented when
one of Amos' owners dies and the widow, in addition to granting Amos immediate freedom, suggests that he establish the
owner's tanning business as his own. Although Amos had
been literally slaving over this business for years, he
"smiled with delight," but refused; "...he had his own pride
and he would accept nothing without fair payment." There
is no mention of the fact, and apparently no realization, that
Amos' whole life and labor had already been given in "fair"
payment--that more had been given than could ever be re-
paid.

As the Revolutionary War approaches, slavery is never discussed as a contradiction to the spirit of that colonial
rebellion.   Rather Amos is given by the author the warped
view that freedom is something you buy with money.

> Amos knew he was never too old to wage his own
> war for freedom in his own way, not with guns or
> valor but hard-earned coinage, buying manumission
> and giving it before it was too late for one he
> loved to die in honor.

The author tells of Amos' struggle to buy freedom for the
three wives he has during his lifetime; but she never refers
to the fact that manumission is part of the institution of
slavery, not a means for combating it.

Perhaps what basically underlies the contradictions
about freedom in this biography is the conviction that dignity
and status can be found only in association with the white
community and culture.   Miss Yates writes:

> As the working member of the Copeland family,
> Amos had his own dignity.   Apart, he would en-
> dure the separateness he knew many of his African
> friends endured because of their lack of status in
> the white man's world.

To say that slavery in a white family is more dignified than
freedom, that it is preferable to "lack of status" as defined
by slave-holders--this argument has more than one destructive element.   It claims a false dependence on whites, and
even worse, it suggests a denial of black identity.

Rejection of identity appears in various ways throughout the book.   One instance is the scene where Amos notices

his old age. He sees his image in a looking-glass, and his
look of surprise is interpreted in these words: "Perhaps he
thought he was white until he saw himself in the mirror. "
Mrs. Richardson shook her head. "Perhaps, but it's more
than that. " The author never rejects the racist implications
of this appraisal. She merely uses the incident as a plot
point, for Amos had been searching for the sister captured
with him in Africa and realizes now that the search is hope-
less--his sister has inevitably grown old like himself.

Several chapters describe Amos' relationships with a
destitute black family. He wants to offer financial assistance,
but his wife Violet says they are "shiftless" and wants the
children to work rather than receive charity. (What work
would be given to children to support a family of six, and
with what remuneration is never discussed.) In the end, with
the family broken up and one child dead, it is suggested that
this was all God's will, that Violet was right and was in fact
under divine guidance.

In more specific terms, this is what happens in these
scenes. Violet wants Amos to buy twenty-five acres of land
with his savings, and she hides the money so he may not use
it to aid this "undeserving" black family. In response to
this theft Amos thinks: "What right had she to oppose him?
Yet it was he who had given her freedom. The word was
meaningless unless in its light each one lived up to his highest and his best. " Even the youngest readers of this biography must be puzzled by this interpretation of freedom and
living up to one's "best": the freedom to deceive one's husband and take exclusive control of the family savings.

Finally the oldest child of the neighboring family is
bid upon in a public auction and taken into the Fortune home
as a servant, but by this time she is so weak and ill she
soon dies. The author describes this event in purely positive terms: "Peace dwelt in her face, a smile hovered over
her lips.... " Then Violet says to Amos, "You've set Polly
free to die happy. " Free in this case is freedom from poverty, the condition this child is forced to die out of, since
Violet made it impossible for Amos to help her family while
there was still hope for its survival.

A case of divine guidance is suggested at this point in
the story. When Violet decided to hide Amos' savings, she
was worried "but something was giving her strength. " Then
as the child is dying Amos prophesies, claiming to see in

her eyes "what was ahead for us": "I've not seen until just
now.... It's good, Violet. It will be worth the waiting
for...." A great destiny for blacks in America is somehow
predicted from the face of a child dying of starvation and
neglect.

The author's statements about this whole series of
events reveal an attitude that stems from the 19th century.
Referring to the failure of New England abolitionists to carry
through the reforms they supposedly advocated, George Fredrickson writes:

> In refusing to [acknowledge]...that most blacks in
> the North as well as in the South were so acted
> upon that there was comparatively little they could
> do to improve their own situation in the ways that
> whites recommended, the abolitionists revealed how
> their underlying commitment to an individualistic
> philosophy of moral reform prevented them from
> perceiving the full dimensions of the American race
> problem. [3]

"Moral reform" in this context refers primarily to
economic progress, to the accumulation of wealth through in-
dustrious competition with your neighbor. Amos Fortune's
wife Violet is made the spokesman for this philosophy when
she insists that the problem in Polly's family is "shiftless-
ness." The author then emphasizes the point by making
Violet's decisions appear God-sent. Amos represents this
viewpoint when, at nearly sixty years of age, he agrees to
buy himself and is glad that his freedom is "achieved by his
own efforts and not through the kindness of any man."

Perhaps something should be said here about the words
put into the mouths of historical characters in children's
books. Many biographical works for children are given the
same kind of fictional treatment we find in Amos Fortune,
Free Man. Events are presented as direct happenings and
it is the author's prerogative to imagine what the characters
would be likely to say and do in the face of these happenings.
The genre includes this technique as a legitimate literary device, but this doesn't mean total license for the author.
The conversations he invents must be credible in view of
what is known about the historical period and event. The
author has the responsibility to show, with as little distortion
as possible, what it felt like to live under certain conditions.
Furthermore, he must make his own response to attitudes

and happenings clear. The narrator's voice adds a great
sense of legitimacy to the ideas presented to a child audience,
whether the work is a fictionalized biography or a biographical novel. The shades of difference between these genres is
slight, and to the child reader probably non-existent. Therefore the writer for children needs to be in some respects
like the kind of teacher described by Jeanne Walton in the
periodical Interracial Books for Children: "...the teacher
needs to accept whatever children have to express, but she
must let children know where she stands. She cannot be
detached or uncommitted. "[4]

In Amos Fortune, Free Man, even if the sayings attributed to the hero could be documented as fact, we are
left with these sayings unchallenged and unexplained by the
author. Her position seems to be one of support for the
ideas voiced by Amos and other characters--the idea that
slavery can be legitimate, that blacks are childish, foolishly
docile, passive, submissive, dependent, easily turned into
speechless "merchandise, " unequal unless they earn equality,
and so on.

But the author is not alone in supporting these assumptions. The history of the book--its reception over the past
twenty years--indicates that thousands of librarians, critics,
and educators have supported them also. Miss Yates was
apparently a very accurate spokesman for her times.

The question now should be, where does the book
stand today? Is it placed on lists of recommended books?
Is it retained in children's collections or moved to research
libraries dealing with American social history? Unfortunately, it is not yet considered a mere artifact for scholars.
It is referred to as a "heroic saga" in the New York Public
Library's comprehensive bibliography, The Black Experience
in Children's Books, published in 1971.

On another influential list, The Negro in Schoolroom
Literature, the annotation reads "highly recommended. "
This list, in its fifth printing in 1970, is published by The
Center for Urban Education, a corporation supported by the
United States Office of Education.

The next Newbery prize-winning book about slavery
was a biographical novel, I, Juan de Pareja by Elizabeth
Borten de Treviño. It was published fifteen years after
Amos Fortune, Free Man, yet it expresses the same white

perspective and contains many of the same attitudes.

Only the setting is different: slavery in Spain rather
than America. Juan de Pareja served in the household and
studio of the Spanish court painter Velazquez, and his story
is cast as a first person account of what slave life was like.
Having the protagonist narrate his own story increases the
illusion of authenticity, and the author's views reach the
child with a great intensity. Amos Fortune was made to
speak for himself often in the Yates book, but now all the
ideas are presented as personal drama and with a sense of
immediacy.

A few quotations will show the general position the
author takes toward slavery. As in the Amos Fortune book,
we find the idea that liberation is something that must be
earned--unless of course one belongs to the ruling class in
the first place. The slave, Juan, receives his freedom after
nearly a lifetime of servitude to Velazquez, and this is how
he describes the event:

> I seized his hand, to carry it to my lips.
>
> "No, no," cried Master, snatching his hand back.
> "You owe me no gratitude, my good friend. The
> contrary. I am ashamed that in my selfish preoc-
> cupations I did not long ago give you what you
> have earned so well and what I know you will
> grace with your many virtues."

In several passages religion is used to rationalize and
render less offensive the institution of slavery. For example, a church friar tells Juan there is much good that he
can do in the world and Juan disputes this because of his
slave status:

> "I am only a slave...a servant," I complained,
> feeling sorry for myself.
>
> "Who is not?" asked Brother Isidro, briskly. "Do
> not we all serve? In any case, we should. That
> is nothing to be ashamed of; it is our duty."

Later in the story Juan describes the dwarfs and
freaks kept at court to amuse the king and relates this conversation with one of them:

"We are brothers," he used to say to me in his
strange, deep voice like a man's, "you and I, because we are enslaved by reason of the way we
were born. You were born strong, a fine normal
being, but black. I was born as I am, a man in
the body of a little creeping child. Why did God
put this burden on us, Juanico?"

"To make us humble, maybe. Our Lord was de-
spised and rejected, you remember. He himself
told us so. And He said, 'He who exalts himself
shall be brought low, and he who humbles himself
shall be lifted up. '"

The self-defamation in this passage is never refuted.
Indeed, the author supports and rationalizes it with an inappropriate line of Scripture--inappropriate because humility
has meaning as a virtue only when exercised voluntarily.
Under the institution of slavery, where a person's life is not
his own, humility cannot be the same as when expressed voluntarily by Jesus.

The author depicts Juan's enslaved life as one of bliss
after he arrives at the house of Velazquez. Freedom, she
claims, is not important to him. He was mistreated by a
gypsy during his journey to the city of his new owner and
therefore says: "Freedom? I had had a taste of it on the
road, and it was cruel to a black boy. "

There is just one exception to Juan's good estimate of
slavery as a way of life, and this has to do with painting.
"I had not really been sad to be a slave, except for not being able to paint. Every life has some drawbacks. "

Is giving up an entire life of free choice and action
just one of those little "drawbacks" that everyone must experience? This suggestion resembles Amos Fortune's alleged view of racism as just one of those "puzzles" of which
there are many "to puzzle a man. "

Contentment in slavery is referred to numerous times
in this story of Pareja: "... in all except that little nagging
wish to paint, I was content, having every reason to look
forward to a pleasant and comfortable life. " If slavery is
this satisfying, or as the writer says, something God ordains
to make us more humble, the child reader must wonder why
people have been so disturbed about it, have argued against

it so vehemently, gone to war over it, objected to its appearance under Naziism and Stalinism and so on.

But only the illegality of painting by slaves disturbed Juan.   It was strictly forbidden under Spanish law for a slave to engage in the arts, and Pareja is in anguish over this throughout much of the story.   Finally, after Juan confesses he has broken this law, the painter Murillo tells him that the law is morally invalid anyway.   Juan then comments on Murillo's attitude:

> In his simplicity, he saw intent as the very essence of the law and could not accept the idea that I had been at fault.

Murillo asks Juan:

> "Is it a sin, then, to paint?"

> "But I am a slave!"

> "Is it a sin, then, to be a slave?"

> "No.   It is an injustice.   But I am a religious man.   I do not expect justice here on earth, but only in heaven.   And I am not a rebellious slave. I love Master and Mistress. "

This is a classic example of white perspective: the claim that blacks have no expectation of justice or a good life here on earth; that they are entirely forgiving, even loving the slaver.   In particular cases this affectionate bond may have developed, but to generalize in this way about Pareja, without any documentary evidence, is to distort history.   The author cannot know that Pareja "loved Master and Mistress," and since it was not customary or natural for the slave to love the slaver, the reader's encounter here is simply with a bias on the side of the slaver.

The most tragic thing about this book is the author's failure to deal with slavery realistically.   She doesn't even seem to be aware of what it is--aware that it denies man his inherent right to make choices, to express his own talents and individuality freely, to have relationships with equals.   Neither Velazquez nor Pareja seem to be conscious of the injustice in their relationship, to see that a normal human association cannot be based on domination.

Juan isn't freed at all until a dramatic complication
arises which forces Velazquez to grant it. His slave has
been caught red-handed, breaking the law against painting,
and only the sudden granting of Juan's freedom will enable
Velazquez to keep him from being taken away and prosecuted.
By making Pareja his assistant, Velazquez in effect keeps
him performing the same services he has been performing
as a slave for years. The king assures Juan after Velazquez' death that the great artist regretted not giving Juan his
freedom sooner. And Juan is willing, according to the author, to think of it as just an oversight! "I never held it
against him that he had been forgetful."

At the end of the book, the author's Afterword includes this statement:

> ...the threads of the lives of Velazquez and Pareja
> are weak and broken; very little, for certain, is
> known about them....
>
> Facts of which I am certain are the bonds of deep
> respect and affection which united Velazquez to his
> sovereign, and, with equal strength, to his slave,
> whom he freed and named his assistant.

This claim would have more credibility if the novel
contained some awareness of how respect and affection depend, at the most fundamental level, upon a respect for human rights. The provision of food and shelter says little
about a deep consideration of others, for these essentials
are no more than what a household pet receives. The asser-
tion in the Afterword that "those two [Velazquez and Pareja]
...began in youth as master and slave,...and ended as
equals and as friends" is not supported in the preceeding
176 pages, for Velazquez never respects Pareja sufficiently
to be sensitive to his needs or wishes. He frees him only
under the stress of circumstances. He sees Juan's "place"
as that of a slave and nothing more. The author clearly intends to show how black and white can live together happily
and peaceably; but she never suggests that it is only without
slavery or domination that this is possible. Equality is mentioned in the last sentence of the Afterword, but never even
glimpsed in the course of the novel itself, never shown as
something valued by the major characters. In this account
of a master-slave relationship, Velazquez can do no wrong,
and his domination of Pareja is therefore presented to the
young reader as something good.

Books like Amos Fortune, Free Man and I, Juan de
Pareja may conceivably be useful to scholars in tracing the
varied manifestations of racism.   But why do librarians still
call them good reading for children?

Notes

1.   Fredrickson, George M.   The Black Image in the White
      Mind; The Debate on Afro-American Character and
      Destiny, 1817-1914.   Harper, 1971, p. 103-106.

2.   Ibid, p. 8.

3.   Ibid, p. 40.

4.   Walton, Jeanne.   "The American Negro in Children's
      Literature," in Interracial Books for Children, Vol.
      1, No. 4, Fall, 1967, p. 6.

PART III

MORE MODERN EXAMPLES

12.   THE CAY: RACISM STILL REWARDED

Albert V. Schwartz

Rather than praise for literary achievement on behalf of "brotherhood," The Cay by Theodore Taylor (Doubleday 1969) should be castigated as an adventure story for white colonialists to add to their racist mythology.   That the major review publications[1] and the five organizations[2] that gave it literary awards--one even for "brotherhood"--so totally misinterpreted The Cay's meaning supports the charge that children's book publishing is indeed a racist institution.

The Cay is the story of the initiation of a white upper-middle-class boy into his superior role in a colonialist, sexist, racist society.   Colonialist, because the people of Curacao and most other people of the Caribbean Isles, where the story is set, are "owned" by outside white powers, which is taken for granted by the author as an acceptable way of life. Sexist, because the only woman in the story is a weak, subservient mother, whose very weakness sets in motion the boy's adventures.   Racist, because the white boy is master and the Black man is subservient throughout the story.   It is incredible that in a book for children today, any writer would be so racially insensitive as to put a Black man in the role of subservience to a white boy--a servant who risks his life for the boy and, in the end, sacrifices his life so the white boy may live.

Specifically, the story is about eleven-year-old Phillip Enright, who is marooned on a small island (a cay) with an elderly West Indian, Timothy (no last name).   Phillip, who relates the tale, has been living in the Caribbean because his father is an oil refining expert on loan to the Royal Dutch Shell from a U.S. company.

The first half of the book sets Phillip up as a young Southern cracker.   The reader knows from the outset that the boy's bigoted remarks are deliberate and that the author will slap Phillip down.   Phillip early in the book declares that his mother was brought up in Virginia and that "she didn't like them."   The "them" are Black people.   Of the

108

Black Timothy, says Phillip, "[his] smell was different and
strong." The Black man's appearance, says Phillip, "is
very much like the men I'd seen in jungle pictures. Flat
nose and heavy lips." Phillip recoils from the touch of Timothy.

Midway in the book Phillip undergoes a conversion--
or so the author would like the reader to believe. This is
the "character growth" of young Phillip that is supposed to
contribute to the literature espousing "brotherhood." If Phillip's racist attitudes were to undergo substantive change,
were Phillip really to have his consciousness raised and
grow in human understanding as a result of his close association with Timothy--all well and good. But this just doesn't
happen. All that changes in Phillip's growth is a shift in the
direction of his racism.

Binnie Tate in an article dealing with authenticity and
the Black experiences in children's books (School Library
Journal, October, 1970) states that, from the Black point of
view, "the author fails in his attempt to show Phillip's
growth in human understanding."

Phillip's "conversion" stems from loss of eyesight after he is shipwrecked, and he comes to depend on Timothy
for help and protection. The conversion comes when Phillip
--remember, now, he is blind--lies down next to Timothy
and says, "[Timothy] felt neither white or Black." Soon he
is saying that Timothy is "kind and strong." Then comes
the question: "Timothy, are you still black?"

Elsewhere in Interracial Books for Children, Ray Anthony Shepard contrasts the interpretations of the Black experience by two author/illustrators, one white and the other
Black. Mr. Shepard makes the point that the stories of the
white author/illustrator are oriented toward the liberal in-
sistence on human similarities and sameness, whereas the
Black author/illustrator celebrates the ethnic differences of
Blacks.

In this light, consider the implications of Phillip's
question to Timothy: "Are you still black?" Phillip is really saying that in order for him to have warm feelings toward
a person, that person must be white. Instead of having
Timothy answer loud and clear, "No, I am not white, I am
Black," he has Timothy disappearing into anonymity.

True to the liberal absurdities of a bygone age, the
New York Times book review of The Cay made this comment
on Phillip's question: "Phillip ... realized that racial consciousness is merely a product of sight." What a racially
unaware remark that is!

One thing we are certain about. Phillip won't grow
up to march with a Martin Luther King (to whose memory
The Cay is dedicated). On the contrary, Phillip will return
to the Islands and, following in his father's footsteps, he
will become a leader in the system that exploits the "natives."

Near the story's end, when Phillip has successfully fulfilled his initiation, he puts on a verbal blackface: "Dis
b'dat outrageous cay, oh, Timothy?" In the end, the white
boy is given control even of the Black man's language!

We will be hearing a lot in the months and years to
come about "Black language." One thing Black language is
not is verbal blackface, and that is the use of apostrophes
and abbreviated word forms to stereotype the language of
America's non-white minorities and, to some extent, its
lower-class whites. The use of apostrophes and abbreviated
word forms is a shoddy literary device used to connote inferior status under the guise of authenticity.

We have said very little about the Black servant. At
the story's beginning and through to its conclusion, Timothy
is very much the invisible man. We know more about him
by omission than by commission. We know that he is good,
kind, generous, resourceful and happy. We know that he is
well schooled in oppression and colonialism. He is very
much aware that the system dictates he call a white boy
"Young bahs." Only when the white boy no longer is afraid
of his servant is Timothy given permission (which is granted,
not assumed) to call the white boy by his first name. Phillip at eleven knows much history. The considerably older
Timothy knows no history. When asked about Africa, Timothy answers: "I 'ave no recollection o' anythin' 'cept dese
islands. 'Tis pure outrageous, but I do not remember anythin' 'bout a place called Afre-ca."

Outrageous? Yes. What should outrage all of us is
that the book's author, its editor, and its publisher should
foist upon our children such an image of a Black man today!

Not only is Timothy denied his color by the act of a

white boy's "conversion. "   He is denied parents, family, children.   He is denied all social ties except one, and that single tie is with a white boy, for whom in the end he is denied his life.

Notes

1. Marilyn B. Singer, School Library Journal; Paul Heins, The Horn Book; Polly Goodwin, Book World; Charles Dorsey, New York Times.

2. Jane Addams Book Award, Lewis Carroll Shelf Award, Commonwealth Club of California Literature Award, Southern California Children's Literature Award, Woodward School Annual Book Award.

13. A NEW LOOK AT OLD FAVORITES:
CHARLIE AND THE CHOCOLATE FACTORY

Lois Kalb Bouchard

It has been seven years since the publication of Charlie and the Chocolate Factory by Roald Dahl (Alfred A.
Knopf, N. Y. , 1964). Since it is still a widely selling children's book, a discussion of its racism in not inappropriate
now. Despite the fact that the Black characters are treated
in an approving manner, whereas several of the white characters are treated harshly, the racism consists of the time-
dishonored stereotypes, childishness and dependency upon
whites, with which the Black characters are presented. (The
Black characters are exploited as workers and dehumanized,
and they are presented en masse with group characteristics
only.)

In this fantasy story, the owner of the chocolate factory, Mr. Willy Wonka, has to find factory workers who
will not steal his candy-making secrets. He finds a tribe of
"miniature pygmies" about the height of a man's knee in "the
very deepest and darkest part of the African jungle where no
white man had ever been before. " It seems to me that the
West has been treated to "dark Africa" too many times and
that it is racism to perpetuate the myth and image of darkness. The people Wonka finds are called "Oompa-Loompas,"
a name that I find offensive because it tries to make fun of
African language sounds. And they are incompetent in jungle
living--they are "practically starving to death. " Wonka (the
Great White Father) saves the Oompa-Loompas by taking
them back home and giving them work.

Wonka offers the Oompa-Loompas cacao beans for
their meals and wages. The fact that the Oompa-Loompas
are delighted and willing to accept the beans shows their
childishness and gullibility. But Wonka says about himself,
"You don't think I live on cacao beans, do you?" Beside
loving candy, the Oompa-Loompas are always laughing. Although they are spirited, they are presented as lacking dignity, as getting "drunk as lords" on butterscotch and soda
and "whooping it up. "

112

The Oompa-Loompas are musical. However, giving
the Black characters the intelligence necessary to write
songs hardly suffices to alleviate the stereotype. The American slaves, too, were musical, and jazz has long been acknowledged a cultural contribution without raising the whites'
esteem for Blacks. The fact that the songs of the Oompa-
Loompas contain the morals and messages of the book is on
the credit side, though (and speaks against any charge that
the author is being deliberately racist). It may not be to the
point that I am made uneasy by the fierce moralism of the
book as embodied in the songs, and that the Oompa-Loompas
seem like Furies:

>   Veruca Salt, the little brute,
>   Has just gone down the garbage chute...
>   We've polished off her parents, too.

Since I do not share an enthusiasm for dumping people down garbage chutes as punishment, I find the Oompa-
Loompas rather like self-righteous children-Furies, little
bogymen. The songs lessen the weight of the book's racism
perhaps, but only momentarily, because after the songs, the
Black characters recede again to childishness, dependency
and dehumanization.

Parenthetically, I dislike these lines from one of the
songs:

>   ... And cannibals crouching 'round the pot,
>   Stirring away at something hot.
>   (It smells so good, what can it be?
>   Good gracious, it's Penelope.)

The name "Penelope" suggests a white girl; the term
"cannibals" suggests Blacks. I find it unfortunate that the
lines are there. Still another miscellaneous racist note is
the fact that the rich girl and her father refer to an Oompa-
Loompa character as "it" instead of "he." The author may
have intended to disparage the father and daughter by their
use of the neuter pronoun; however, leaving such a thing
questionably in the air is, at best, insensitivity.

As workers in the factory, the Black characters are
exploited. The owner clicks his fingers sharply when he
wants a worker to appear. The Oompa-Loompas are made
to test various kinds of candies, sometimes with unfortunate
effects. For example, one man sprouts a beard that never

stops growing.   The only comment on this is, "In the end
we had to use a lawn mower to keep it in check!   But I'll
get the mixture right soon!"   The following example is worse
still:

> "I gave some to an Oompa-Loompa once out in the
> back yard and he went up and up and up and disap-
> peared out of sight!   It was very sad.   I never
> saw him again."
>
> "He should have burped," Charlie said.
>
> "Of course he should have burped," said Mr.
> Wonka.   "I stood there shouting, 'Burp, you silly
> ass, burp, or you'll never come down again!'   But
> he didn't or couldn't or wouldn't, I don't know
> which.   Maybe he was too polite.   He must be on
> the moon by now."

It cannot be said that the Oompa-Loompas are treated
any worse--in a satiric or caricature sense--than the white
characters.   The white children suffer fates, in my opinion,
far worse than their vices deserve (the girl who chews gum
turns purple and remains purple; the T.V. watcher is ten
feet tall at the end).   But the children's parents are concerned about their fates, and the children suffer individualized fates.   But a Black man floats away to his death stupidly silent, and no one among his family or friends misses
him, as far as the book is concerned.   The Oompa-Loompas
are still laughing.

The paternalism toward the Black workers is given a
resounding finale.   Says Mrs. Wonka: "Someone's got to
keep it (the factory) going--if only for the sake of the Oompa-
Loompas..."   It is this ending to the book that makes clear
the racism present throughout.   The entire plot is based on
Wonka's quest for an heir--he has invited five children to
his factory so that he can choose one.   No Black child is a
contender, although there are 3,000 Black people, many of
them children, inside his factory.   He searches the outside
world for a child to become the owner.   And although in the
story he searches the "whole world," only preponderantly
white-populated countries--Russia and England--are mentioned
by name.   The children who find the golden admission tickets
are never designated white in words, but the Oompa-Loompas
are designated Black, and the illustrations show white children.   Thus, the implication is that Black characters are for-

ever dependent upon the white boss.   I believe this message comes across in a particularly strong manner, because it is not verbalized and yet the whole plot rests upon it.   (If someone should say that the Oompa-Loompas are ruled out as heirs due to their size, not because of their color, I must answer that this is not what comes across.) I suspect, also, that in our cultural context of racism, the small size of the Black characters becomes a symbol of their implied inadequacies.

14. THE PERSISTENCE OF UNCLE TOM:
     AN EXAMINATION OF THE IMAGE OF
     THE NEGRO IN CHILDREN'S FICTION SERIES

Paul C. Deane

Bette Banner Preer believes that since about 1940, and definitely since 1945, the Negro in children's fiction has been losing his stereotype.

> The familiar Negro character who is too meek, too lax, too superstitious, too eager to be content with "leftovers" which society has to offer, is slipping into the background ... In the earlier books there was a definite attempt to show the Negro boy and girl content with his lot in life, accepting defeat, unambitious, menial, inferior in all respects.[1]

What she says may be true of certain children's books; hopefully it is. But she does not read the series, and that fact is especially significant, for the fiction series--the Bobbsey Twins, the Hardy Boys, Tom Swift, and the like--by any standard, dominate children's reading from grade two to grade six, when children are between seven and twelve. Inexpensive enough to be bought by children themselves, readily available in Five-and-Ten's, supermarkets, and drug stores, and widely traded, they have a huge reading public, the extent of which can only be guessed. They are also the one major kind of children's reading designed to be read by children themselves, not by adults; hence adult censorship and expurgation are not generally possible.

During the entire history of the children's series since 1899 (the year that the Rover Boys first appeared), the image of the Negro has not changed. He lost his dialect in the 1950s, and certain descriptive or identifying words with unpleasant connotations ceased being used at about the same time. But these are superficial changes; his position in society, his general character, and his personality have never really varied.

The change in the use of dialect is dramatically re-

vealed in the Bobbsey Twins.   Since the series began in
1912, the Bobbsey family has had Dinah, a cook, maid, and
mammy, and her husband, Sam, a handyman and driver.
When the family visited Washington in 1919, Dinah's dialect
was as strong as that of Uncle Remus: "What's aa dish
yeah I heah Nan say? ... What you gone and done to yo' l'il
broth' an' sistah?"   Sam's is identical: "I'll put back de
hay fo' yo' all.   'Tain't much, an' it won't take me long. "
By 1953 Sam was speaking quite differently: "Well, I don't
know ... Folks say that if a horseshoe is thrown so that it
lands with the two ends pointing toward you, that means
good luck. "   (The Horseshoe Riddle, p. 1).   When the Bobbseys went to Pilgrim Rock in 1956, Dinah used the phrase
"mighty careful"; that was as close as she ever came to dialect again.   Clearly, phonetic spelling had disappeared; both
Dinah and Sam put g's on words ending in ing; "yo'" has become "you"; d's are now th's.

Until the 1950s, when agitation for civil rights became
a major issue in the United States, the Negro in children's
fiction always spoke in dialect.   In the earliest series with
which this study was concerned, The Rover Boys, the Rover
family had a Negro servant, Alexander Pop.   Aleck never
lost his dialect or even modified it ("yo' is a sight fo' soah
eyes, deed yo' is, " he says in The Rover Boys in the Mountains), despite his having lived in the North for decades.
The dialect seems an element of race, not geography.   When
the Rover Boys actually went into the South (The Rover Boys
in Southern Waters), they found that all Negroes used dialect.
Almost a quarter of a century later in 1924 (The Rover Boys
Shipwrecked), Aleck was saying, "Can't say as I's much
younger, but I ce'tainly doan feel no older. "

The Tom Swift series introduced a comic Negro, Eradicate Andrew Jackson Abraham Lincoln Sampson, always
called Eradicate, because he eradicated dirt.   Like the
Rover Boys, the Tom Swift series lasted until 1930, and as
long as Eradicate was in it, he spoke dialect: "Suffin's
gwine t' happen, " he says early in Tom Swift and His Motor-
cycle (1910); later he adds, "I trabled all ober and I couldn't
get no jobs. "   By 1928, Eradicate declares: "An' ef I
kotches de feller what done planted it I--" (Tom Swift and
His Talking Pictures).

Eva Knox Evans discovered that even Negro children
are conditioned to expect Negroes to speak in dialect in the
pages of books.   Her book Araminta's Goat was read to her

kindergarten class as she was writing it; not until the final
book appeared could the class see that Araminta was a Negro:
the illustrations revealed the fact.   The children protested
that Araminta did not speak as Negroes are supposed to speak
in books.   When it was pointed out that the class, all of
whom were Negro, did not speak in dialect, they answered
that in books colored people do. [2]   Other writers, Adelaide
Rowell, for instance, feel that "dialect is the folk flavor in
the speech of all people of all nations."[3]   Since the early
1940s, controversy has existed over dialect in juvenile literature.   It is practically gone from series books, and since its
use in these books was almost invariably degrading--it was a
source of humor and an indication of inferiority--one is in-
clined to applaud its passing.

The Bobbsey Twins began two years after Tom Swift,
in 1912, and introduced Sam and Dinah immediately.   Their
dialect lasted until the year 1950, when a new version of
volume two, In the Country, re-written and published in that
year presented Dinah suddenly without dialect; in fact, her
speech in general underwent a considerable transformation:
her grammar also improved.   By 1953 her speech was in-
distinguishable from that of white characters.   Negro dialect
is heavy in Bunny Brown and His Sister Sue in the Sunny
South and in Grace Harlowe's Overland Riders Among the
Kentucky Mountaineers, both published in 1921.   In the former, Bunny and Sue meet a porter on the train who tells
them, "De do' am done closed," and a Negro woman at their
destination warns a boy playing in the street by saying, "Dat
freshy l'il niggar suah will be splatter-dashed."   On Grace
Harlowe's trip South, she and the Overland Riders pick up
Washington Washington, whose dialect is incredible: "He
war peekin' at yuh-all, an' when he seed ah sawed him, he
snooked an' ah didn't sawed him no moah."   His speech is
twice imitated by Emma Dean, who also shies a pebble at
him.   In both cases, fun is made of him because of his manner of speaking.

Negroes in the Hardy Boys books Hunting for Hidden
Gold (1928), The Sinister Sign Post (1936), A Figure in Hiding (1937), and The Twisted Claw (1939) all speak in dialect;
all of Sue Barton's Negro patients in Visiting Nurse (1938)
do also; and in the Nancy Drew series, Negroes, when they
appeared, spoke in dialect through the 1940s and as late as
The Mystery of the Tolling Bell (1946).

If his speech has undergone change and improvement

in the last seventeen years, the Negro's position, his role in society, his character and personality have not. In the first volume of the Bobbsey Twins, Flossie has a Negro doll named Jujubl; she used to explain to her friends, "He doesn't really belong to the family, you know. " Indeed, so secure were authors and publishers of series that children would recognize Negroes by their jobs that they often did not bother identifying the race. In The Twisted Claw, a Hardy Boys mystery, for example, a Negro is merely called "the porter," but the work he does, his dialect, and the fact that he calls Joe and Frank "massa" meant that no one was expected to miss the point. This situation occurs under identical conditions in another Hardy Boys book, Hunting for Hidden Gold.

Negroes have remained servants and slaves, always in inferior positions. They are porters in Herbert Payson's Boy Scout series, the Hardy Boys, and Nancy Drew; they are maids and cooks in the Bobbsey Twins (in volume one, Sam and Dinah lived "in some pleasant rooms over the stable"); they are handymen and butlers in the Rover Boys; and they are mammies in Bunny Brown and the Bobbsey Twins; in the Grace Harlowe series they are ineffectual servants, ranch hands in the Honey Bunch books, laborers and cleaners in Tom Swift; Negroes are elevator operators and grease monkeys in the Rover Boys books; they are washroom attendants in Nancy Drew and Don Sturdy books. As late as 1953, Sam was still saying, "I can help my folks [i. e. , the Bobbseys] in and out of coaches. " Dinah was called "the faithful servant" in 1942 (Land of Cotton), and when the Bobbseys go South to visit Colonel Perry, they find that "everyone was fond of the 'master,' as he was affectionately called; they also learn that "We all depend on [Mammy] Liza here at Great Oaks. " Bunny Brown and his sister, Sue, also find a mammy, Mammy Jackson in The Sunny South. Both Don Sturdy (Port of Lost Ships) and the Rover Boys (In New York) were called "boss" and Tom Swift was "Massa Tom" all through his series.

As Negroes are awarded inferior social and occupational status, so are they supplied with traits of character and personality calculated to develop their inferiority further. By way of example, when Sue Barton takes a job as a visiting nurse, she is sent, in chapter eleven, to Harlem. "You'll love working with colored people, " she is told. "They're so willing to cooperate, and so eager to learn. " Sue concludes that "she was not there to exploit the colored people, or to be grandly feudal, but to help them stand on their own feet. "

Yet she persists in treating the families to whom she is assigned like children or babies, and they respond by saying,
"Yes, ma'am.   Thank you, ma'am. "   On the Bobbsey Twins'
trip South in 1942, they found that all Negroes "had a re-
spectful word or smile for Colonel Perry. "

If they appear as subservient to Whites, Negroes are
also presented as lazy, ignorant, good natured, cowardly;
they are consistently patronized.   In Sue Barton, Visiting
Nurse they have "enchanting black babies. "   Dinah smiles
and grins through fifty-eight volumes of the Bobbsey Twins:
In the Country shows her as "full of fun"; the Twins are carried to bed in Land of Cotton by "a smiling Negro butler";
and when they awaken next day, "one thing that interested
the Bobbseys was the large number of Negroes they saw
about the place.   All looked healthy and happy"; the face of
Dinah's Aunt Emma "was crisscrossed with wrinkles that
made it seem as if she were smiling all the time. "   Bunny
Brown and Sue, also visiting in the sunny South, meet "a fat,
jolly-looking colored woman, " Mammy Jackson; and their
father says, "I'll see if I can get one of these easy-going
colored boys to drive me uptown. "   A Negro applicant for a
housemaid's position in Nancy Drew and the Mystery Inn arrives "dirty, slovenly in appearance and [with] an unpleasant
way of shuffling her feet when she walked ... answered in an
unsatisfactory manner. "   Washington Washington in the Grace
Harlowe book Among the Kentucky Mountaineers is the most
offensive portrait of a Negro in any series.   He is dirty and
refuses to wash; he is futile and stupid in emergencies;
throughout the book he is an abject coward.   Aleck Pop, the
Rover Boys' servant, is invariably fooled by plays on words
and by the most basic references, his ignorance being revealed thereby.   And Eradicate Sampson in the Tom Swift
series is so abysmally stupid as to be only a caricatured
comic fool.

None of these pictures of the Negro is improved by
the terms which, until the 1940s, were liberally applied to
him.   They shock a modern reader, but the completely mat-
ter-of-fact tone with which they are delivered suggests that
they were taken for granted by writers and readers.   "Nigger" is quite common.   It may be used as part of a phrase,
such as "nigger in the woodpile, " as it is in The Boy Scouts
at the Panama-Pacific Exposition, or directly applied to a
Negro, as in Don Sturdy in Lion Land, and in the Tom Swift
series, where Eradicate calls himself "nigger" frequently;
the term may be found as "They told us you had to make

them work like niggers" in The Rover Boys on Land and Sea;
when Bunny Brown is in the sunny South, a Negro woman
refers to a young Negro boy as "dat fresh l'il nigger."

Sometimes the word is used in dialect, as "niggah,"
the manner used by Washington Washington to refer to himself in Among the Kentucky Mountaineers. A Negro is called
"darky" twice in Bunny Brown and His Sister Sue in the Sunny South and twice in Tom Swift and His Motor Cycle, where
he is also called "coon" twice, and he is a "black rascal"
in Tom Swift and His Airship. An amazing irony arises in
The Bobbsey Twins in the Country, as that book was re-
written in 1950 to bring it up to date, according to the author's claim in the Preface: in the revision, dialect was
practically removed, but in one scene, a pigeon is described
as making a noise like "see-de-coon, see-de-coon." Negro
children are referred to as "pickaninnies" in the Grace Harlowe series.

Other means of debasing the Negro's status are accomplished by the use of certain stereotypes, a device which
further equates all Negroes. The majority of Negro women,
for example, are fat: Dinah and her Aunt Emma, Mammy
Jackson, are only two. Dinah and Sam have "kinky heads"
in The Bobbsey Twins at the Seashore, and they love water-
melon. Eradicate Sampson carries a razor as a weapon of
defense in Tom Swift and His Airship. Washington Washington plays the harmonica.

There are three notable exceptions to what has been
said--the number is absurdly small; one is an attempt to remove some of the onerous clichés mentioned above; one
other, an attempt to individualize the Negro by making him
a villain. The first occurs in Sue Barton, Visiting Nurse,
"All the apartments [of Negroes] were clean ... They had a
tradition of cleanliness and were proud of it. An apartment
was seldom cluttered ... no speck of dust lingered anywhere." After the Hardy Boys are attacked by three criminals in Hunting for Hidden Gold, suddenly two Negroes appear: the same criminals had earlier run over their chickens.
One is "an enormous Negro"; he and his friend proceed to
beat up the hoodlums; throughout the scene they act fearlessly
and with considerable ability. The only use of Negroes as
villains occurs in a late Tom Swift book, Tom Swift and His
Talking Pictures (1928). There Tom is captured by two Negroes and taken to see some movie moguls who wish to steal
Tom's television machine. They speak well, without dialect--

in fact, their language is superior to that of the heroes.
Tom is so struck by the fact that "the language of the Negroes was above the average"--note the assumption, however
--that he comments on it: "They did not talk like poor old
Eradicate. Rather their talk was that of the man who has
seen service in wealthy families. " (Note also that although
they can learn from Whites, Negroes are still servants.)

    Only one attempt is made to portray the Negro's hous-
ing situation realistically. This occurs in Sue Barton, Visiting Nurse: "The moment a Negro family moved into a tenement, the rent would go up. "

    In general, then, the Negro, with one exception, is
never presented in a children's series as bad, so of course,
he can never really be good. Never is he allowed to develop
as a real character, a real person; instead he is revealed
always as a century-old cliché.

    Children, as Ruth Viguers points out in her contribu-
tion to A Critical History of Children's Literature, are not
aware of racial, national, or religious intolerance; economic
and social fears that create intolerance in the world of adults
are not natural in the world of children. Clearly, however,
children may take attitudes and prejudices that they see displayed, and as Spencer Brown put it, children's books may
become a "fertile breeding ground for prejudice through
stereotypes. "[4] Eleanor Nolen is even wiser in pointing out
that the prejudices and attitudes a child forms through reading may be more serious than actual contacts with minority
races. The child, for example, may never know a Negro
except through the pages of a book. "The place to combat
race prejudice is with the child's first books and first social
relationships. "[5] Except for removing dialect, the series
books are maintaining the traditional image of the Negro.

Notes

1.   Bette Banner Preer, "Guidance in Democratic Living
       through Juvenile Fiction, " Wilson Library Bulletin,
       XXII (May 1948), 680.

2.   Eva Knox Evans, "The Negro in Children's Fiction, "
       Publishers' Weekly, CXL (October 18, 1941), 650.

3.   "Negro Dialect in Children's Books, " Publishers' Weekly,

CXL (October 18, 1941), 1556.

4. Spencer Brown, "The Dilemma of Liberal Censorship,"
   The Education Digest XXX (September 1964), 4-6.

5. Eleanor W. Nolen, "The Colored Child in Contemporary
   Literature," The Horn Book, XVIII (September-Octo-
   ber 1942), 349.

15. CRISPUS ATTUCKS, BOY OF VALOR:*
A BOOK REVIEW[1]

Jean Dresden Grambs

It is not usual to accord a lengthy review to a book
written for 4th or 5th grade students in American schools.
This is unfortunate. Public and school libraries have shelves
of such books; the market is good and is growing with each
new injection of Federal money.

One portion of this market, growing faster than any
other, are books which have anything to do with Negroes, today or yesterday. The volume reviewed here is a 'natural'
for enjoying a wide and profitable market; for young children,
it is a book about a Negro whose name occurs in American
revolutionary history, but is not controversial. Thus, we
are teaching Negro history and can tell Black Power leaders
to hush.

Many educators, white and Negro, are justly critical
of American history for its continuing distortions of the history and influence of Negroes, both individually and as a major ethnic group. We are naturally eager that these distortions be corrected, the blank places filled in, and the appropriate data reported accurately. In an effort to overcome
the ignorance of Negro and white teachers and historians,
new books and articles devoted to Negro history, African his-

---

*Editors' Note: Ironically, reviewer Jean Grambs criticizes
author Dharathula Millender for distorting history and showing "how happy slaves were with their New England masters;"
while in another article in this anthology, Dharathula Millender criticizes Harper's Weekly and other publications for this
stereotype: "the 'true Negro' ... is of a contented and happy disposition ... docile-unambitious .... " Perhaps some of
the problems in this biography of Crispus Attucks arise from
the widespread tendency of children's book authors to over-
simplify and idealize history. They employ a literary con-
vention which is of questionable value. "

tory, or biographies of Negroes are appearing at a great rate. It is to be hoped that librarians and educators will see to it that these volumes take their place with other works on American history, and that the data reported become a standard part of students' historical study of America from the very earliest grades.   Hopefully, too, textbooks will reflect balanced versions of the African, British, and Spanish Caribbean backgrounds of American Negroes, a more realistic view of the demeaning aspects of slave life prior to the Civil War, a reasonable as well as accurate discussion of the Reconstruction period, and a balanced report of the struggle by Negroes and other ethnic minority groups to gain full access to the privileges and responsibilities of American citizenship.

The contribution of the book reviewed here, however, is a major disservice to these commendable goals.   Works of this kind assign to history a dubious name in education and to the Negro an equally dubious role in American life.   To change our sentimental view of the past it is one thing to present authentic, historic material, but it is quite another matter to twist or invent material.   That the Negro has been ignored or lied about in American history does not justify our telling other historical lies to repair the damage.   Unfortunately, that is exactly what Millender does in her "biography" of Crispus Attucks.

Despite the absence of historical data regarding Attucks' life, Millender reconstructs a complicated family, complete with conversations purporting to show how happy the slaves were with their New England masters.

Historical reviews of Attucks' life indicate no authentic data, other than an advertisement to pay a reward for his capture as an escaped slave, his appearance and sudden death in front of the Boston Customs House on March 5, 1770, and disputed, contradictory evidence at the trial of the British soldiers involved.

Questions may be asked, too, about the kind of "history" which has Attucks' father, in the book by Millender, recounting to his son his own life in Africa.

'...Tell me about your father. '

'Well, my father was known best for his efforts to make the people of his kingdom prosperous.   He encouraged them to be farmers and to trade with other people.' ...

'My father told his people that they needed to go
to school in order to learn how to be prosperous
or successful. Our schools were different from
the schools in this country, but they were suited
to the needs of our people. They taught our people how to read and write our own language. We
had doctors and scientists, too, and many other
kinds of workers.... Then one day my father was
killed and I was sold as a slave.'

'How awful, Father!'

'No, not awful, son. Anyone captured during a
war was thought of as a slave. That's the way
things were in those days. Slaves were the property of the chief of a tribe or the head of a family, and could be kept or sold as the owner wished.
Most of them became trusted members of the tribe
or family and were free to carry on many activities. But others were sold and taken to other
countries. I was one of these.'

'What happened to you?'

'I was sold to some traders from the West Indies,
who brought me here.'

The father explains that now they are the property of Colonel
Buckminster. Crispus does not seem to like the idea, but
this father remonstrates:

'Not many slaves have their own cottages,' Prince
[Attucks' father] explained. 'I have my own plot
of ground just as I might have had in Africa,
though not as large. You have always been happy
here and you can keep on being happy. The important thing is that you are my son and I'm proud
of you...' (p. 33-35).

Where are the horrors of the Middle Passage? What
about the less than gentle slave trading resorted to by African tribal chiefs? What a delightful picture of the life of a
slave in colonial Massachusetts! One wonders just what kind
of history Millender was writing, and for whom? Such a
benign picture would warm the hearts of book selection com-

mittee members from Texas to Mississippi.

Millender provides no footnotes or lists of references to indicate the sources from which she has reconstructed the home and family of Crispus Attucks as he grew up. It would appear that the author has done some study of the lives of Indians, colonial customs, and the incidents leading up to the Boston Massacre. But what is "true" and what has been fabricated by the author cannot be untangled. To pretend that his book provides an authentic story of the life of Crispus Attucks is to mislead in the grossest possible fashion.

In writing the "biography" of Crispus Attucks, Millender closes her volume by saying

> Much has been written about the beginnings of the American Revolution. Strangely enough, few United States history books have ever given sufficient attention or credit to Crispus Attucks, the first to fall for American Independence (p. 187).

What Millender fails to point out, as we will document below, is that Crispus Attucks became a martyr for the evolving American Revolution by an accident of history.

But Miss Millender is not alone in desiring a larger-than-life role for her "hero." Unfortunately, other historians have similarly distorted the role of Attucks. For instance, according to C. Eric Lincoln:

> Crispus Attucks, a Negro sailor who sought to rally the confused Americans in the face of the British fire, was the first to give his life for America.[2]

Another eminent Negro Historian, John Hope Franklin, also falls into the chauvinistic trap:

> Attucks could hardly be described as a saucy boy. [By whom?] Nor was he deserving of the other harsh things John Adams had to say about those who fell in the Boston Massacre. He was more than forty-seven years old and had made his living during the twenty years after he ran away from his Framingham master by working on ships plying out of Boston harbor. As a seaman he probably [sic] felt keenly the restrictions which England's new

navigation acts imposed. He now undertook [sic]
to make the protest in a form that England would
understand. Attucks's martyrdom is significant not
as the first life to be offered in the struggle against
England.... The significance of Attucks's death
seems to lie in the dramatic connection which it
pointed out between the struggle against England
and the status of the Negroes in America. Here
was a fugitive slave who, with his bare hands, was
willing to resist England to the point of giving his
life. It was a remarkable thing, the colonists reasoned, to have their fight for freedom waged by
one who was not as free as they. [3]

On what basis Franklin dismisses John Adams' comments and produces his own probabilities one cannot discern.

Quarles, unlike some of his colleagues, does not let
being Negro distort his historical appraisal:

John Adams later [after the event] observed that
the men who lost their lives that night were 'the
most obscure and inconsiderable that could be
found upon the continent.' His remark had some
justification. Crispus Attucks, 'the first to defy,
and the first to die,' was a Negro of obscure origin, with some admixture of Indian blood. Presumably he had been a slave ... Attucks's obscur-
ity prior to the Boston Massacre was in dramatic
contrast to his role on that occasion...

Whatever Attucks actually did that night, his prominent role in the Boston Massacre owed much to
John Adams, who, as counsel defending the British
soldiers, chose to make him the target.... It was
Attucks 'to whose mad behavior, in all probability
the dreadful carnage of that night is chiefly to be
ascribed.'[4]

Quarles argues that there is little historical evidence
that Attucks was motivated by patriotic principles, and that
in all likelihood--as John Adams in the defense of the British soldiers states--Attucks was merely part of an unruly
and drunken mob enjoying the prospect of goading the nerv-
ous British. Yet, he continues, it is historically possible
that he was influenced, as were other Bostonians, by anti-
British sentiment. But all of this is inference, as Quarles

admits. [5]

In his collection of first-hand accounts of events in
Negro history, Katz summarizes the events of the mob action
which resulted in the Boston Massacre by reporting:

> A group of Boston patriots met a company of Brit-
> ish soldiers, but this time the usual name-calling,
> scuffling, and throwing of snowballs ended in blood-
> shed.
>
> The leader of the crowd of Boston men and boys
> was Crispus Attucks, a tall runaway slave who had
> become a seaman. When Attucks waved his cord-
> wood club and urged the crowds forward, someone
> gave the order to fire and the British muskets cut
> down Attucks and four other Bostonians. [6]

The actual "eyewitness" account, however, does not
quite jibe with the above summary. Katz quotes an observer,
also a Negro, who stated in court:

> ...a stout (heavy set) man with a long cordwood
> stick, threw himself in, and made a blow at the
> officer; I saw the officer try to ward off the stroke,
> whether he struck him or not I do not know; the
> stout man then turned around, and struck the gren-
> edier's gun at the captain's right hand, and im-
> mediately fell in with his club, and knocked his
> gun away, and struck him over the head, the blow
> came either on the soldier's cheek or hat. This
> stout man held the bayonet with his left hand, and
> twitched it and cried kill the dogs, knock them
> over; this was the general cry; the people then
> crowded in, and upon that the grenedier gave a
> twitch back and relieved his gun, and he up with
> it and began to pay away on the people. [7]

From the eyewitness account, it sounds as though Attucks was foolhardy in the extreme; had the soldier not re-
trieved his bayonet and fired, it is likely that he would have
been the one lying dead. Katz, the author of page 44, should
read his own page 56. There is absolutely no supporting
evidence that Attucks was a 'patriot,' except in the sense
that he was the first man to fall, mortally wounded, in a
brawl with the British soldiers in Boston in 1770. This fact,
however, does not quality him <u>as an individual,</u> Negro or

white, for elevation to the Hall of Fame.

By contrast, the classic history of the United States of Charles and Mary Beard provides this comment, and only this comment, on the Boston Massacre:

> ...school children (of Boston) now emulated their elders by jeering at soldiers and officers; indeed, one of the first Americans killed in the conflict was a school boy shot by an informer who resented childish ridicule.
>
> This affair was shortly followed by the 'Boston Massacre' of March, 1770, starting in comedy as some youths threw snowballs and stones at a small body of British regulars and ending in tragedy with the killing and wounding of several citizens. [8]

In writing her fantasy biography of Crispus Attucks for children, Millender has him attending the trial of Richardson, who shot the taunting schoolboy. Nothing in the historical record would indicate that Attucks would do such a thing, particularly since his official status as a runaway slave would make such public appearance rather dangerous. Courthouses, in those times, were not large and impersonal places; a person of Attucks' appearance would have certainly drawn comment, whereupon his former master could have had him seized; Millender ignores the other 'probabilities' of history in order to invent those more suited to her purpose of inflating an individual tragedy to the level of heroic martyrdom.

A more recent "popular" history of the United States summarizes the Boston Massacre in these terms:

> The Townshend Acts bore most heavily on Massachusetts, and for its protests against them that colony's General Court was dissolved in 1768. Violence broke out soon after when a mob attacked customs agents trying to collect Townshend duties from John Hancock's sloop, Liberty. This prompted the governor to ask for troops. On March 5, 1770, a snowball attack on some of the soldiers brought the unfortunate order to fire, and after the melee four [sic] Bostonians were lying dead.
>
> New England seethed over the 'Boston Massacre';

but when the new Lord North Ministry repealed all
duties but that on tea, quiet seemed to have been
restored... [9]

The charge that the Beards and William Miller, being
white, are thus insensitive to the role of the Negro might be
worthy of further examination.   One might pick up any current American history and find similar quotations.   Few general histories today do an adequate job of placing the Negro
in perspective throughout our history, and indeed, one could
cite the absence of Crispus Attucks in "white" history books,
and school textbooks.   Suffice it to say that, historically,
those who died provided a rallying cry for the American pa-
triots.   Yearly, the anniversary was

> duly observed... in a public ceremony, which took
> on a ritualistic pattern.   Bells would toll during
> the day, and at night lighted transparencies depict-
> ed the soldiers and their victims, giving a sub-
> stance of sorts to the 'discontented ghosts, with
> hollow groans' summoned to solemnize the occasion.
> The highlight of the evening was a stirring address
> by a leading citizen which, as the contemporary
> historian David Ramsay observed, 'administered
> fuel to the fire of liberty, and kept it burning with
> an incessant flame.'   The propaganda value of the
> Boston Massacre cannot be minimized.... [10]

Is it not a bit ironic for another Negro historian
proudly to quote George Washington: "Remember it is the
5th of March and avenge the death of your brethren,"[11] when
that same Washington was most reluctant to allow Negroes,
free or slave, to be recruited and treated as regular soldiers?

The necessary question remains: must we make a
hero out of Crispus Attucks?   At a critical point in American colonial history, a traumatic event occurred whose prop-
aganda value, as Quarles indicates, played a useful role in
rallying wavering colonial sentiments and stiffening the resistance to British rule.

One small nagging question might occur to the careful
reader: what about those other Bostonians killed along with
Attucks?   John Adams, in supporting the defense witness who
stated that it was to Attucks' "mad behavior, in all probability, the dreadful carnage of that night is chiefly to be ascribed," added "...a Carr from Ireland and an Attucks from

Framingham, happening to be here, at the head of such a
rabble of negroes, etc. etc. etc., as they can collect together, and then there are not wanting persons to ascribe all
their doings to the good people of the town."[12] No one, however, in writing the history of the Irish in America makes
much claim for Patrick Carr for having lost his life in the
same fracas. The backgrounds and forebears of the others
who died have faded into the fogs of history. Why such efforts to resurrect Crispus Attucks?

Perhaps the important point is that when Negroes have
appeared in these small but critical points in American history they have somehow become 'white-washed.' The impression conveyed to the innocent and the ignorant is that Negroes appear in American history as slaves, over whom the
states quarreled and therefore had a bloody and unnecessary
war, and who then, after living in animal conditions for
decades, once more (circa 1954) have become visible and vol-
uble on the American scene.

A reasonable request might be, then, to "color them
black" when, indeed, black faces appear as they do throughout our history. But is it necessary to go further and create
heroes out of non-heroes, black, white, or in-between? The
life of Crispus Attucks by Millender is only one in a series
of over 100 titles published by the same firm. One can justly ask what kind of historical authenticity guides the produc-
tion of these volumes, and what kind of publishing responsibility is demonstrated?

At a time when authentic history is more essential
than ever, we must refrain from creating non-history. We,
who tittered over the revisions of Russian history to discredit Stalin and then Khrushchev, have perhaps a little
housecleaning to do at home. Indeed, the usually-impeccable
Encyclopedia Americana might do well to review its reference to Crispus Attucks as "American patriot and leader of
the demonstration that lead to the Boston Massacre...."[13]
An impressive list of textbook studies over the years shows
that educators have been well aware of the errors of omission and commission existing in books of all kinds, and particularly in history books.[14]

Future historians can, however, at least settle the
problem of Crispus Attucks by turning to the definitive discussion of the incident in a recent essay by Fleming. As
Fleming persuasively argues, the true import of the event

was not who did or did not provoke the bloodshed, but that a
bloody confrontation had indeed taken place, and furthermore,
that men who were to play leading roles in the ensuing evolu-
tion of the American Revolution took opposing sides in the
trial of the British soldiers: Samuel Adams and the Liberty
Men against his cousin John Adams and the rule of law and
reason.   John Adams, reviled by other Bostonians for taking
on the defense of the British, won the case through his skill
with courts and procedures, and thus gained time for the
coming revolution to mature.   He and Sam Adams became
friends though they never agreed on tactics.   In the end,
Fleming observes:

> That John [Adams] won the larger place in history
> should not be surprising to anyone who penetrates
> beyond the patriotic myth to the interior drama of
> this great but little-understood trial. [15]

Are these subtleties of history too difficult for little
children?   Must we, then, give them fantasy?   I for one
would opt for genuine make-believe, the great myths and
fairy tales, the sagas and ballads, Paul Bunyan and Ulysses.
Let youth, in all good time, ponder some of these obscure
and dramatic by-ways of authentic history, from which last-
ing ethical and moral insights may, in all truth, also be
gained.

Notes

1. Of Crispus Attucks, Boy of Valor, by Dharathula H.
    Millender.   Indianapolis: Bobbs Merrill, 1965.   200 p.
    $2. 50.

2. C. Eric Lincoln, The Negro Pilgrimage in America.
    (New York: Bantam Books, 1967), p. 18.

3. John Hope Franklin, From Slavery to Freedom, 2nd ed.
    (New York: Alfred A. Knopf, 1965), p. 127.

4. Benjamin Quarles, The Negro in the American Revolu-
    tion.   (Durham: University of North Carolina Press,
    1961), p. 5-6.

5. Ibid. , p. 8.

6. William L. Katz, Eyewitness: The Negro in American

History. (New York: Pitman Publishing Co., 1967), p. 44.

7. Ibid., p. 56.

8. Charles and Mary Beard, The Rise of American Civilization, Rev. ed. (New York, Macmillan Co., 1934), p. 221.

9. William Miller, A New History of the United States. (New York, George Braziller, Inc., 1958), p. 102.

10. Quarles, op. cit., p. 7.

11. Charles H. Wesley, "Editorial," Negro History Bulletin, 30, No. 3, March 1967, p. 4.

12. Thomas J. Fleming, "The Boston Massacre," American Heritage, XVIII, No. 1, December 1966, p. 6-11ff.

13. Encyclopedia Americana (New York: The Americana Corporation, 1967), vol. 2, p. 662.

14. Barbara Finkelstein, Loretta Golden, and Jean D. Grambs, "Textbooks in Social Context: a Bibliography of Studies of Textbook Contents," College of Education, University of Maryland, 1968. (Mimeographed).

15. Fleming, op. cit., p. 11.

PART IV

SOME EARLY EXAMPLES

16.   MARK TWAIN'S JIM IN THE CLASSROOM*

Donald B. Gibson

The great concern of the Negro in our time with his
social image has caused the question to be raised with increasing frequency about whether Adventures of Huckleberry
Finn should be taught in high school and college.   Most teachers would agree that it should be taught; Mark Twain's novel
remains one of the mainstays of the English curriculum.   I,
too, agree that it should not be discarded.   At the same
time, however, those who oppose its being taught have a case,
and people teaching the novel need to pay attention to that
case, for opponents of the book have seen something in it
which is really there and needs to be dealt with. [1]

The case against the novel centers around the character of Jim.   Opponents of the novel feel that Jim is a stereotype, a minstrel show figure, who in his actions and attitudes
proves often to be less than human.   Such is the case in the
first chapters of the book, in which Jim is presented as lacking dignity, as superstitious, ignorant, and comical.   Indeed,
a slave such as Jim might well in fact have been undignified,
superstitious, ignorant, and comical, but the problem is that
he is presented as being nothing but these things.   Conse-
quently, even granted that Jim appears otherwise later in the
novel, the fact is that at the beginning of the novel Mark
Twain sees Jim as being no different from the "minstrel
show nigger" or the comical darky of plantation literature.

---

*Editors' Note: Professor Gibson is speaking to high school
and college teachers in this article, but his discussion of racial stereotypes in Huckleberry Finn is important to public
and school librarians at every level.   This book is often inappropriately given to children and junior high school students who are ill-equipped to handle either the irony in Mark
Twain's treatment of characters or, as Professor Gibson
states, "the limitations imposed upon his sensibilities by a
bigoted early environment. "

The same case can be made about the presentation of
Jim during the final chapters of the novel. Whatever happens
in the relation between Huck and Jim during the central episodes of the novel, it is clear that Jim (frequently referred
to by critics as "Nigger Jim" though he is never once called
this in Huck Finn!) is seen by Huck and Mark Twain alike
as only an object and not human, a pasteboard, one-dimen-
sional figure. At the novel's end, Tom turns Jim into an
unreal object of his imagination. Huck and Jim go along
with the farce, and Mark Twain does too, for despite the
limitations imposed on him by his choice of point of view, he
is always able, when he wants, to indicate disparity between
his attitudes and the attitudes of his characters. [2] The tone
of the final section suggests that no such disparity exists.

Opponents of the novel also feel that the relation between Jim and Huck is essentially demeaning. Despite Huck's
decision to go to hell rather than turn Jim in, a strong
point in his favor, he could only assume the role of leader,
protector, and provider in relation to a person whom he considered and who considered himself to be his dependent.
Thus, the usual roles of child and adult are reversed, and
Jim assumes the inferior role.

One need only compare Huck's reactions to every
other adult he encounters in the novel to see this. All other
adults in Huck's world embody authority, but Jim, stripped
of authority and, indeed, masculinity by social consensus,
appears to himself and to Huck as less than an adult. [3] Thus,
the general social conception of the proper relation between
white and black in regard to authority is carried onto the
raft and persists even at the very moment Huck decides to
go to hell rather than turn Jim in. The very conditions
creating the possibility of the decision stem from Huck's authority.

As a corollary to the preceding, no escaped slave, it
is argued, would subject himself to domination by a child to
the extent of allowing himself to be led deeper and deeper
into slave territory and further and further away from freedom on the Illinois shore. Viewed from the perspective outlined here, the journey downriver is more than a failure of
execution. It was only possible at all as a result of the reversed child-parent relation between Huck and Jim.

When the relation between the two characters is described by most critics, the irony and ambivalence so often

expressed in Huck's attitude toward Jim is generally overlooked. Most critics see a certain progress, a positive development in Huck's character when in the chapter, "Fooling
Poor Old Jim," Huck says finally, "It was fifteen minutes
before I could work myself up to go and humble myself to a
nigger; but I done it, and warn't sorry for it afterward neither." Indeed there does occur development in Huck's character at this point, for presumably he has never before apol-
ogized to a "nigger" and was never capable of it. The fact
of positive development cannot be denied.

Yet the statement also indicates that despite Huck's
moral growth, he continues to see Jim as a "nigger," a "nigger" to whom he feels the personal necessity to apologize.
Hence, Huck sees with a certain duality of vision. Jim is
at once an individual, a discrete personality, to whom respect is due--but at the same time a "nigger." Which view
is the true one? Critics almost invariably see the positive
view as the true one. But why, opponents of the novel ask,
is the one view more true than the other?

Moral growth likewise takes place during the central
episode of the novel in which Huck decides to go to hell
rather than turn Jim in--at least within the limitations outlined. The salient issue, however, is that the conflict within Huck between heart and conscience reflects the same essential conflict in Mark Twain himself, only he did not resolve it quite so clearly and decisively. As a result, the
novel's ending serves to obviate all that has preceded and
Huck's decision becomes finally meaningless. For those,
who might have missed the point, Mark Twain tells us at the
end that Jim was free anyway. If Huck's decision is meaningful in any sense, the fact remains that Mark Twain specifically intended to undercut its meaningfulness by telling us
that Jim was free all the while.

From this perspective the ending implies Mark Twain's
own personal decision not to go to hell, but to set things
right, to square himself with the values of the society which
Huck rejects in deciding to "take up wickedness." The recon-
ciliation means among other things turning Jim into the stage
clown he was at the beginning of the book. Thus the central
episode of the novel is unambiguous only if we look at it in
isolation, apart from the context of the novel.

Further, what is to be made of the episode during
which Huck meets Aunt Sally and explains why it has taken

him so long to get to the Phelps' farm? "We blowed out a
cylinder head," Huck says. "Good gracious! Anybody hurt?"
Aunt Sally asks. "No'm. Killed a nigger." "Well, it's
lucky; because sometimes people do get hurt." This passage
could conceivably be described as simply an instance of a
failure of tone, an instance in which Mark Twain sacrifices
character for the sake of humor, for certainly the author at
this point intends to ridicule Huck and Aunt Sally because
both assume that a Negro is less than human. At the same
time, however, Huck's feeling here is not the least bit incon-
sistent with his character. Though his attitude toward Jim
may change somewhat, there is no reason to feel that he is
able to see a single Negro other than Jim as simply and only
a "nigger," and toward Jim his attitude is at best ambivalent.

Those antagonistic toward the novel ask whether there
isn't something wrong in the view describing Jim as "noble,"[4]
as Huck's "true" father,[5] or as "the conscience of the novel,
the spiritual yardstick by which all men are measured."[6]
These terms are indeed true and fitting insofar as they describe the spiritual man, Jim. But what of the social man?
Is Jim a model human being in any but a spiritual way?
Such terms do not describe the character fully enough. Is it
noble for a man to allow a child to usurp his authority? Is
a "true" father one who is led by his child? It is all well
and good to see Jim as "white on the inside," but isn't it
luxurious indulgence to believe that his spiritual state, given
Jim's circumstances, should be so much more important
than his social condition? Are his saintliness and nobility
so clearly positive qualities in light of the fact that their
price is his masculinity?

If we take into account Mark Twain's ambivalence
about so many things, examined in detail in Van Wyck Brooks'
The Ordeal of Mark Twain, it is not surprising to find him
seeing Jim at once as human, capable of deep feeling and
compassion, of loyalty and sincere friendship, and as simply
a character from a minstrel show. It is not surprising to
find Mark Twain concerned in this novel with the theme of
man's inhumanity to man while at the same time giving tacit
approval to the institution of slavery which is the primary
cause of Jim's predicament. Of course Huck, incapable as
he is of dealing in abstractions, could not very well con-
demn slavery. But Mark Twain indicates his own feelings
and they are that slavery is all right as long as slaves are
not treated badly. The Phelps farm, for example, is a happy place. Further, Jim's only justification for running away

from Miss Watson is her cruel intention to sell him down the
river and separate him from his family. The extreme degree of ambivalence in the novel calls into serious question
the adequacy of most criticism about it, for critics habitual-
ly treat it as though its meaning were monolithic. Yet we
can find the opposite within the novel of nearly every thought,
ideal, feeling, or idea presented there. [7]

Hence, it should be acknowledged by those opposed to
the novel on the grounds outlined above that if the book says
the one thing--Jim is a "stage nigger," etc. --it also says
the opposite. Though the descriptive terms applied to Jim
by critics do not define him totally, he is in truth morally
superior to anyone else in the book (including Huck). If the
image of the Negro presented in the book is of importance,
the episode in Chapter 6 need be recalled during which Pap
describes a Negro who is educated, knows six languages, is
a college professor, respected and free. The novel's expression of the value of freedom should also be acknowledged.
At least Jim seeks freedom when his condition becomes ut-
terly intolerable. This distinguishes him from Harriet B.
Stowe's long-suffering Uncle Tom, who acquiesces to the pain,
misery, and hardship of his life in hope of a glorious life in
heaven. Though it is sometimes difficult to distinguish between them, they are not precisely the same persons.

The basic problem, the problem underlying the question whether the novel should be taught, is the matter of how
it is taught. Too often critics and teachers ignore the implications arising from Mark Twain's ambivalence toward
Jim, either through lack of attention to this aspect of the
novel's meaning, or through too great commitment to particular critical schemes. A survey of recent criticism of Huck
Finn reveals the operation of one or both of these factors in
most of it. For example, all of the criticism justifying the
last section of the novel ignores or glosses over the problem of the presentation of Jim as stereotype. Likewise, a
significant number of critics seeing the ending as a limitation of the novel deal with it in terms other than the moral
or sociological. [8] Problems about whether the novel should
be taught are bound to arise if the moral and sociological
ramifications of the book are ignored.

If the novel is taught truly, as it is, rather than as
a vehicle for the practical application of various limiting critical notions, the problem of whether it should be taught will
not arise. It should not be presented as simply a great nov-

el by a great author, as non-evaluative critical approaches usually imply, but as a novel written by a man limited like the rest of us in his inability to be constantly charitable and always to think and feel the right thing. It should be presented as the work of a man whose intentions were in large measure good, but who was not entirely able to overcome the limitations imposed upon his sensibilities by a bigoted early environment. It should be shown to be a novel whose author was not always capable of resisting the temptation to create laughter though compromising his morality and his art. In short the problem of whether to teach the novel will not exist if it is taught in all its complexity of thought and feeling, and if critics and teachers avoid making the same kinds of compromises Mark Twain made.

Notes

1. Edward Wagenknecht's response to objections to the novel on racial grounds is characteristic: "When Negroes object to Jim in Huckleberry Finn, one can only regret that they are behaving as stupidly as white folks often do, for surely Jim is one of the noblest characters in American literature." Mark Twain: The Man and His Work (Norman: University of Oklahoma Press, 1961), p. 222.

2. One of many such examples occurs in Chapter 22 in which Mark Twain shows Huck's inability to distinguish between illusion and reality at the circus. A more subtle instance occurs in the title of Chapter 8, "I Spare Miss Watson's Jim." The note of condescension is clear.

3. It is significant to note that Jim has been described as Huck's "spiritual" father, his "mother," and even as a homosexual. He is none of these, though he might appear to be because he does not possess the dominant characteristic of masculinity in our society, authority. He is a child and does not have even the limited authority of a mother.

4. Wagenknecht, op. cit.

5. Lionel Trilling, Introduction to The Adventures of Huckleberry Finn (New York: Rinehart, 1960), p. ix.

6. James M. Cox, "Remarks on the Sad Initiation of Huckle-
    berry Finn," Sewanee Review, 62 (Summer 1954) 404.
    Reprinted in Barry A. Marks' collection of essays,
    Mark Twain's Huckleberry Finn (Boston: D. C. Heath
    and Co. , 1959), p. 73.

7. This statement could be made in relation to the ending
    which many feel reverses the novel's meaning.   But
    there are more specific examples available.   One is
    Mark Twain's shift in attitude toward the Widow Doug-
    las in the opening pages.   As first she is seen as
    Huck's tormentor, then that role is assumed by Miss
    Watson and the Widow becomes a positive force.   Note
    also Mark Twain's shifting attitude toward Colonel
    Sherburn from Chapter 21 to Chapter 22.

8. The prominent exception is Leo Marx whose view of the
    novel and of criticism of it implies the importance of
    the question dealt with here.   Marx specifically refers
    to Jim at the end of the novel as "the submissive
    stage Negro, " and points to its source as a "lapse of
    moral vision" on Mark Twain's part.   The preceding
    quoted phrases are implied to have the relation I sug-
    gest.   "Mr. Eliot, Mr. Trilling, and Huckleberry
    Finn, " American Scholar, 22 (Autumn 1953) 423-440.
    Reprinted in Marks, op. cit. , p. 53-64.

17. THROUGH A GLASS, DARKLY (Excerpt)

Dharathula H. Millender

For centuries, literature has been valued for introduc-
ing readers to each other. Books describe the physical appearance of other people, explain customs, modes, and ways
of living, and illustrate graphically how others are supposed
to look, live, and seem to be.

Tragically, however, books have often planted false
images in the minds of readers. Certainly, much is being
said today about the damage the early books about Negro life
for children have done to foster misunderstanding between the
races. With little or no contact between the races in the
early 1900's, books were the only medium of introduction.
Yet they often explained customs and modes and ways of living not as they normally were, and often showed grotesque
stereotypes in illustrations portrayed as "true" representa-
tions but certainly not genuine. They introduced readers to
people, but not real people or normal situations. Unfortunately authors seldom knew the subject about which they wrote,
and those who did know were seldom allowed to make the in-
troductions. The result was irreparable damage.

Yet one must remember that books are just a mirror
of the times...they present life as it is interpreted to be by
authors who can convince publishers that they have something that will sell. Most authors successful in having stories for children published in the early 1900's had no real way
of knowing the Negro about whom they were writing, but they
wrote about Negroes, nevertheless, and people believed their
farcical presentations. At that time in our country's history,
it was accepted that the Negro lived little better than in his
plantation days, that he wanted nothing, had nothing, and
looked like nothing that resembled other humans of the day.

The Negro author, who could have made a valuable
contribution to human relations at that time, writing truthful-
ly and plausibly about his own people, seems to have been
unacceptable to most publishers. So separated were the
races in the early 1900's that few whites knew that many Ne-

143

groes lived in much the same way that they themselves lived.
Unaware of the Negro society within the crowded ghettoes
they did not know that the Negro was trying to provide for
his young people many of the same kinds of opportunities and
advantages for growth that the whites provided for their
youngsters.   Few outside the ghetto knew what life went on
within the narrow confines of the Negro's partially unim-
proved area, usually down by the railroad tracks or in the
slums of the inner city, which had been destroyed and left
by others who had moved on to a second try at decency.
Few knew that within such areas the Negro was providing for
his youth opportunities for leadership and development, and
preparing him to be ready for acceptance when it came; that
the Negro was constantly looking up and struggling for a better way of life; or that, without fanfare, the Negro was edu-
cating his youth to take jobs that were not even available
then... but merely hoped for at this point.

Books did not mirror this kind of life, the life that
really was, but revealed instead another and alien existence.
How different life might have been for all if they had really
mirrored the times, and the outside world could have seen
in them the struggle of the Negro to survive under tremendous odds... ever moving forward with hope when at that time
he found most doors closed to him.   Many who could have
opened those doors were ignorant of the fact that the Negro
wanted a chance and was not content to do, be, and want
nothing but idleness and pleasure.   Without books to reveal
the true life and aspirations of the Negro, progress in race
relations was set back years.   Those who chose to promote
the inferiority of the Negro went unchallenged by the masses
--who had no way of finding out for themselves.

In the early 1900's publishers, I'm sure, really wanted stories that mirrored the thinking of the day and times.
They, too, had little or no contact with Negroes, and were
perhaps governed by the way public opinion was shaped by
the leading news media of the day.   Scribner's Magazine,
Vol. XXXIV, Aug. , 1903, No. 2, had a story entitled, "The
County Fair," by Nelson Lloyd, illustrated by Edwin B.
Child.   On page 142 of that issue, a "representative" illustration of Negroes was shown.   Apparently the reader was to
think that these Negroes were on their way to the Fair.
Nothing in the story revealed this.   Each other illustration,
previously shown with its appropriate caption, portrayed the
text of the story; yet the grotesque illustration of the Negroes
had nothing to do with the story, nor was the picture caption

included in this story on "The County Fair." The three hor-
rible, apish-looking, black, creatures did have a small boy
with them who looked normal. The picture caption was:
"Dey's somfin' goin' on." Typical of the times, the Negro
was usually portrayed by whites in books and articles speaking the unknown tongue of a dialect no one but the author understood. Also, typical of the times, the Negro was portrayed as a caricature or joke, as afraid, lazy, docile, and
unambitious.

Here again, the news media planted this stereotype,
and the books that followed merely mirrored this concept.
Harper's Weekly, Editorial Section for the week ending May
16, 1903, in its comment on various articles summarized
thus: One of the best authorities on Negroes and the Negro
problem is Mr. Alfred H. Stone of Greenville, Mississippi,
who had many deliverances about the "Southern Blacks." He
declares, said Harper's, that mulattoes weren't Negroes as
such and achieve only because of their Caucasian blood, for
the "true Negro," according to Mr. Stone, "...is of a contented and happy disposition...docile-unambitious...with but
few wants and those easily satisfied."

About 1903 many articles were written to explain the
supremacy of the white man and justify the disenfranchise-
ment of the Negro. True, the 14th Amendment had given
the Negro paper citizenship, and the 15th Amendment guaranteed him the right to vote, but there were whites who had
to keep before the public the image of his inferiority. Though
the Constitution said the Negro was a citizen, he was portrayed, cruelly, as a servant with no real rights; and, there
was a school of thought that theorized the Negro, though le-
gally a voter, was not capable of exercising that Constitution-
ally guaranteed right. The July 18, 1903, Vol. XLVII of
Harper's, on the "Negro Problem," reported that Dr. Lyman
Abbott, editor of Outlook, explained equality of the Negro
thus: "Equality does not mean that all men, black and white,
are to govern as state executives, as sheriffs, as members
of a legislature, or as voters. We are reminded that a boy
16 years of age is equal before the law with a man of 60;
but the boy can not vote and the man can." Thus the practice of referring to the Negro always as a "boy" was firmly
implanted in the minds of people across the country, and to
this very day, to many whites, even the most outstanding
educated Negro scholar is still just a boy. Comparably, the
Negro woman is a "girl," no matter what her age. The
idea of calling all Negro men, even gray-haired old men,

"boy," was a carry-over from the days of slavery, and the articles in the early news media insisted that Negroes should not mature to functioning adults, even though they were.

About the time that the 1903 article appeared in Harper's, the era of the Negro in the U.S. Congress, State Legislatures, and in high positions in government, had just passed. The molders of public opinion had to eradicate the memory of the fact that the Negro had led commendably... even, at one time, signing the paper money issued by the U.S. government before it could be spent. (Blanche K. Bruce, a Negro, was Register of the Treasury under President Garfield).

The white protective societies were flourishing with the old black codes, though supposedly outlawed, to back them up to help "keep the Negro in his place." But, as these societies flourished unchecked, there was a ray of hope for the Negro. White philanthropists and their agencies poured money into the improvement of Negro education in the South... a South menaced by the devastating cancer of hatred. This hatred of the Negro was probably fostered by the unspoken realization that the exploitation of the Negro was beating their consciences. As the middle class and poor whites fought to regain some of what they had lost by the ravages of the Civil War, they lashed out openly at the Negro whom they blamed for all their ills. Inwardly, they must have beaten themselves for what they knew they had done to make the situation so bleak. All this was reflected in books and writings of the times for adults, but children got a different kind of story; yet subtly, stories for children added little happiness and joy to the reader's life. Books were mirroring the sadness, frustration, and fear of truth.

In books for children, authors of this frustrated background wrote all sorts of plantation stories and little "ditty" stories purported to show the Negro they told publishers they "knew." Because these authors "played" with them in Alabama, or "grew up" with them on such and such plantation of a relative, they were supposed to know the Negro. Now this was the early 1900's, I must remind you, and down to and through a part of the 1930's we still had only the "plantation" story that showed Negro life to the boys and girls.

The times, certainly, were in turmoil for all people. There was confusion, then a spurt of prosperity, and then depression. All this took its toll. Books were sorely needed

about all kinds of children. People wanted books about the
Negro, who was really a puzzle to many. The southern
white saw the Negro migrate to the north by the thousands.
The northern white often met those hordes of people with
subtle and open resentment. In the south the Negro was
drawing his circle tighter as he kept from the whites his
plans to advance above the menial status of the past to one
of leadership and status as the new citizen he was. In the
north the whites pushed the Negro into ghettoes and drew a
tight band around that area from which he had few ways and
means at his disposal to escape. So, the Negro closed the
whites out as he made a way of status for himself.

Needed at this point were stories of the happiness
within the Negro communities, north and south. The Negro
always found a way to give hope to his youth and show the
brighter side of a very bleak life. This spirit often gave the
outside world the wrong impression. Often the writings in
the journals and news media of the day portrayed the Negro
as always joking and laughing and taking nothing in life seri-
ously. It would be hard to explain the philosophy of life
taught incidentally and sometimes purposefully to the little
Negro child and reemphasized daily as he went out to meet
a hostile and fearsome world. It is almost impossible to explain the humor of the Negro and what it really means. The
impression portrayed in news media and books of the early
times might have mirrored the life and aspirations of a small
percentage of the Negro; yet certainly not the average nor
the whole. Handed down to us, however, were many false
stereotypes of Negro life. The children of the early 1900's
are the grandparents who taught the parents of today, and
who are often parents of the open-minded youth of today who
don't want to buy the old half-truths.

The books our grandparents of today read to our parents of today were what the publishers thought the people
wanted to read. The larger and more established publishers
who could afford to gamble on the market did include a few
books about Negro life for children by authors who were supposed to know the Negro. The stories were blown up as
good literature, and the public accepted them and passed
them down.

A sampling of a few of the books for children might
emphasize what was available.

1890: Pendleton, Louis. <u>King Tom and the Runaways.</u>

Appleton.   Gr. 7-8.   Life in the south before the war--
Georgia.

1922: Lindsay, Maud. Little Missy. Lothrop. Gr.
4-6. Southern life before the war. --Alabama.

1924: Perkins, L. F. Colonial Twins of Virginia.
Houghton. Gr. 4-6. Plantation life with a note that the author got her "local color" by staying on a Virginia plantation.
(in 1920?)

1929: Bannerman, Helen. Story of Little Black Sambo. Stokes.

1930: Pyrnelle, L. C. Diddie, Dumps, and Tot, or
Plantation Child Life. Harpers.

1931: Knox, Rose B. Miss Jimmy Deane. Doubleday. Plantation life before the Civil War.

1932-1935: Hogan, Inez. The Nicodemus books.
Dutton. The New York Times in its review stated, "...
amusing pictures of the little darkey... the excellence of the
drawings and their humor help to make up for the somewhat
commonplace quality of the text. " So even then, reviewers
realized that they had no stories... no real contribution to
literature, and that is how they explained it all... that the
illustrations of the little pickininny would make up for the
lack of story.

1935: Credle, Ellis. Across the Cotton Patch. Nelson. Gr. 3-5. Plantation life with "black twins" whose
names were "Atlantic" and "Pacific"... not even human beings
with real children's names.

1936: Bannerman, Helen. Story of Sambo and the
Twins. Stokes.

1935-1938: Evans, E. K. Araminta, Araminta's
Goat, and Jerome Anthony. Putnam. City-bred children
visit "down home" in the country. These were not the typical plantation stories, and not too bad for the times. This
author really seemed to be trying to present the public with
acceptable stories.

1937: Braune, Anne. Honey Chile. Doubleday.
Plantation life again.

1938: Evans, E. K. Key Corner. Putnam. The author was trying to show Negro professional life, but the little
stereotypes crept in, and it was, I'm sure, unintentional.
One writes only what he thinks is so, if he is a sincere writer, and I believe this was a sincere attempt to show that Negroes could be teachers. A new teacher comes to the Negro
school which has had a stern, white one, and this Negro
teacher immediately exhibits unconventional behavior... she
sits on the desk "swinging her legs like a little girl," doesn't
hear giggles and whispers in the back of the room, and generally shows the laxity Negroes were said to exhibit. She
does bring a better type of education, eventually, for that
area and inspires the youth to move up; yet typically this
story, though better than most at that time, had to throw in
subtle untrue stereotypes.

1938: Nolan, E. W. Shipment for Susannah. Nelson.
Back again to the plantation.

1938: Lattimore, E. F. Junior, a Colored Boy of
Charleston. Harcourt. While this was not a plantation story,
the stereotypes that presented a false image of general Negro life were portrayed... deprivation and lack of a strong
father figure are here and were what the news media of the
times portrayed, so one would expect a publisher to accept
such a story. The author, I'm sure, was sincere, but just
didn't know enough about many Negro families.

While the Negro was being portrayed on the plantation,
or stories of the Civil War life were being rehashed in books,
there was just as little progress in the concepts presented in
books about white children. Stories for children were more
or less regional, it seemed, and told of the life of the past,
also, with rare exceptions. Stories about Arizona told of Indians and Mexicans; Arkansas, Ozark Mountain people; Colo-
rado, ranch life; Idaho, pioneering; Indiana, Quakers, Dunes,
New Harmony; Iowa, farm life; and Kansas, lumbering or
the history of the Kansas territory. Stories about New York
and California included children in modern settings, showing
the fascinations of Hollywood or San Francisco, or the wonders of New York City.

Since books were the only way some children could
learn about the Negro, as they were the one way they could
learn about children in other states, it is unfortunate that
stories of plantation life, Civil War days, deprivation in the
south, and general poor living conditions were the only stories

available.   White children may have had a rash of regional
stories that also presented life of another day, but they did
have actual contact with all kinds of white children living
normal life-situations in normal family and community settings where there were laughter and good times.   It is a sad
commentary, however, that from the early 1900's up to the
1940's all that seemed known about Negro life was how he
had lived on the plantation some 50 years before.

It was the Negro author who was most frustrated during this period.   He could and did create, but as he ap-
proached publishers with his stories, he was rejected as having nothing of value for the market of that day.   Those who
wrote for the adult market met with slightly better success,
but many manuscripts that could have given a true picture of
Negro life went unpublished, while often the manuscripts that
showed what people wanted, were accepted, though the life
was not really that of the average.

Finally the Negro author grew so upset about the image constantly fostered in books and the news media that he
found a way to make a contribution.   In 1927 a Negro, A. H.
Fauset, published For Freedom (Franklin Press), a biographical story of the American Negro.   Carter G. Woodson published a history of the Negro, incorporating African culture,
entitled Negro Makers of History, but Dr. Woodson, who pro-
moted the study of Negro History, started an association for
the study of Negro Life and History, and had to, also, form
his own publishing company (Associated Publishers, still in
existence today) so that authentic books about Negro life and
history could actually reach the public.   After that, more
books about the true history and culture of the Negro were
published.

In 1933 Charles C. Dawson, a Negro, published a book
for young children, ABC's of Great Negroes, a series of al-
phabet pictures of outstanding Negroes, incorporating linoleum
cuts with a brief text.

Friendship Press, which today publishes material on
the Negro, began as early as 1936 accepting material on the
Negro.   We Sing America, by the Negro, Marion Cuthbert,
was one of the contributions of Negro Americans to the culture and development of this country.

Recognizing the frustrations of Negro children in trying vainly to find books with material about their people, a

few writers saw that the time was ripe for elementary histories on the Negro for children.   Jane D. Shackelford's
Child's Story of the Negro (Associated Publishers, 1938) filled
a great need for children and teachers.   After its publication
Mrs. Shackelford, who was a teacher in Terre Haute, Indiana, published My Happy Days, showing through photographs
and some text that some Negro families could live much the
same as any other family.   This was her sister's family.
The sister was a housewife, her husband, a fireman; they
lived in a modest, but clean and well-kept home in a Negro
neighborhood.   The children had what any other family of
equal means could afford--nothing elaborate, but a life typical of many other such Negro families.   This truly mirrored
the times, for though many Negroes didn't fare as well,
many lived just as this family lived.   (This was my home
town.   I knew the family and the author.)

     Several other books of photographs of Negro life ap-
peared at this time.   Stella Sharpe's Tobe showed a farm
family in North Carolina which, I'm told, presented a true
picture of that type of farm life.   Books showing the Negro
in his school appeared about this time, and added much to
the changing concept of the Negro.   Many whites did not
know that the Negro went to school in the South, which seems
hard to believe, but when races are so separated, it is no
condemnation that we do not know each other and how each
other lives when there are no books to help us.

     As publishers began to accept some of the many manu-
scripts presented them, Negro authors and others kept trying,
and with the 1940's more books for children on Negro life
succeeded in reaching the public.   A few were fictional, but
most were nonfiction biographies, probably published in an
attempt to show in true lives what had been achieved despite
tremendous odds.   Or perhaps the publishers were playing it
safe in printing mainly true stories.   But whatever the reason, the publication of Negro biographies began to dispel
many of the myths and stereotypes that had branded the Negro as an inferior non-achiever with few capabilities similar
to others, and generally wanting nothing.

     Those few fictional works and stories that were pub-
lished, often were objectionable in that they insulted the
average Negro who lived just as simply as any other average
citizen.   The Negro who had little to eat; fought off rats and
rodents; froze in unheated, decaying, overcrowded kitchenettes;

turned to dope and the cut-throat life of the streets; had no father-figure, but a mother with eight or nine children who turned to Welfare for aid were the types of stories people wanted to read.   And isn't this true today?   This is the kind of story that gets the rave notices, even today.   This kind of story gets in the movies....

18. PORTRAYAL OF THE BLACK
IN CHILDREN'S LITERATURE (Excerpt)

Jessie M. Birtha

... Let me clear up one question which may be in
your mind, as it is the question which I have been asked
most often when people approach me on the subject of book
selection. "What do you think of Little Black Sambo?" I
think that the story of Little Black Sambo was and is an entertaining story for small children, but the development of
circumstances concerning the Sambo tradition has been unfortunate. The usefulness of Little Black Sambo is dead. The
acceptability of Little Black Sambo is dead. The story itself
is not about an African child. It is about a child in India,
and contains little in the slight plot that is objectionable, although as racial sensitivity and pride grew, the book has
been dissected and all manner of symbolism attributed to its
motivation, including sexual. However, a librarian will
never offer this book to a black child if he stops to realize
that the name Sambo has been used so often to refer to a
Negro in a derogatory sense. Remember that the end man
in the minstrel show, the stupid one who was the butt of all
the jokes, was Sambo. The ventriloquist's little black, red-
lipped dummy was named Sambo. Webster's Third New International Dictionary defines Sambo as "Negro, mulatto,
perhaps from Kongo nzambu, monkey. Often capital: NE-
GRO--usually used disparagingly."

The argument has been offered, children don't know
or care about the background of a name. They only listen
to the story. But it has been proved--and experienced--
that if a story of this type is used in an integrated story
hour or classroom, there is a certain amount of discomfort
and--yes, inferiority feeling--for a black child when white
classmates look at him and giggle, later teasing him by calling him Sambo. No matter how entertaining a book is, one
group of children should never be entertained at the expense
of another group's feelings.

The same is true of another once popular classic,
Epaminondas and His Auntie, by Sara Cone Bryant. The il-

153

lustrations portraying a stupid, trifling, big-lipped black boy
and his equally worthless looking aunty, spoil for Negro children and their parents the same story line which they happily
accept when presented in the Lazy Jack version. The two
books mentioned were written long ago, but are still available.   (A new edition of Epaminondas by Eve Merriam, illustrated by Trina Schart Hyman, offers a change from the
original edition.)

       I am not saying that I advocate destroying all of the
existing copies of such books.   These books have been classics in children's literature and as such have value for adults
in tracing the development of black children's literature.
However, I feel that at this time, their existence should be
relegated to the historical collection in the children's library.
To these, I might add Dr. Dolittle and Mary Poppins in their
original form, and I have never really advocated rewriting a
book to improve its acceptability once it has been in circulation.   Mark Twain, Booth Tarkington, and Harriet Beecher
Stowe's Uncle Tom's Cabin may be considered from a somewhat different viewpoint.   Children are older when these are
read, and should be encouraged to evaluate the stories in the
light of the time in which they were written.

PART V

RACISM AND PUBLISHING

19. THE ALL-WHITE WORLD OF CHILDREN'S BOOKS*

Nancy Larrick

"Why are they always <u>white</u> children?"

The question came from a five-year-old Negro girl who was looking at a picturebook at the Manhattanville Nursery School in New York. With a child's uncanny wisdom, she singled out one of the most critical issues in American education today: the almost complete omission of Negroes from books for children. Integration may be the law of the land, but most of the books children see are all white.

Yet in Cleveland, 53 per cent of the children in kindergarten through high school are Negro. In St. Louis, the figure is 56.9 per cent. In the District of Columbia, 70 per cent are Negro. Across the country, 6,340,000 nonwhite children are learning to read and to understand the American way of life in books which either omit them entirely or scarcely mention them. There is no need to elaborate upon the damage--much of it irreparable--to the Negro child's personality.

But the impact of all-white books upon 39,600,000 white children is probably even worse. Although his light skin makes him one of the world's minorities, the white child learns from his books that he is the kingfish. There seems little chance of developing the humility so urgently needed for world cooperation, instead of world conflict, as long as our children are brought up on gentle doses of racism through their books.

---

*Editors' Note: This article first appeared in 1965 and was of great importance in alerting public opinion to the scope of racism in children's books.

For the past ten years, critics have deplored the blatant racial bias of the textbooks. Last August, Whitney Young, Jr., executive director of the National Urban League, attacked the trade books as well. In a nationally syndicated column, he berated American trade book publishers for omitting Negroes from their books for children. As an example, he singled out a Little Golden Book, entitled A Visit to the Zoo, which pictures New York's Central Park Zoo in realistic detail except that no dark face is shown. "The entire book-publishing industry is guilty of this kind of omission," charged Mr. Young.

Are the publishers guilty as charged? To find the answer, I undertook a survey of more than 5,000 trade books published for children in 1962, 1963, and 1964. Surely the effect of Little Rock, Montgomery, and Birmingham could be seen by this time, I reasoned.

As a start, I turned to the seventy members of the Children's Book Council who published trade books for children in each of these three years. Sixty-three of them--90 per cent--completed my questionnaire; many gave anecdotal information as well.

Analysis of the replies and examination of several hundred books led to the discouraging conclusion that the vast majority of recent books are as white as the segregated zoo of Golden Press. Of the 5,206 children's trade books launched by the sixty-three publishers in the three-year period, only 349 include one or more Negroes--an average of 6.7 per cent. Among the four publishers with the largest lists of children's books, the percentage of books with Negroes is one-third lower than this average. These four firms (Doubleday, Franklin Watts, Macmillan, and Harper & Row) published 866 books in the three-year period, and only 4.2 per cent have a Negro in text or illustration. Eight publishers produced only all-white books.

Of the books which publishers report as "including one or more Negroes," many show only one or two dark faces in a crowd. In others, the litho-pencil sketches leave the reader wondering whether a delicate shadow indicates a racial difference or a case of sunburn. It would be easy for some of these books to pass as all-white if publishers had not listed them otherwise.

The scarcity of children's books portraying American

Negroes is much greater than the figure of 6. 7 per cent would
indicate, for almost 60 per cent of the books with Negroes
are placed outside of continental United States or before
World War II, an event as remote to a child as the Boston
Tea Party. There are books of African folk tales, reports
of the emerging nations of Africa, stories laid in the islands
of the Caribbean, biographies of Abraham Lincoln and Jeffer-
son Davis and historical stories about the Underground Railroad.   Most of them show a way of life that is far removed
from that of the contemporary Negro and may be highly dis-
tasteful to him.   To the child who has been involved in civil
rights demonstrations of Harlem or Detroit, it is small comfort to read of the Negro slave who smilingly served his
white master.

       Over the three-year period, only four-fifths of one
per cent of the children's trade books from the sixty-three
publishers tell a story about American Negroes today.
Twelve of these forty-four books are the simplest picture-
books, showing Negroes in the illustrations but omitting the
word from the text.   Examples are Benjie by Joan M. Lexau
(Dial Press); Tony's Birds by Millicent Selsam (Harper &
Row); The Snowy Day and Whistle for Willie by Ezra Jack
Keats (Viking).

       Those for readers of twelve and up mention the word
Negro, and in several the characters tackle critical issues
stemming from school integration, neighborhood desegregation, and nonviolent demonstrations.   But these books are
usually so gentle as to be unreal.   There are no cattle prods,
no bombings, no reprisals.   The white heroine who befriends
a Negro in high school enjoys the support of at least one
sympathetic parent and an admiring boy friend.

       Several books do have outstanding literary merit.
Among them are Roosevelt Grady, by Louise Shotwell (World),
the story of a Negro boy whose parents are migratory workers; I Marched with Hannibal, by Hans Baumann (Henry Z.
Walck), a boy's report of the brilliant Carthaginian general;
Forever Free: The Story of the Emancipation Proclamation,
by Dorothy Sterling (Doubleday); The Peoples of Africa, by
Colin M. Turnbull (World); and The Peaceable Revolution, by
Betty Schechter (Houghton Mifflin), a beautifully written report of three phases of the nonviolent revolution as seen in
the work of Thoreau, Gandhi, and the American Negro today.

       But these notable titles are the exceptions.   "Really

fine books are still scarce," says Augusta Baker, coordina-
tor of Children's Services in the New York Public Library.
Most of the books depicting Negroes are mediocre or worse.
More than one-third have received unfavorable reviews or
been ignored by the three major reviewing media in the juve-
nile book field--The Horn Book, School Library Journal, and
Bulletin of the Children's Book Center of the University of
Chicago.

How well do recent children's books depict the Negro?
To answer this question I enlisted the help of four Negro librarians who work with children in New York, Chicago, and
Baltimore.   They rated 149 of the books "excellent" and
thirteen "objectionable" in their portrayal of Negroes either
through illustration or text.

Among those listed as "objectionable" are three edi-
tions of Little Black Sambo.   Another is The Lazy Little
Zulu, which a reviewer in School Library Journal rated as
"Not recommended" because it "abounds in stereotypes. "

The identification of Negro stereotypes in adult fiction
is vividly spelled out in the unpublished doctoral dissertation
(1963) of Catherine Juanita Starke at Teachers College, Columbia University.   By analyzing the work of popular American novelists of the past hundred years--from James Feni-
more Cooper to James Baldwin and Ralph Ellison--Dr. Starke
shows how the Negro in fiction has changed from the ridiculous stock character to the emerging individual who is first
a human being and second a Negro.

Early novelists called the Negro "gorilla-like," gave
him a name that ridiculed his servile status (Emperor, Cae-
sar, or Brutus, for example), and made his dark skin and
thick lips the epitome of the ludicrous.   The Negro mother
was described as uncomely and ungraceful, clothing her stout
body in gaudy calico.

Concurrently there were protest novels which showed
the "counter stereotype"--the Negro of unsurpassed grace
and beauty, poetic language, great wisdom, and unfaltering
judgment.

In the 1920s The Saturday Evening Post was building
circulation on the Irvin S. Cobb stories of Jeff, the comic
Negro menial.   Twenty years later, the Post was still doing
the same with stories by Octavus Roy Cohen and Glenn Allan,

who wrote of Negroes who ridiculed themselves and their
race.

Perhaps the public opinion which applauded this kind
of adult fiction in the forties was responsible also for the
1946 Caldecott Medal award to The Rooster Crows: A Book
of American Rhymes and Jingles, illustrated by Maud and
Miska Petersham and published by Macmillan. Apparently
the librarians who selected this book as "the most distinguished American Picture Book for Children published in the
United States" in 1945 were not bothered by four pages showing Negro children with great buniony feet, coal black skin,
and bulging eyes (in the distance, a dilapidated cabin with a
black, gun-toting, barefoot adult). White children in this
book are nothing less than cherubic, with dainty little bare
feet or well-made shoes. After eighteen years enough com-
plaints had been received to convince the publisher that the
book would be improved by deleting the illustrations of Negro children. In the new edition of The Rooster Crows (1964)
only white children appear.

The 1964 Caldecott Award went to The Snowy Day,
written and illustrated by Ezra Jack Keats and published by
Viking. The book gives a sympathetic picture of just one
child--a small Negro boy. The Negro mother, however, is
a huge figure in a gaudy yellow plaid dress, albeit without
a red bandanna.

Many children's books which include a Negro show
him as a servant or slave, a sharecropper, a migrant worker, or a menial.

On the other hand, a number of books have overtones
of the "counter stereotype" observed by Dr. Starke--the Negro who is always good, generous, and smiling in the face
of difficulties. The nine-year-old hero of Roosevelt Grady
is one of these. Cheerfully and efficiently he looks out for
the younger children or works alongside his parents in the
fields, does well at school when there is a school to go to,
never loses his temper, and in the end finds a permanent
home for the family. The book won the Nancy Bloch Award
for the Best Intercultural Children's Book for 1963, although
it includes no whites except the teacher, the social worker,
and the owner of the trailer camp. Only the pictures indicate
that the Gradys and their friends are Negroes.

When the Cleveland Board of Education recommended

Roosevelt Grady for children's reading, a Negro newspaper
deplored this choice because one picture shows a work-gang
leader grappling with a fat knife-toting Negro who has threatened a young boy. "This is a gross stereotype," was the objection. "But the main story shows beautiful family life
among Negroes," was the reply, and Roosevelt Grady remains on the Cleveland list.

It is not unusual for critics to disagree as to the ef-
fectiveness of the picture of the Negro in a book for children.
For example, one of the librarians who helped me gave Tolliver, by Florence Means (Houghton Mifflin), a rating of "excellent" for its picture of the Negro. Another criticized it
as a modern story set in Fisk University as it was twenty-
five years ago. "There has been a revolution down there
since then," she wrote. "As a result the book seems somewhat condescending."

Whispering Willows, by Elizabeth Hamilton Friermood
(Doubleday), also brought mixed response. It tells of the
friendship of a white girl who is a high school senior in the
class of 1911 and a Negro girl who works as a domestic in
a white home. One librarian gave the book top rating. Another objected to the stereotype of the gentle Negro serving-
girl who "knows her place."

These divergent opinions point up the dilemma faced
by publishers of children's books. As Albert R. Levinthal,
president of Golden Press, explains it, "Golden Press has
been criticized from both sides.... Almost every time we
reissue Little Black Sambo we receive mail deploring it.
When it is not available in our Little Golden Book series,
we have had letters asking why we do not keep this classic
in print!"

One irate Mississippi mother (white) denounced a Little Golden Book of Mother Goose rhymes in a long letter to
the Jackson Clarion-Ledger. She was aroused by the old
rhyme, "Three babes in a basket/And hardly room for two/
And one was yellow and one was black/And one had eyes of
blue."

"I bought one of the Little Golden Books entitled Counting Rhymes," she wrote. "I was horrified when I was reading to my innocent young child, and, behold, on page 15
there was actually the picture of three small children in a
basket together... and one was a little Negro! I put my child

and the book down and immediately called the owner of the
drugstore and told him he would not have any more of my
business (and I buy a lot of drugs, for I am sick a lot) if he
didn't take all the rest of his copies of that book off his
shelves. "

The illustration shows the Negro baby looking down at
a mouse. Determined to get the whole truth about basket integration, the Mississippi mother said she got in touch with
the author, presumably Mrs. Goose herself. She said the
author gave this explanation of the black child: "He was
aware he didn't belong there, and he was looking down in
shame because somebody (a symbol for the outside meddling
yankees) has placed him in the same basket with the white
child, where he didn't really want to be. Also he was looking down at the mouse as if he recognized some kinship to
animals. "

It's an amusing story. But the sad fact is that many
publishing houses are catering to such mothers of the South
and of the North. As one sales manager said, "Why jeopar-
dize sales by putting one or two Negro faces in an illustration?"

Caroline Rubin, editor of Albert Whitman, tells of
three books brought out in the 1950s: Denny's Story, by Eunice Smith, which shows Negro children in illustrations of
classroom activity; Fun for Chris, by Blossom Randall, with
Negro and white children playing together; and Nemo Meets
the Emperor, by Laura Bannon, a true story of Ethiopia.
"The books won favorable comment," writes Mrs. Rubin,
"but the effect on sales was negative. Customers returned
not only these titles but all stock from our company. This
meant an appreciable loss and tempered attitudes toward
further use of Negro children in illustrations and text. "

Jean Poindexter Colby, editor of Hastings House,
faced similar opposition in 1959 when she told her salesmen
about plans for A Summer to Share, by Helen Kay, the story
of a Negro child from the city who visits a white family in
the country on a Fresh-Air-Fund vacation. "Galleys on the
book had been set and art work was in preparation," Mrs.
Colby wrote in the April 1965 issue of Top of the News, published by the American Library Association. "I told the
salesmen present about the book and immediately encountered
such opposition that I felt we either had to cancel the book
entirely or change the book to an all-white cast. I wrote

apologetically to the author and artist, explaining the situation. They were both cooperative and the racial switch was
made. " A Summer to Share came out in 1960 with the Negro child turned into another white one.

Mrs. Colby's experience with New Boy in School, by
May Justus (1963), was quite different. This is a simple
story for second and third graders about a Negro boy who
enters an all-white class. "We had a great deal of trouble
selling New Boy in School in the South," she writes. "Ed
Jervis, our southern salesman, reported that one big jobber
would neither stock nor sell it. Another one would only fill
special orders. " But then favorable reviews began to come
in--from School Library Journal, the New York Times, the
Chattanooga Times, the Savannah News, the Raleigh Observer,
and the Tulsa World, among others. "Now it is a real best
seller!" she reports.

Mrs. Colby is also feeling pressure from those who
deplore a story that shows the Negro as a slave, a servant,
a railroad porter. "Slavery has been practically taboo for
many years now as a subject for children's literature," she
writes, "and depicting the Negro an anything but perfect is
not welcome either. White children and adults can be bad,
but Negroes cannot. So my job has been to tone down or
eliminate such people and situations.... But when can we lift
the shroud from the truth?"

Not all editors speak as frankly as Mrs. Colby. One,
who asks to remain anonymous, says it took her two years
to get permission to bring out a book about children in a minority group. Another reports a leading children's book
club rejected a 1961 book "especially because Southern sub-
scribers would not like the way this heroine tackled the problem of prejudice. " Although no other publisher commented
on bookclub selection, this is undoubtedly an important influence in editorial decisions.

When the directors of eight children's book clubs were
questioned about the books they have distributed since September 1962, they listed only a tiny fraction that includes
Negroes. Four hard-cover book clubs offered 230 books of
which only six mention Negroes. Four paperback book clubs
distributed 1,345 titles with Negroes included in fifty-three.

Not one of the fourteen Negro books on the ALA list
of Notable Children's Books in 1962, 1963, and 1964 won the

more lucrative award of book-club selection.

        In the two Negro books distributed by the Weekly Reader
Children's Book Club--Long Lonesome Train Whistle, by Virginia Ormsby (Lippincott), and Skinny, by Robert Burch (Viking)
--the Negro characters are Aunt Susan, her son Matt, a fireman, and the handyman, Roman.   Richard R. RePass, director of this hard-cover book club, says, "These I would consider neither germane to the plot, nor particularly flattering
to our Negro citizens.   The main reason why there are not
more books with Negro characters among our book club selections is the general dearth of good candidates. "

        It should be explained that the hard-cover book clubs
send the same book to every child while the paperback book
clubs ask each member to choose one title from a list of
ten to a dozen.   Perhaps for this reason the paperback clubs
have distributed certain titles which the hard-cover book
clubs would not take a chance on.   One of these is Mary
Jane, by Dorothy Sterling, published by Doubleday in hard
cover and given a two-star rating by School Library Journal.
It also received the Nancy Bloch Award for 1959.   This is
the realistic story of a Negro girl who is the first to enter
an all-white junior high school that bristles with prejudice.

        Mary Jane has not been selected for hard-cover book
club distribution.   But after several years of deliberation,
the Arrow Book Club, one of the paperback clubs, offered
Mary Jane to its fifth- and sixth-grade members.   By December 1964, 159,895 copies had been sold.   "Only six letters of complaint were received," reports Lilian Moore, Arrow Book Club editor, "all from adults in the South.   And
many warm comments have come in from the children who
read Mary Jane. "

        By March 1965, Mary Jane had been published in
Swedish, Dutch, Czech, German, and Russian editions.   According to Publishers' Weekly, the Children's Literature
House of Moscow reports 100,000 copies of Mary Jane have
been printed there and are stirring up "lively interest. "

        Obviously not all children's books can or should in-
clude Negroes.   The story of a family in Plymouth Colony or
in modern Sweden would be distorted if Negro faces were
shown.   Certainly no author or artist should be required to
follow any formula for integration.

But, consciously or unconsciously, most writers and
artists have long been following the formula for pure white
books. Some of the distortions caused by this formula are
ludicrous. For example, We Live in the City, a simple pic-
ture-book by Bert Ray (Childrens Press, 1963), tells of
Laurie and Gregg looking over the city of Chicago--a city
that apparently has no Negroes.

Only white people appear in Your Brain, by Margaret
O. Hyde (McGraw-Hill, 1964). In books of science experi-
ments, it is usually a white hand that holds the thermometer,
a white arm reaching for a test tube, white children feeding
the guinea pig. In books of poetry it is a white face smiling
over the first stanza.

While making a survey of G. P. Putnam's books of
the past three years, Putnam's juvenile editor Tom MacPher-
son came upon an illustrated novel about professional football,
with not a single Negro player among the professionals.
"That embarrassed us considerably," he wrote.

Several juvenile editors expressed similar concern.
"I was surprised," wrote Virginie Fowler, editor of Knopf's
Borzoi Books for Young People, "to realize how few books
we have on our list that accept an integrated society.... as I
look at my titles and think of the books [I realize] in many
instances they could easily have been books about a Negro
child or could have been shared books of child and friend. "

Executives at Golden Press analyzed the Little Golden
Books of 1962, 1963, and 1964 and decided that thirteen of
their all-white books could have included Negroes in a per-
fectly natural, realistic way. One of these is A Visit to a
Children's Zoo, cited by Whitney Young, Jr. ("He is certainly right," said the Golden Press editor. "A missed opportunity for a natural handling of the situation. ")

In the meantime, the Negro market has expanded to
at least $25 billion in consumer purchasing power, according
to John H. Johnson, publisher of Ebony. The Negro school
population and the number of Negro teachers are growing
rapidly, particularly in the large urban centers. With vastly
increased funds available through government sources, a huge
economic force is building up for integrated schools and integrated reading materials.

Lacking good children's books about Negro history,

many school libraries are purchasing the $5.95 adult book,
A Pictorial History of the Negro in America, by Langston
Hughes and Milton Meltzer (Crown). Boards of education in
both New York and Detroit have written and published their
own paperback Negro histories for young readers.

The integrated readers produced by the Detroit Board
of Education and published in 1964 by Follett for in-school
use are now being sold in paperback in the bookstores--
where parents are reported to be buying eagerly.

The market that most publishers are avoiding is being cultivated by--of all corporations--the Pepsi-Cola Company, which has produced an excellent LP recording Adventures in Negro History. This has been made available to
schools through local soft-drink distributors. The first pressing of 10,000 copies was grabbed up almost immediately, according to Russell Harvey, director of Special Market Services. After a year, 100,000 copies had been distributed and
a second record is being made. (The first record, filmstrip,
and script may be purchased for $5 through the Special Mar-
kets Division of Pepsi-Cola, 500 Park Avenue, New York,
N. Y. 10022).

What about the children's books coming out in 1965?
According to reports from editors, about 9 per cent of their
1965 books will include one or more Negroes. This is 1.5
per cent above the average for 1964.

In addition, there will be a continuing trend to up-
date or reissue earlier books that include Negroes. Among
those re-issued in the past three years: My Dog Rinty, by
Ellen Tarry and Marie Hall Ets (Viking); Black Fire: A
Story of Henri Christophe, by C. Newcomb (McKay); Famous
Women Singers, by Ulrich (Dodd, Mead); The Story of the
Negro, by Arna Bontemps (Knopf); and The Barred Road, by
Adele DeLeeuw (Macmillan). Ladder to the Sky, by Ruth
Forbes Chandler (Abelard), which went out of print for sev-
eral years, has returned in 1965.

This year Doubleday is launching its new Zenith Books,
"to explain America's minorities. " These books are planned
for supplementary reading in high school English and social
studies classes. The accompanying Teacher's Manual puts
them more definitely with textbooks than with trade books.

Many juvenile editors who state determination to pre-

sent a completely fair picture of Negroes in our multiracial
society add the reservation: "where it seems natural and
not forced."

"We don't set about deliberately to do these things,"
writes Margaret McElderry, editor of children's books at
Harcourt, Brace & World, "but take them as they seem natural and right."

"We plan to continue to introduce Negroes where it
can be handled in context and illustrations in a normal way,"
says Margaret E. Braxton, vice president of Garrard Publishing Company. "Artificial books forcing the racial issue
are not a part of our future plans."

"Most publishers are eagerly looking for manuscripts
that deal with integration and the problems faced by Negroes
in our country," writes Mrs. Esther K. Meeks, children's
book editor of Follett Publishing Company. "If we found
twice as many publishable books that included Negroes in a
natural and sympathetic manner, we should be happy to publish them." South Town, by Lorenz Graham, winner of the
Follett Award of 1958, is one of the few books for young
people that tells a realistic story of the violence resulting
from racial prejudice.

Fabio Coen, editor of Pantheon Books for children,
makes this comment: "A book even remotely discussing racial problems has to deal with the subject with the same
spontaneity and honesty that is basically required of any book.
To my mind, it is therefore impossible to commission one."

The newly formed Council on Interracial Books for
Children operates on the principle that, given encouragement,
authors and artists will create good children's books that include nonwhites, and that given the manuscripts, publishers
will produce and market them. The Council, sponsored by
a group including Benjamin Spock, Ben Shahn, Langston
Hughes, Mary Gaver, Alex Rosen, Harold Taylor, Harry
Golden, and Sidonie M. Gruenberg, will offer prizes for outstanding manuscripts and will negotiate with editors for their
publication.

The crisis that brought the Council into being is described by one of its organizing members, Elinor Sinnette,
district school librarian for the Central and East Harlem
Area of New York: "Publishers have participated in a cul-

tural lobotomy.   It is no accident that Negro history and Negro identification have been forgotten.   Our society has contrived to make the American Negro a rootless person.   The
Council for Interracial Books for Children has been formed
to relieve this situation. "

        Whether the Council gets many books into print or not,
it can accomplish a great deal simply by reminding editors
and publishers that what is good for the Ku Klux Klan is not
necessarily good for America--or for the book business.
White supremacy in children's literature will be abolished
when authors, editors, publishers, and booksellers decide
that they need not submit to bigots.

20. THE DAWNING OF THE AGE OF AQUARIUS
     FOR MULTI-ETHNIC CHILDREN'S LITERATURE*
     (Excerpt)

     David Gast

     I'd like to make a few observations on the present
state and possible future of multi-ethnic children's literature,
hoping, of course, that my comments might serve to elicit
discussion. Let me start out by disclaiming any great ex-
pertise in the field of children's literature. My training has
been in the social scientific and philosophic foundations of
education. With this background I made my now reasonably
well-known study in children's literature. Of course, I got
hooked on it. So you're listening to a fellow who divides
his academic interests between philosophy of education and
children's literature, at first thought, an unseemly combination, but in reality a rather delightful one. My comments
are random rather than organized.

     First, let me say that we educators and scholars find
ourselves all too often on the trailing edge of innovation in
education and society. Quite often we know what needs to be
done but we are seldom innovators partly because we see our
role as objective interpreters of what passes for reality,
partly because we fear taking a stand, partly because we

---

*Editors' Note: Professor Gast's doctoral dissertation,
"Characteristics and Concepts of Minority Americans in Contemporary Children's Fictional Literature," which he refers
to in this article as a "reasonably well-known study," contains this conclusion: "traditional, non-complimentary stereotypes have largely disappeared from the literature." This
conclusion is somewhat misleading because Dr. Gast's study
overlooked numerous forms of insidious racism. He did not
attempt to show the simultaneous presence of complimentary
stereotypes and racist attitudes in a majority of books. In
the article reprinted here he lists some of the typical ways
that minorities are represented in current publications.

have little direct influence, and partly because we might lose
our heads and our academic respectability in going for a
"cause." The real innovators can mainly be found in the
creative arts. Surely the search for tomorrow is taking
form in the heads and hearts of those who risk their respectability by disavowing belief in a deterministic world dominated by old myths.

Our problem with children's literature and teaching
materials (and with all other areas of education as well) is
that of keeping the human spirit and potential in stride with
our free-wheeling technology and the social implications this
technology has. Because, as we ought to know, technology
is a two edged sword. Among other things, technology has
made us aware of poverty in a consumer-product oriented
America and our ability to do something about it if we decide
to. So we have increasing educational concern in our day for
the social imperative voiced about 200 years ago by Immanuel
Kant: "Man is to be treated as an end, not a means."

You are probably in agreement with this last sentiment
or you would not be concerned that educational literature
should reflect a viable past, present, and future for minority Americans. And I surely believe most of you are interested in dispelling old myths about minorities.

Children's literature is a conservative medium in a tra-
ditionally conservative social institution. But as a number of
scholars have shown, children's fictional literature has been
a more flexible, up-to-date vehicle for mirroring social reality than the media of textbooks. This will probably continue
to be the case for some time even though some publishers
are giving up "mint julep" editions of their various lines of
textbooks. So we have hope. But we also have some problems. How do we presently view minorities in children's
literature? How will we view them in the future?

Let's take a look at some past, present, and possible
future approaches to the treatment of minorities in the literature. The categories that I enumerate here are not mutually
exclusive. I've been somewhat factitious in labeling them
but I think you'll recognize them.

1) The Invisible Man Approach. Perhaps the worst
treatment of minorities is no treatment at all. A number of
studies have indicated that our literature is guilty of sins of
ommission. The minority American is the man who just

doesn't enter into the picture when we reflect upon our society.

2) The Noble-Savage Approach. Since Rousseau, Western man has had a fondness for the ideal of the noble-savage,
the simple natural man who lives a rugged and virile life
close to nature without the bonds of complex social restric-
tions. Of course this is a hopelessly romantic view that
overlooks actual hardships and implies a separatist existence
with little interest on the part of the minority portrayed as
desiring integration or holding dominant American values.
American Indians and Mexican-Americans have typically been
portrayed in this way. It's interesting to note that many liberal middle-class whites now view Negroes in this light,
somewhat jealous of the alleged black freedom of physical
expression.

3) The White Man's Burden Approach. A familiar approach in older texts and children's literature is the explicit
or implicit idea that the minorities portrayed are dependent
upon white benefactors. This view is inherent in darky-on-
the-old-plantation settings. It is also the message when history books talk of immigrants as being social problems. Recent literature has largely moved away from this kind of pa-
tronizing.

4) The Minstrel Show Approach. Largely limited to
children's books about Negroes, this approach portrayed the
Negro as a happy-go-lucky, tattered, "coon." Low comedy
was achieved through situational farces and stereotyped dialect. Inez Hogan's Nicodemus books were typical of this
category and were printed up until 1945. We no longer tol-
erate such books.

5) The Queer Customs Approach. Literature in this
category is usually a well-meaning attempt to illustrate the
unique cultural traditions and beliefs, generally of American
Indians, Spanish-Americans or Chinese-Americans. Most
books about Indians fall into this category as well as books
like Leo Politi's Pedro, The Angel of Olvera Street and Moy
Moy. At worst, such books stereotype minority Americans
in regard to dress, occupation, and life style. At best, children should not be fed a steady diet of these books. A related and disturbing fact is that many teachers assume that
books dealing with life in the land of national origin will provide sound generalizations for understanding a minority American. I'm thinking particularly of reading about life in Mex-

ico in order to understand a bicultural person, the Mexican-American.

6) The Multi-Ethnic Dick and Jane Approach. This is a new approach and in many ways a viable one. In primary and easy reading books children are portrayed in multi-ethnic settings in school. They are all getting along well with one another. This approach illustrates an ideal but is subject to the same kind of criticism leveled at Textbook Town--too aseptic, too goody-goody, and artificial.

7) The Reversed Stereotype Approach. We are still trying to overcome occupational and life-style stereotypes that have dominated the literature for many years. One sure-fire but questionable way to do it is the stereotype switch. We've seen this in the media of television and in some books. For example, showing all blacks as middle-class professionals is likely to cause problems of reader identification among ghetto children. One must say however that such books are in the American tradition of encouraging middle-class values and virtues.

8) The Tell-It-Like-It-Is Approach. This category is perhaps the most popular genre in children's literature today. Few punches are pulled. Ghetto and tenement living is shown. Discrimination, racial conflict, family hardships are all dealt with in a realistic fashion usually devoid of moralizing. Dorothy Sterling's Mary Jane was one of the first books about Negroes with this approach. Clyde Robert Bulla's Indian Hill shows the problems of Indians trying to make a life for themselves in the city.

9) The Remanufactured Past Approach. Although we have a great distance to go in honoring the historical contributions of various minorities to American arts, letters, and science, some pitfalls are apparent. We must avoid the hastily contrived out-of-context appendix to history. And we must also avoid giving the false notion that minority American inventors, professionals, and artists were as numerous and prolific as their white counterparts. Let's face it, social conditions didn't always foster minority contributions. History has been interpreted, rewritten, and fictionalized as long as man has been on earth. It's a natural part of man's tendency to seek mythic support for his beliefs. The question is how scholarly and objective do we wish to be.

I am sure that you can think of other categories, es-

pecially possible categories of future depictions.   And that
brings me to another consideration.   What are the present
and future taboos in children's literature dealing with minority Americans and multi-ethnic portrayals?   An advertisement of Houghton Mifflin Company Children's Book Department claims, "So far as we know there is no taboo against
fantasy, sex, booze, integration, mischief, and mayhem..."
But surely there are taboos dictated by present attitudes and
tastes, sales appeal, reading level, maturity level of reader.
What are the taboos?   At what grade levels and in what ways
can social problems and conflict situations be introduced?
Or should conflict situations be the only thematic vehicle for
bringing about inter-group understanding?

    Some of our recent Tell-it-like-it-is books are hard
hitting accounts of social realism including topics of: black
power, poverty, fierce racial pride, integration, inner-city
living, and family disorganization.   When are we going to
approach interracial dating and marriage, mixed marriages,
Oriental war brides and Eurasian children?   I've just taken
note of a new book by John Neufeld entitled Edgar Allan
about a white family which adopts a Negro boy.   To what extent are these areas taboos?

    In closing I'd like to say that children's literature can
be an effective means of transmitting values and attitudes
about minorities and their relationship with white Americans.
You all realize its tremendous potential in what we might
call "culture therapy" and also bibliotherapy.

    We should not forget that children's literature has a
mythic quality and function.   Otfried Müller has told us that
myth is a narrative that unites the real with the ideal.   We
have cultural ideals and we have manifest cultural reality.
We need to unite the two.   And it seems to me that this is
part of the reason for producing and using children's literature.   Any culture in which reality and ideal are greatly
separated is a culture which suffers from what Durkheim
called anomie with the resultant alienation of individuals and
social groups.   We'd hope that literature could help prevent
cultural disintegration by reflecting a rapprochement of the
ideal and the manifest culture in acceptable mythic form.

    Yet, there are some cautions.   Back in 1908 Georges
Sorel suggested that myth was the most effective political
and ideological weapon known to man.   Ernst Cassirer re-
iterated this view in 1945 when he said that myth is "a thing

of crucial importance.   It has changed the whole form of our
social life. "

So for those of us interested in the minority Americans in children's literature--teachers, scholars, authors,
publishers, librarians--the basic questions remain philosophi-
cal: What ideals do we wish to promote?   How far beyond
the present social status quo do we go in depicting the future
reality our children will be living with?   How can we help
promote the good life and the good society for all citizens?
In short, ladies and gentlemen, it is the dawning of the age
of Aquarius for multi-ethnic portrayals in children's literature.   We've all got a lot to live.   So--Where are we going?
How will we get there?   And how will we know we've ar-
rived?

21. THE SOUL OF LEARNING (Excerpt)

Dorothy Sterling

I have had a general impression, which perhaps you
share, that there has been an outpouring of books about Negroes for young people. The impression has certainly been
bolstered by an outpouring of book lists. In Erwin Salk's
handy Layman's Guide to Negro History (McGraw-Hill), he
notes more than a dozen bibliographies prepared by public libraries in New York, Chicago, Philadelphia, Milwaukee, by
American Friends Service Committee, the American Jewish
Committee, etc. While doing my homework for this confrontation, I discovered several others, including two that I think
you'll find particularly useful: "Books by and about the American Negro," selected by Young Adult Librarians at the Countee Cullen Branch of the New York Public Library, and "Bibliography of Materials by and about Negro Americans for
Young Readers," prepared by Atlanta University, for the
U.S. Office of Education.

But aside from the lists, what about the books themselves? Are there enough books--and enough good books--
that present honestly the Negro experience in the United
States?

Thirty years ago--and indeed for a long time before
that--books about Negroes were, to borrow a phrase from
Hollywood, box-office poison. There were exceptions, of
course. Uncle Tom's Cabin sold well. A century after its
publication, Ralph Ellison won a National Book Award for Invisible Man (Random House). In between a handful of Negro
writers managed to break into print.

In an article titled, "Uncle Remus, Farewell," Arna
Bontemps tells of haunting the public library in Los Angeles
when he was a youngster, seeking a recognizable reflection
of himself and his world. "What I found was of cold comfort, to say the least," he writes. "Nothing more inspiring
than Our Little Ethiopian Cousin was on the shelves, and I
read almost every book in the room to make sure. Moreover, Our Little Ethiopian Cousin was not me and his world

175

was not mine. "

Two decades later, when his children were growing
up, all he could locate for them was The Pickaninny Twins.
Trying to provide them with something less damaging, he began to write children's books with Negro characters and
themes.   In the thirties he had the field almost to himself.
His first book, You Can't Pet A Possum, published in 1934,
was marred by stereotyped illustrations, but he continued
with Sad-Faced Boy, Lonesome Boy, The Fast Sooner Hound
(all Houghton Mifflin) and others.   In addition to fiction, he
edited Golden Slippers (Harper), an anthology of Negro poetry
for young people, wrote We Have Tomorrow (Houghton), a
book of biographies, and The Story of the Negro (Knopf).

Langston Hughes collaborated with Bontemps on Popo
and Fifina, a story with a Haitian setting, and prepared a
collection of his own poetry for young people, The Dream
Keeper (Knopf).   Then Jesse Jackson came along with some
boys' stories: Call Me Charley (Harper) and Anchor Man
(Harper), Ellen Tarry wrote My Dog Rinty (Viking), about a
boy and his dog in Harlem, and Ernest Crichlow and Jerrold
Beim collaborated on Two Is a Team (Harcourt), the first
"integrated" picture book, and for a long time the only one.

In 1947, Shirley Graham won an award for the "best
book combatting intolerance in America" with There Was
Once a Slave (Messner), and thousands of people encountered
Frederick Douglass for the first time.   I know, because I
was one of those people.   With my children, I continued to
read her groundbreaking string of biographies--of Phillis
Wheatley, Benjamin Banneker, Jean Baptiste du Sable, George
Washington Carver, Booker T. Washington.   I remember listening to a radio adaptation of her Story of Phillis Wheatley
(Messner) with a Negro friend.   My friend burst into tears
during the program.   "Why didn't somebody tell me about
this?" she sobbed.

In addition to these Negro authors, a small number of
white writers--people like Marguerite de Angeli, Adele De-
Leeuw, Florence Means, Hope Newell (I think they're all
white)--began to tackle the problems of prejudice and explore
Negro history.   In 1951 Elizabeth Yates won the Newbery
Medal for Amos Fortune, Free Man (Dutton), a biography of
a slave in eighteenth-century New England who earned his
freedom.   It's a well-written, carefully researched book, but
I was a bit suspicious about the thinking behind the award.

Almost until the end, Amos Fortune kept saying "No, I'm
not ready for freedom--don't give it to me yet. " I couldn't
help wondering if his humility wasn't a part of the book's appeal.   However, it is described enthusiastically in the Atlanta
University bibliography, so perhaps I'm wrong.   Still, if I
were a teacher in a ghetto school, I wouldn't put it on my
reading list.

Around the time of the Supreme Court decision on
school integration there was a flurry of interest in books
about Negroes.   Gwendolyn Brooks published her Bronzeville
Boys and Girls (Harper), Langston Hughes wrote Famous
American Negroes (Dodd) and Famous Negro Music Makers
(Dodd).   Emma Gelders Sterne revived the Amistad case in
The Long Black Schooner and followed this with a biography
of Mary McCleod Bethune.   I wrote Freedom Train, The
Story of Harriet Tubman (Doubleday) and a year later came
Ann Petry's excellent biography, Harriet Tubman: Conductor
of the Underground Railroad.

The flurry didn't last long.   The white South, you will
remember, soon reacted to the Supreme Court with a loud
"Never!"   This was the period when White Citizens Councils
mushroomed, when the Klan was revived, and southern librarians were attacked if they displayed a copy of Garth Williams' The Rabbits' Wedding (Harper), a picture book describing the marriage of a black rabbit and a white rabbit.

I can speak at first hand about these years.   In 1955
I went to South Carolina to work on a biography of Robert
Smalls, a slave who became a Civil War hero and, later, a
Congressman from South Carolina.   The reconstruction period, as it emerged from my research, was totally at variance
with the then cherished notion of "the tragic era. "   When my
editor read the manuscript of Captain of the Planter (Doubleday), she was frankly reluctant to publish it.   It was one
thing to write about Harriet Tubman who fought against slavery.   By 1955 even White Citizens Council members admitted
that slavery was wrong.   But to tell the often brutal, truly
tragic story of Negro disfranchisement and the birth of Jim
Crow was something else again.   All southern markets would
be closed to the book, and she wasn't at all sure about northern ones.   Fortunately for me, she sent the manuscript to
Arna Bontemps for his opinion, and he was so enthusiastic
that it was finally published.   Although it has never been a
best seller, it is still in print.   In fact, it is now on the
list of books approved for schools by the South Carolina State

Department of Education!

     After I finished Captain of the Planter, I traveled
through the mid-South to talk with the Negro and white children who were entering integrated schools for the first time.
Myron Ehrenberg, a photographer, accompanied me and together we turned out Tender Warriors, a picture and text
report of the unbelievably brave young people who were walking through screaming mobs to go to school.   The text con-
sisted largely of the students' own words, along with interviews with their parents.   It was really a moving little book
and the first thing of its kind.   Few people were interested,
however, and it soon went out of print.

     I mention it now only to tell you of a curious incident
connected with it.   Tender Warriors was published by Hill
& Wang in 1958.   Months before its publication, the publishers were informed by the U.S. Information Agency that the
book was disapproved for export under the informational media guaranty program.   This is the program that guarantees
dollars instead of francs, marks, etc. to U.S. publishers
who export books.   Without the guarantee, of course, it's
scarcely worthwhile to attempt to sell a book overseas.   The
Hill & Wang people were sufficiently piqued about the rejection of a book before it had been read that they pursued the
matter further.   In reply to a series of letters, the U.S. Information Agency informed them that the disapproval was
on the description of the book in their catalogue.   Therefore,
when the book finally appeared a copy was sent to the clear-
ance officer at the Information Agency for re-review.   His
answer came promptly: "We regret to inform you that this
publication is not eligible for export under the informational
media guaranty program."   No reason was ever forthcoming.
Was the book disapproved because of its subject matter?
Your guess is as good as mine.   However, I think the incident sheds some light on the national mood in the late '50s.

     Tender Warriors was intended for adults and young
adults, but I was so emotionally involved with the children I
had met in the South that I went on to write Mary Jane
(Doubleday), a fictional account of a Negro girl's first year
in an integrated school.   My editor at Doubleday winced when
I told her about it.   "Couldn't you set it in the North?" she
asked.

     I couldn't.   I wrote it as I saw it and, after some
backing and forthing, Doubleday published it in 1959.   At a

cocktail party that fall--sometimes you learn more at a party
than at an editorial conference--a salesman told me that although he liked some of my books he wouldn't dare enter a
bookstore in Chicago with a book that had a picture of a Negro on its jacket. But this story has a happy ending, for
Mary Jane won a few awards, sold well in 1959, and is selling better now, even in Chicago. And, as a footnote for the
U.S. Information Agency, it has been published in seven
European countries.

　　　　I was lucky. My publishers were willing to gamble.
Other writers were not as fortunate. The same year that
Mary Jane appeared, an acquaintance wrote a far less controversial book about a Negro child visiting a white family
for a Fresh Air Fund vacation. Her book was already in
galleys when the sales department heard about it. They were
so dead set against it that she was obliged to revise it,
transforming the Negro youngster into a white one. At still
another publishing house, an editor reports that during the
'50s she brought out three books in which Negroes appeared.
"The books won favorable comment," she said, "but the effect on sales was negative. Customers returned not only
these titles but all stock from our company. This meant an
appreciable loss and tempered attitudes toward further use
of Negro children in illustrations and text."

　　　　Of course, there wasn't a total white-out of books
about Negroes during these years. Arna Bontemps wrote
Frederick Douglass: Slave, Fighter, Freeman (Knopf); Henrietta Buckmaster, Flight to Freedom (Crowell); Jean Gould,
That Dunbar Boy (Dodd); Mimi Levy, Corrie and the Yankee
(Viking); etc. But no one was holding out a carrot or swinging a stick to induce authors and editors to enter the field.

　　　　Then came the student sit-ins and freedom rides, the
Birmingham bombing, the Civil Rights Acts, the struggle
against de facto segregation in the North. In every section
of the country there has been a growing awareness of civil
rights and a growing demand for picture books, stories, biographies, history about Negroes. We have seen a number
of severely critical studies of the history textbooks used in
schools, as well as blistering attacks on the Dick-and-Jane
type readers that show only middle-class white suburban
families.

　　　　I won't pretend to be an expert on primers but, from
newspaper stories and an NAACP study on "Integrated School

Books," I gather that Dick and Jane have been making new
friends--and some of them are black. The Bank Street Readers series, the Skyline series, and others show children in
urban as well as suburban settings and dark faces appear increasingly in spellers, science, and math books. Some of
these changes are a bit mechanical. At the Education and
Labor Committee hearings I learned of one textbook publisher
who instructed his artist to make every tenth person a Negro
in his illustrations. Another temporarily solved his market-
ing problems with three editions of a primer. In one, all
the children portrayed are white. In the second, some are
brown. In the third, the children are white, but the teachers pictured wear nuns' garb. One edition for the South, one
for urban schools in the North, one for parochial schools!

     The picture is far less bright in the field of history
texts. Adult readers can find new interpretations of the
slavery period, the anti-slavery movement, reconstruction,
and so on. A little of this "new history" which should be
more correctly called "true history," has begun to trickle
down to school texts. A study made by Irving Sloan for the
American Federation of Teachers shows that generally the
history texts of 1966 are an improvement over 1956. But
not much. Some now have inserts describing the death of
Crispus Attucks at the Boston Massacre. Harriet Tubman
and Frederick Douglass are mentioned. Readers are told
that 200,000 Negro soldiers fought in the Civil War. There
is a slightly more balanced but still woefully inadequate
treatment of reconstruction, and a few books have a supplement covering the civil rights movement and the Negro today.
Among the thirteen books Sloan analyzed, only one Land of
the Free (Crowell) by John Hope Franklin, John W. Caughey,
and Ernest R. May, comes close to presenting the "true history." And the picture is even darker than Sloan paints it
because schools don't buy new textbooks every year. Many
are continuing to use the same old distorted ones. I went
through the textbook assigned to the seniors in the high school
in my community--it's called History of a Free People by the
way--and found it disappointingly full of misstatements,
omissions, and bias.

     As you undoubtedly know, textbook publishing is a
multi-billion dollar industry. Each text represents a large
capital investment so that asking a text publisher to rewrite
a history book is a little like asking General Motors to de-
sign a new car. Trade books, however, are issued in much
smaller editions. Because there is less money riding on an

individual book, trade publishers are able to respond more
rapidly to new ideas, new programs, new audiences....

Let's play a numbers game for a minute. There were
roughly twelve thousand children's trade books issued in the
seven-year period from 1960 through 1966. If we say that
eighty, perhaps one hundred and twenty, dealt with the Negro
past and present in the United States, that means that at best
1 per cent of the total output of books for young people are
devoted to the Negro.

Is this possible? Have I made a mistake in arithmetic? I don't think so. Two years ago Nancy Larrick, former president of the International Reading Association, jolted
the publishing world with an article in Saturday Review titled
"The All-White World of Children's Books." She sent a
questionnaire to the seventy members of the Children's Book
Council. From sixty-three replies she found that out of
5,206 children's books issued between 1962 and 1964 only
6.7 per cent included a Negro in text or illustrations. Her
figure is higher than mine because the questionnaire replies
included books that showed Negroes only in illustrations, as
well as books about Africa, the Caribbean, etc. When she
subtracted these and the histories and biographies she reported that only four-fifths of 1 per cent of the books told a
story about American Negroes today.

Since it takes a year or two to write a book, and another year before publication, perhaps the situation has
changed since her article appeared. Twice a year Publishers' Weekly puts out a special Children's Book Number reporting on forthcoming books. Their issue of July 10, 1967,
describes the children's books that will be published this fall.
I always go through these special numbers with a sinking feeling, afraid that the books I would like to do have already
been done by others. I needn't have worried. From the ads
and thumbnail descriptions of more than five hundred books
I found just fourteen about Negro Americans. And that really
gave me a sinking feeling.

Four are biographies, two collective biographies, one
an anthology of poetry. The fiction includes two sports stories about boys who want to become boxers, one about inte-
grating a school, one about two girls who go from a city
slum to a summer camp, and one about a boy living in a
mixed neighborhood in Brooklyn. Good enough as far as it
goes, but it doesn't go very far, does it?

Only 2.8 per cent of the current output of books for
young people are concerned with the most burning issue of
our time.   When Arna Bontemps' grandchildren go to the library they won't have to read every book on the shelves and
find only Our Ethiopian Cousin.   But they will have to read
ninety-seven books before they discover three that speak to
them.

And it is not only Negro youngsters who are being deprived.   As Nancy Larrick says, "The impact of all-white
books upon 39,600,000 white children is probably even worse."
How can they understand the news on television and in the
newspapers?   Increasingly isolated from their darker con-
temporaries, how well are these white children being prepared for the larger adult world in which they are globally
a minority?

I'd like to carry this discussion a step further by asking "Why?"   Are editors and authors less liberal, more prejudiced than the rest of American society?   Certainly not.
Those I know, at least, are probably more concerned, more
open to new ideas than the average citizen.   Are they then
only interested in money?   The dollar is a factor, of course.
Both writers and publishers must be paid for their efforts.
But the economic picture has changed radically since the
1950s--and most radically since the passage of the Elementary and Secondary Education Act of 1965, which released
millions of dollars to libraries and schools for the purchase
of books for the educationally deprived.   There's gold in
them thar hills now.   I doubt if any trade publishers or book
salesmen would turn down a reasonably well-written book because it portrayed a Negro.

Then why?   President Johnson has said "You do not
wipe away the scars of centuries by saying 'Now you are
free to go where you want.'   You do not take a man who,
for years, has been hobbled by chains, liberate him, and
then say, 'you're free to compete with all the others.'   It is
not enough just to open the gates of opportunity."

He was speaking of Negroes, but his words could also be applied to editors and writers.   You do not take minds
that have been hobbled by centuries of racism and say, "Now
you're free to write the truth."   What is the truth?   Most
white people and many Negroes don't know.   And there's
more than that, of course.   When you begin to write the
truth, you bump into all sorts of obstacles.   Consider the

rule of the happy or at least upbeat ending. Should we tell
the children that in real life people do not always live happily ever after?

I faced this problem when I was writing Mary Jane
and didn't really solve it properly. I compromised by letting
her make one friend in school and ending with the hope that
she would make more next year. When the book was published the bright, warmhearted little girl who lives next door
asked, "Is it really that bad?" "Much worse," I answered.
"Why today's paper tells about the bombing of the home of
an eight-year-old boy because he went to a 'white' school."
"Oh, don't tell me about it!" she said and ran home.

Should she be told? I think so.

Even more ticklish are the rules of American society.
A policeman is a boy's best friend. Is he? Does a black
boy in Philadelphia, Mississippi, think that about Sheriff
Rainey, accused of conspiring to kill Chaney, Schwerner, and
Goodman in 1964? Does a boy in Newark or Detroit think
so? Not according to what I see in the newspapers.

Recently I've read two books that every high school
student should read. One is Mississippi Black Paper (Random), published in 1965, with a foreword by Reinhold Niebuhr and an introduction by Hodding Carter III. It consists
of the testimony of fifty-seven Negro and white civil rights
workers on the breakdown of law and order, the corruption
of justice, and brutality of the police in Mississippi. The
other is The Torture of Mothers by Truman Nelson. Nelson
tells, largely through tape-recorded interviews, of the arrest
of six Harlem boys for a murder they did not commit, of
beatings administered by the police, and of slanted stories in
the press. There is plenty of raw material for books for
young people here--really raw.

Books that tell it like it is--and nothing less will be
acceptable today--must challenge all sorts of hitherto cherished beliefs. You were probably as shocked as I was, a
couple of years ago, by the plot to blow up the Statue of Liberty. I'm still not sure there really was such a plot, but
think how the Goddess of Liberty welcoming the world's poor
and oppressed must look to a Negro teen-ager. When I was
growing up, I recited the pledge of allegiance, "with liberty
and justice for all," with real emotion. I was not aware--I
had no way of learning--that the Goddess of Liberty was say-

ing "But not for you" to large numbers of my fellow citizens.
We have to tell young people about this, particularly white
youngsters.

History must be completely rewritten, not just revised
with supplements tacked on to the end. Seven biographies of
George Washington Carver, three of Harriet Tubman, two of
Frederick Douglass, one of Benjamin Banneker--it's like a
giant jigsaw puzzle with most of the pieces missing. There's
a scrap of blue sky, the top of a tree, but you can't even
guess what the whole picture looks like.

Where is Paul Cuffee who built up his own fleet of
ships in the Eighteenth Century and carried Negroes back to
Africa when he couldn't find justice in his home state of
Massachusetts? And James Forten, sailmaker for the U. S.
Navy and Revolutionary War veteran, who was penning anti-
slavery pamphlets as far back as 1812? And Forten's son-
in-law, Robert Purvis, handsome, well-educated, wealthy,
who sheltered thousands of escaping slaves? And William
Still who kept the records for the Pennsylvania branch of the
underground railroad? And black abolitionists like the Re-
monds and Henry Highland Garnet, William Wells Brown,
Alexander Crummell, whom you read about in Souls of Black
Folk?

I'm out of breath and I'm barely up to the Civil War.
Why has so little been written about the twenty-two Negroes
who served in Congress during Reconstruction and after?
The black Populists? The men and women of the early twen-
tieth century who spoke, wrote, fought for Negro freedom?
It's time for young people's biographies of W. E. B. DuBois,
A. Philip Randolph, Marcus Garvey.

I can think of a dozen episodes from history that
should be written about, not only because they demonstrate
Negro courage or the Negro's contribution to American society, but also because they would make darn good stories.
And there are hundreds more.

Who will write these books? And who will write about
today's young people in urban ghettoes and the rural South?

I believe that publishers are ready to bring out the
books. However, they are somewhat in the position of a
manufacturer who puts a sticker--a small one--in his window
announcing that he is an Equal Opportunity Employer and then

says, "But no Negroes have applied." Not many Negroes are
likely to apply. The welcome mat has been out for such a
short time that they have not had a chance to see it.

Whitney Young of the Urban League has proposed a
"more-than-equal" program in which employers seek out qualified Negroes for jobs and train those who lack qualifications.
"For more than three hundred years the white American has
received preferential treatment over the Negro," he says.
"What we ask now is that there be a deliberate and massive
attempt to include the Negro citizen in the mainstream of
American life." I'm asking editors to make a deliberate and
massive effort to seek out Negro writers and manuscripts
with Negro themes. By this I don't mean that only Negro
writers can do the job. I happen to be hooked on Negro history, and I don't plan to give up my addiction. But from
my comfortable suburban home, I cannot write a story about
a girl in Harlem or a boy in Lowndes County, Alabama--and
doubtless other white authors feel the same way.

I can almost hear rumbles from editorial offices....
You can't write books to order.... You can't commission
books.... You'll only get formula books with pat solutions
.... Nonsense! Books are written to order all the time.
Three of my books--not about Negroes--were written because
Doubleday salesmen said there was a need for them. I've
just completed a book suggested by my editor--and the suggestion, I'm glad to say, was that I write about the civil
rights revolution. I am definitely not asking for formula
books with pat solutions. That's why I believe Negro writers
should be sought out and convinced to try their hand at books
for young people.

An organization that feels as I do about this is the
Council on Interracial Books for Children, which was founded
by a group of children's book writers and children's librarians, along with such concerned citizens as Harry Golden,
Benjamin Spock, and Harold Taylor. They are currently
sponsoring a contest for the best children's books by Negroes,
with $500 prizes for the best manuscript for ages three to
six, seven to eleven, and twelve to sixteen.

There are also two Negro organizations turning out
reference books. The Negro Heritage Library is planning a
twenty volume encyclopedia and has already issued seven volumes, one a Negro Heritage Reader for Young People which
reprints folk tales, songs, poetry, and prose by Negro au-

thors. The other books in the series--none too difficult for
high school readers--include Profiles of Negro Womanhood,
A Martin Luther King Treasury, The Winding Road to Freedom, Negroes in Public Affairs and Government, etc. The
Association for the Study of Negro Life and History which,
for too long a time, was the only group that knew there was
such a thing as Negro history, is preparing an International
Library of Negro Life and History (Books, Inc.). Their
first five volumes cover Negro Americans in the Civil War,
The History of the Negro in Medicine, Anthology of the
American Negro in the Theatre, Historical Negro Biographies,
and The Negro in Music and Art.

     Aside from these, Doubleday is, I believe, the only
trade book house that has begun to make the sort of deliberate effort I am suggesting, with its Zenith series which, incidentally, was initiated by a Negro editor. Ordinarily I dislike series books. They tend to be pedestrian and, over the
years, to run downhill. The Zenith series is uneven. Some
of the books are very good and some only fair. But in this
long, hot summer of 1967 wouldn't you rather give a youngster a fair book that tells the truth, instead of a pretty good
one about, say, a talking mouse? Let's face it. Not all of
the books published each season contain deathless prose--
and these books that were written to order stand up very
well. ...

     The fantastically difficult and yet hopeful job that con-
fronts us as teachers and writers is to provide the young
with the vision of conciliation, and the frame of mind and intellectual materials which will make conciliation possible.
And perhaps I have hit quite by accident, on the significant
word of the immediate future--conciliation. The concept of
"soul," no matter how many ways you define it, expresses
the growing Negro reaction against oppression and rejection
on one hand, and against assimilation or absorption on the
other.

     Integration, in the light of Negro experience since
1954, has lost considerable credibility among Negroes, as a
goal which is either attainable or desirable. But conciliation
remains applicable, not merely as a semantic convenience
but as a social process; because it means the coming together of antagonistic equals to resolve their antagonisms on a
footing of mutual respect. If this happens, and only when it
happens, will America stand a chance of becoming "the dream
the dreamers dreamed"--

> The land that never has been yet--
> And yet must be--
> The land where every man is free.

We are among those who have to help it happen.

22. BOOK PUBLISHING:
     A RACIST CLUB?

Bradford Chambers

The publishing industry was embarrassed several years
ago when, after it had given its top accolades to The Confessions of Nat Turner by a white author, William Styron, the
book was taken severely to task by Black critics; the publishing world was slow to admit that it had on its hands a very
racist book.

The same thing has happened again. Sounder, a story
about a family of Black sharecroppers--also written by a
white author--won the 1970 Newbery Medal, the most coveted
award in all of children's book publishing. A growing number of Blacks are now pointing out that, while the book does
indeed present some of the horrors of the Black Experience,
the story's positive points are negated by its racial stereotypes and white bias.

If we give our highest awards to books that try to de-
lineate the minority experience, yet, upon reexamination,
turn out to be inherently racist, what does this say about the
publishing industry?

It wasn't long ago that minorities were invisible in
books, particularly in books for children. This now is changing. A basic problem is that, with increased visibility, conscious and unconscious racism is also coming to the surface,
especially in commercially-oriented books which exploit the
new market represented by minority themes.

A superficial analysis might suggest that, in the rush
for profits from the so-called minority market, insufficient
care is taken in the editorial supervision of the books. That
is part of the answer, but a small part only. Books produced with elaborate editorial care can be just as guilty of
racial bias as books that are handled with little editorial
care.

In the course of these articles prepared for Publishers'

Weekly, we will examine the structures of publishing that our
Council believes are responsible for racism within the publishing industry.   A great deal is talked about along these
lines by editors and publishers in the privacy of their offices
and living rooms; but it needs to be brought out into the open
and faced with candor by all of us.

We will explore, for example, why book publishing
has been the least responsive of all the communications media to the practical and moral pressures to open its doors to
previously excluded minority groups.   We will examine a complaint of minority groups--a complaint which gains increasing
urgency--that establishment publishers are exploiting minorities by the profits they make from minority movements.

Last summer, Time magazine estimated that of the
6000 editorial personnel employed by American book publishers, only six editors were members of ethnic minorities.
In the children's book field, the area we know best, not a
single major publisher's book operation is directed by a minority editor.   Of the 80-odd publishers who belong to the
Children's Book Council--the publishers' trade organization--
we know of only one minority editor who heads a department.
There are as yet no complete statistics to verify this.   But
in cooperation with Publishers' Weekly, our Council is now
conducting a detailed survey of publishing recruitment practices as they affect minorities.   In a later atricle we shall
report on this survey.

Publishers are very much aware of the all-white structure of the industry, and it is a matter of record that they
have in fact taken some steps to open up the industry to minorities.   The question is: Do these steps add up to a commitment, to a sincere desire to change the structure of publishing?   Or are they tokenism only?   The record very definitely indicates the latter, that publishing as an industry has
acted mainly to counter publicity adverse to its image.

The record of an industry-wide move to recruit minority talent does not begin until early 1969, barely two
years ago.   Critics will comment that two years ago was
late to make such a move.   The time was late, and publishers realized it.   When at last the decision came, a sense of
extraordinary urgency seemed to impel it.

The record begins with two separate meetings, both
held in January 1969, in midtown Manhattan, both initiated by

official committees of the American Book Publishers Council
(since reorganized as a part of the Association of American
Publishers). The first meeting was held at the Waldorf-Astoria on January 15 and was widely reported in the press.
This meeting proposed an industry-wide minority recruitment
program. The second meeting was held later that month at
the Time and Life Building. The latter meeting, which was
closed and received no publicity, resulted in a proposal for
the industry to finance minority-owned-and-staffed publishing
houses.

        The Waldorf-Astoria meeting was a day-long seminar,
called by the ABPC's committee on management and adminis-
tration, to consider ways and means to recruit and train minority personnel within the publishing establishment. It resulted in a resolution adopted on May 6 at the annual meeting of the ABPC, held in Miami, Florida, to set up a minority manpower clearing house, with a budget of $25,000 to
$30,000 for a director's salary, secretary, travel and pub-
licity. The clearing house, to be called the Office of Minority Manpower, would seek out personnel primarily from
Black colleges and high schools. It would also establish and
coordinate on-the-job training and job-upgrading programs
within member publishing houses.

        Three months after the adoption of that resolution, a
representative of our Council spoke with a representative of
the ABPC staff, to inquire whether the Office of Minority
Manpower had been set up. The ABPC spokesman said,
"We regard the office as so critical and so desperately needed that we don't want to rush into it headlong, but want to
set it up gradually." The spokesman added that candidates
for the office would be interviewed in a few weeks, and that
a director would be hired to start recruiting on colleges and
campuses in the fall of 1969.

        A year later, in mid-August 1970, still no Office of
Minority Manpower. The delay this time, we were informed,
was caused by procedural difficulties involved in the ABPC's
merger with the American Educational Publishers Institute.

        The facts presented so far appeared in a report pre-
pared by our Council in late August 1970. The report was
presented to, among others, Publishers' Weekly. It became
the basis for an editorial in PW, August 28, criticizing the
publishing industry for dragging its heels on help to minorities. The editorial used nicer words. "Hope offered," it

stated, "has been deferred."

Two weeks following that editorial, the Association of American Publishers announced (on September 15) that it was launching the Office of Minority Manpower, and that it was hiring Edward B. King, Jr., to direct it.

In reviewing the sequence of events that finally led to the Office, one is hard put to find any degree of commitment, and the events since then indicate even less commitment than at first appeared. It says something for the AAP that it had the courage to hire a founder of so controversial an organization as SNCC (Student Nonviolent Coordinating Committee), and indeed Mr. King was one of the first field directors of SNCC. He was assistant to the president of Hofstra University at the time he was hired by the AAP. The fact remains that the publishers' association moved into the recruitment field very, very late; and once it did, the association moved with a shocking lack of alacrity, and then only under outside pressure. If the Office had been conceived of as a substantial one, with various departments devoted to an all-out recruitment and publicity drive--as indeed it should have been--one might understand why it would take nearly two years to establish it. As it turns out, the Office of Minority Manpower is strictly a one-man operation, without even benefit of an assistant.

The original appropriation for the Office, it will be recalled, was $25,000 to $30,000. At the time that sum was originally announced, many people in the publishing world laughed that so small an amount would be expected to cover a director's salary, an assistant's salary, traveling expenses, the cost of a national recruitment publicity program, and, in addition, the cost of setting up on-the-job and job-upgrading programs. What was laughable then is concern for tears now.

As this article goes to press, the facts about the operation of the Office are these. Working alone, and with only a part-time secretary promised for 1971, Mr. King has been devoting his time to the daily routine of interviewing people who want jobs. In three and a half months, he has interviewed 65 candidates and has made 25 referrals to 13 publishers. The record, for placing minority personnel, is unhappily par for the course. Six jobs placed: two receptionists, one salesman, one indexer, and one free-lance editor, and one office clerk.

Clearly, the Office of Minority Manpower is strictly a

token gesture.   The manner in which it was established and
the priorities subsequently given the Office indicate that it
was never meant to be anything more.

Suppose the concept of integrated publishing had been
given top priority.   Suppose that minority editors were recruited to make up, say, 15 per cent of the total book publishers' editorial manpower.   Would there be any change in
the quality of the books from the point of view of providing
substantially more ethnic authenticity than now prevails?

This was the question posed at another publishers'
meeting two years ago.   The place was the Time and Life
Building.   The date was January 21, 1969, one week after
the Waldorf-Astoria meeting that led to the publishers' recruitment program.

The Time-Life meeting proposed to capitalize minority
publishing houses.   The meeting originated some months before when, to the board of directors of the ABPC, Arthur
Wang, president of Hill & Wang, stated that it was about
time the book industry, as an industry, met "the challenge
of the ghetto. "   The board agreed that indeed the time had
come and voted to refer the matter to its Reading Development Committee.   This committee then set up a subcommittee and gave it the responsibility for determining what the
publishing industry should do.   It gave the subcommittee a
charter and the title of the Subcommittee on Urban Development and Publishing.

It was this subcommittee that called the January 21
seminar at Time-Life.   A. Edward Miller, chairman of the
subcommittee, who was at the time president of World Publishing Co. , recalls the original intent of the seminar:

> Our first thinking was to develop ways of distribut-
> ing books to children in the ghettos, and we called
> publishers and welfare workers together to find out
> how to make the books available.   We didn't know
> how to distribute the books.

Black leaders at the seminar asked the publishers
whether they were serious in their idea that giving away a
few books would meet the horrendous problems of the ghettos.
Was this a way to assuage the white liberal publishers' guilt?
Anyway, they asked, what books would be given away?   How
many books had been produced that relate in any real way to

the lives of ghetto children?

Another topic of the seminar was job apprenticeship
and training minority youth as a way to the future integration
of publishing.   It was during the discussion of editorial training that Black literary agent Ronald Hobbs made this rejoin-
der:

"We all want more Black editors everywhere," Hobbs
said.   "But," he asked, "what qualitative difference to the
lives of minorities will integrated establishment publishing
bring about?   The decisions at the highest levels will still be
made by whites, and as long as white people make the decisions, books will never be ethnically honest."

Hobbs asked another provocative question.   Is it fair
that establishment publishers make big profits from minority
movements?   "Since so many books, including bestsellers,
are about Blacks or by Blacks, shouldn't the Black communities be getting a piece of the action?   What we need are
independent black publishers."

From that point on the dominant theme of the seminar
was on ways to bring into existence minority-owned-and-man-
aged publishing houses.

A report by the subcommittee describing the seminar
frankly stated:

"The seminar's biggest surprise for the publishers
was the strong plea made by many of the minority group leaders for our industry to assist in the creation and support
(counseling and investment) of Black books publishing enter-
prises--companies designed to be creatively independent and
profitable."   The report went on: "It is the position of your
subcommittee that this is altogether appropriate--that there
are pluralist means for achieving the desired harmonious so-
ciety--working like hell to integrate our 'traditional' houses
at the same time we lend a hand with emerging Black-owned
and managed enterprises.   Another reason for the new Black
houses deserving the support of the book industry is the
'part of the action' point.   Blacks and Spanish-Americans
comprise roughly 15 per cent of the population that account
for a mere 1/10th to 2/10ths of 1 per cent of the nation's
business investment.   Philosophically, then, it seems to your
subcommittee that it is appropriate--almost in a compensatory
way--for the book industry to help professionally qualified

Black entrepreneurs share some of the profits on the best
sellers on the Black experience. "

Throughout 1969, the subcommittee--henceforth to be
known as the committee on minority publishing--met at least
ten times in formal session, sometimes in the offices of the
members, sometimes on the premises of the ABPC. Additional meetings were held with aspiring minority publishers.
Volunteers from publishing houses, like Bill Mayo of Intext,
helped prepare presentations and financial projections. According to its own estimate, the subcommittee spent "400
hours" of work from the original January 21 meeting to the
time that it submitted--on August 19, 1969--a formal plan to
the ABPC for aiding the minority publishers.

The plan was this: that the ABPC co-sponsor, with
the New York Urban Coalition, a major one-day forum at
which "existing and forming minority group publishing houses
be invited to make 45-minute presentations of their plans and
people. " To this forum, publishers and bankers and Wall
Street investment houses would be invited as prospective back-
ers.

The forum plan--soon to be referred to as the "slave
block auction"--was officially approved by the ABPC's board
of directors, and on September 23 a call went out to the minority publishers that the subcommittee had already screened.
Part of the plan was to advertise the forum in trade and community newspapers, so that additional groups might have the
opportunity to seek the platform. No such ads were ever
placed.

It is crucial to know how the subcommittee thought the
new publishers would be capitalized. For all during this
time, hopes among the minority publishers were running high.

One way to raise the capital would be to levy on each
of the ABPC member companies an assessment proportionate
to its annual volume of business. This is the way the association raises its annual dues. It is the way the association
raises supplemental funds for special purposes, as when the
Right to Read Committee recommends that the association appear as an amicus curiae in censorship court cases involving
publishers, booksellers, and book wholesalers. It is the
way the association raised a war chest in 1969-70 to pressure the U. S. government to restore Federal appropriations
for the purchase of books and other educational materials by

schools and libraries.

According to Ed Miller, at no time did the subcommittee consider asking the AAP to raise capital by the levy of an assessment on association members. All funds for capitalization were to be strictly voluntary. The assumption was that, once the subcommittee did its job of finding the minority publishers and helping them present their cases, the money would somehow appear. Events would soon show the fallacy of the assumption. Individual publishers, investment houses and bankers--First National and Morgan Guaranty Trust, to name two--had expressed enthusiastic interest in funding minority publishers. The commitment which was by inference only, proved illusory.

The forum was postponed at least once and then abandoned altogether. All along, Ronald Hobbs had had his own misgivings. To him the forum plan held odious connotations of an auction block. Not only was the forum idea demeaning, it was unnecessary, Hobbs said recently. Somehow, he had been led to believe--as had other Black leaders--that the AAP had funds available for the capitalization program.

By now publishers were feeling the pressures of a tightening national economy, and the AAP leadership was having second thoughts. There was the probability that the publishers and investment houses attending the forum might fail to come up with loans and investments substantial enough to capitalize the new publishers. Then the AAP would itself be embarrassed. Good intentions in our economy are as a rule overwhelmed by the practical pressures of the profit motives and perhaps the AAP could not have been expected to rise above the self-interest of its members. No one will admit it, but "high visibility embarrassment" was what finally dashed the minority publishers' hopes.

On December 18, Ed Miller, in his position as chairman of the Reading Development Committee, wrote the following letter to a number of individuals who had been working with the subcommittee (note the absence of any reason for the change in plans):

> We have altered some of our plans for the minority publishing project. After careful thought and discussion the members of the board met with several other publishers who have indicated their interest in helping minority group publishers. It had become

apparent to all of us that an open meeting or forum
might not be the most effective procedure for the
proposals we have in hand and expect.   The banks
and investment counsel we consulted shared in this
view.   Therefore, we shall attempt to bring prospective publishers together with established publishers on an individual basis, perhaps through the
major banks that have agreed to work with us.

This was the subcommittee's last recorded letter.
Late in December Ed Miller left World Publishing to become
president of Berlitz Publications.   In January another member of the subcommittee, Carter Smith, left his position as
assistant president of Time-Life Books to launch his own
company.   Carter Smith's views on the sequence of events
that led to the collapse of the publishing industry's negotia-
tions with the minority publishers will be found below.   Arthur Wang, president of Hill & Wang, was the third member
of the subcommittee.   Sometime between January and the
summer of 1970, Arthur Wang must have considered as a
last resort the levying of an assessment on AAP members,
for below, too, appears his explanation for what must now
be regarded as one of the more shocking episodes in the an-
nals of American book publishing.

In the strict legal sense, at no time was a written
promise of a loan or other financial help made to a minority
publisher, but in making the original commitment and in offering assistance, hopes were raised very definitely.   In the
moral sense, the offer was indeed a promise.

To date, not a single establishment publisher, not a
single investment broker, not a single banker has loaned
money to any of the minority publishers whom the subcommittee sought out during its period of extensive activity.

A New York Times story of June 26 chronicled the
hopes and disappointments of Joseph Okpaku in launching the
Third Press, a Black enterprise begun last summer with the
publication of "Verdict!" a pictorial essay on the trial of the
Chicago Eight.

Okpaku told the Times reporter that he and many other
Blacks had been led to believe that white publishers were eager to help Blacks get into the field, but that when he was
ready with the presentation and all the financial projections
he had been requested to submit "no one returned my calls. "

He said that on one occasion a publisher sent him to a bank that, he was told, was "very interested." Describing his meeting with the bank official, Okpaku said: "They told me they were sorry, but they were interested only in fried chicken franchises."

Another time, Okpaku said, a bank executive told him he would help, but because of "tight money," he would need one of his white publisher friends to co-sign. No one would co-sign the note.

The experiences of Oswald White--who sought funds for his venture, the Buckingham Learning Corporation--were similar. Mr. White last summer told a representative of our Council: "I was informed, after we made our applications, that members of the American Book Publishers Council were prepared to make a substantial capital investment to help us get off the ground. Nothing whatsoever came of it."

Mr. White said that he was told to visit Chemical Bank. "I went to Chemical and they told me the government would have to guarantee a loan, but that unfortunately the government was not guaranteeing any loans to publishing companies.

"My whole experience with white publishers was a bad dream. I was made to feel that I was invading a world where I was not wanted."

Here is the statement of another Black publisher, that of Alfred Prettyman, president of Emerson Hall:

> Whether or not one is clubbable is far more important in the American book publishing industry than is one's talent for the trade. The majority of the industry is interested in fads not causes, in opportunistic self-advertisement, not in enduring commitment, in maintaining a male white hegemony at all levels of operation which are neither clerical nor janitorial. The industry will shift its weight to the other foot now and then, but it will not be moved. And any member of a minority who would challenge it must expect to be systematically impeded and routinely discredited.

And so we approach the end of a chapter of our story.

A recruitment program for minorities that spells tokenism
only.   A funding program for minority publishers that ends
in default on promises.   Listen to Arthur Wang, who sparked
the conscience of the AAP board of directors when he made
his plea for action.   The following statement was given to
our Council last summer:

> Our intentions were the highest, but as we consid-
> ered the issue further we realized that our com-
> mittee was without the power to lay an assessment
> on member publishers to raise working capital for
> the Black publishers who came to us for help.   All
> we could do was to ask publishers to voluntarily
> help them.   And now, with tight money, publishers
> feel that they are no longer in a position to be of
> financial help.   The whole issue now is dead.

A compelling statement was given to us in January,
1971, just as this article was going to press, by Carter
Smith:

> I am embarrassed personally and professionally that
> the special subcommittee on minority publishers of
> the AAP Committee on Reading Development turned
> out to be another well-meaning but impotent instru-
> ment of a well-meaning but monolithic establish-
> ment.   Despite the fact that publishers have experi-
> enced lean times in the past eighteen months, the
> AAP had no problem raising a war chest to lobby
> for Federal funds for the book industry.   When,
> however, it came to the question of helping to fi-
> nance the well-qualified minority publishers our
> committee worked with, all the establishment raised
> was false hopes.

What are the consequences when so prestigious an industry as book publishing takes a stand on what is perhaps
the most critical issue of our times and then defaults?   One
consequence is to further polarize the white from the minority communities, as one more indication that the Man makes
empty promises.   Another consequence is to discredit the
private profit concept, for if good intentions on so critical
an issue are destroyed by the practical considerations of the
profit system, then how can that system be at all creditable?
We will consider these and related questions in later issues
of this series.

Right now our Council believes that the movement to support independent, self-determining minority publishers must come from forces outside the publishing industry; and so in recent months we have been calling on individuals, community control groups and other organizations to offer the new publishers the support they need--ranging from such measures as grant-loans from foundations to the direct purchase of books by schools and librarians from the minority publishers' lists.

23.   RACISM IN BOOK PUBLISHING

Hoyt Fuller, Joseph Okpaku
and Alfred Prettyman

Excerpts from a Press Conference, March 15, 1971,
Sponsored by Publishers' Weekly and The Council on
Interracial Books for Children

HOYT FULLER: ... For many years now--since it became
possible and popular to publish works by and about Black
people at the beginning of the so-called revolution--the publishing industry has gone out and commissioned sociologists
and leaders of various other disciplines to throw together
books about Black people.   Most of the people who have been
engaged in doing this have been white people, the so-called
authors or experts on Black life, on Black history, on Black
culture.   We consider that dangerous to the Black image.
We have been trying for the last ten years to combat that,
even though the resources which we have been able to bring
to bear were pale compared to the power of the New York
publishers.   So this morning I wrote a statement, which I
think you all have, and which I am now going to read.   It
gives my perspective on the whole question of Black publishing.

The first thing I would like to make clear is that I
am not present at this "Racism in Book Publishing" press
conference either to plead for financial support from establishment publishers for Black publishing firms nor to be-
moan the prevailing racism among establishment publishers
which serves to discourage--if not to throttle--the efforts of
Black publishing firms.

I agree with the Chicago book publisher who wrote
Publishers' Weekly, in response to Bradford Chambers' ini-
tial article in Publishers' Weekly on racism in publishing,
that it is simply ridiculous to expect established publishers
to underwrite their own competition.   That is like asking the
United States to finance Russia's exploration of the moon.
Whatever the myths of book publishing in America, the fact
is that book publishing is a capitalistic competitive endeavor,

organized to make money for entrepreneurs, managers and investors. Book publishers--like other businessmen--are concerned about problems of minorities only when those problems, in some way, overflow the ethnic enclaves and threaten the accepted order of things.

Nor do I waste my time or anybody else's chiding established publishers about their racist attitudes and practices. America is a racist society. Racist attitudes and practices are the norm. I know of no reason why book publishers should be expected to be less racist than, say, a razor blade manufacturer or the United States State Department.

I am here because I am a Black man who is deeply engaged in the struggle to seize control of the Black image from those who have never respected it and to place that image in the hands of Black people, where it belongs. For far too many centuries now, the Black image has been imprisoned and manipulated by white men. And, of course, a key instrument of that imprisonment and exploitation has been the publishing industry. The Black image has been systematically defamed; Black History has been distorted; Black Literature has been crippled and maimed by being forced in a form designed for other races, cultures and colors; and the Black Experience has been degraded so that its degraders would not have to deal with the monstrousness and guilt of the White Experience.

I am here to take advantage of the opportunity of a press conference staged by the most influential organ of the American book publishing industry to say that Black people will no longer meekly submit to the benevolent paternalism and sly opportunism inherent in the recently inaugurated practice of employing a token or two Black editorial staffers as proof of absence of racism. Black people are not deceived. As one of the Black book publishers has pointed out, Black people are at the very least 22 million strong in this country, constituting a nation far greater and infinitely more able than many formal nations in the world.

In more than a half dozen of the major cities in America, Black people make up more than half the total population; and in even more cities, the percentage of Black children in the schools exceeds that of any other ethnic group. In those cities where Black children are in the majority, it is fair to say that the days of Dick and Jane are numbered as the sub-

jects of stories in textbooks.   Black children in Detroit and
Atlanta and Harlem are going to read about Little Leroy and
Edna Mae, stories written by Black authors, illustrated by
Black artists, in books published by Black firms.   Black
people are going to control their own image.

Now, in stating the above, I want it known that I am
fully aware of the practical considerations involved in transferring the power of image from white to Black hands.   I
know that I am talking about snatching millions of dollars out
of the pockets of white people and transferring that money to
Black people, and I know very well that white people do not
take lightly to the prospect of losing money--particularly to
Black people.   I know full well that the struggle to effect
this transformation will be long, arduous and dangerous, and
that even some influential Black people will be enlisted
against Black forces in the struggle.   That is the way it
goes.   But, as a Black man, engaged in the struggle for
Black autonomy and survival, I know that there is no alter-
native.

JOSEPH OKPAKU: It is understandable that some white publishers might resent having to deal on an equal level with
Black publishers.   It is the nature of a confused white liber-
alism to see Black enterprises as poverty neighborhood op-
erations.   As long as this is so they do not have to deal
with the possibility of having to compete with, and perhaps
lose to, a Black publisher.   The American public needs the
broadest perspective of information possible.   Without this a
healthy dialogue is impossible, and unnecessary hostilities
can not be averted.   It is for this reason that the Third
Press believes strongly that as many minority publishers as
possible should be launched.

The American reading public and the book industry
desperately need Black publishers.   Of course, we also need
lots more Black editors.   But we can have 5,000 Black editors in white houses, and it will not make the crucial difference.   The Black editors in white houses fight hard to make
a dent.   In fact, but for them there would be little to talk
about today.   And there have been a few white editors, too,
with insight, especially some of the younger ones.   But editors, even the most influential, are not publishers.   An editor has no final say on what gets published and how, and it
is in these aspects that publishing dominates the minds of
the reading public.

ALFRED PRETTYMAN: I think it is important to bear in
mind that the majority of Black publishers are operating out
of their own pockets, and that they actually see themselves
continuing to do this. The perdurable core of minority publishing consists of those persons who will refuse, whether
for lack of capital from foundations, banks or other money
resources, to permit themselves to be squeezed out of this
publishing industry simply because of the greater resources
of larger minority publishers. And I think that in view of
the movement in this country, on several levels, for paying
more and more attention not just to ethnic concerns but to
regional concerns--I think that this is a ground-swell which
you really have to pay attention to because this is where
your real change is going to come from.

     I never believed that the Association of American Pub-
lishers would keep its commitment to help capitalize minority
publishers. I never believed they were sincere. I myself
never asked them for money. And in a way, I find it an
interesting and sophisticated effrontery to promise funds to
a minority publisher contingent upon those monies being
matched by another publisher. And I think that's something
we ought to bear in mind....

     It might be well for us to remember what [Whitney
Young] said in one portion of his last atricle, which appeared
in the Saturday edition of the New York Times. He calls attention to a problem of American people when dealing with
minorities, which is a problem that American businessmen
find the most reprehensible of habits among others. It's the
matter of not having staying power. Young said, in brief,
"Hard-headed businessmen are reflecting the same qualities
that they find so reprehensible in others: lack of staying
power and dilettantism. " Young was speaking about pledges
of investment in the ghettos. But I think this is something
that is pervasive in American business society, and in American life in general. It seems to be an enormous drain to
be concerned about minorities, about the poor. It seems to
be one of the things you can only be concerned about in
spurts, because it wears you out, or it is just too depressing,
and there are other things that you'd like to get on with; and
since they are so readily at hand and since your life revolves
around so many other things aside from being concerned with
minorities and the poor, it's very easy to switch off. I
think this is going to continue to be the case. America will
switch us on and off. And I don't think that you can solve
any of the most pressing problems of this society living at
the will of that kind of switch.

NOTES ON CONTRIBUTORS

RAE ALEXANDER is a doctoral student in early childhood
education at Columbia University--Teachers College,
and the compiler of the anthology What It's Like to be
Young and Black in America.

AUGUSTA BAKER is the Coordinator of Children's Services
at the New York Public Library, and the compiler and
editor of The Talking Tree and Other Stories and The
Golden Lynx.

JESSIE M. BIRTHA is the children's book selection specialist at The Free Library of Philadelphia.

LOIS KALB BOUCHARD is a free lance writer, and author
of the children's book The Boy Who Wouldn't Talk.

BRADFORD CHAMBERS is the chairman of the Council on
Interracial Books for Children, and the compiler and
editor of Chronicles of Black Protest.

PAUL C. DEANE is a professor in the Department of English, Bentley College.

HOYT FULLER is president of the Johnson Publishing Company, the publisher of Negro Digest and Black World
Magazine.

DAVID K. GAST is a professor in the Department of Education, San Diego State College.

EVELYN GELLER is the former editor-in-chief of The
School Library Journal, and a member of the editori-
al committee of the Council on Interracial Books for
Children.

DONALD B. GIBSON is a professor in the Department of
English, University of Connecticut, and author of Five
Black Writers; Essays on Wright, Ellison, Baldwin,
Hughes, and Leroi Jones.

JEAN DRESDEN GRAMBS is a professor in the Department of Education, University of Maryland.

NANCY LARRICK is the former president of the International Reading Association, and the author of many books in the field of education and children's literature.

JULIUS LESTER is an author, editor, folk singer, and song writer. His book To Be A Slave was a runner-up for the Newbery Prize.

DONNARAE MacCANN has been a children's librarian in California, and a lecturer on children's literature at the University of Kansas. She is the co-author of The Child's First Books.

DHARATHULA H. MILLENDER is the librarian at Pulaski Junior High School in Gary, Indiana.

JOSEPH OKPAKU is the president of Third Press, the publisher of the Journal of African Literature and the Arts.

ALFRED PRETTYMAN is the president of the Emerson Hall Publishing Company, and chairman of the Minority Publishers' Committee of the Council on Interracial Books for Children.

ALBERT V. SCHWARTZ is a professor of Language Arts, Richmond College, New York.

DOROTHY STERLING is the author of Tear Down the Walls! A History of the American Civil Rights Movement, Captain of the Planter, and many other books for children and young people.

ISABELLE SUHL is the librarian at Elisabeth Irwin High School in New York City.

BINNIE TATE has been a children's librarian in California, and is now teaching in the School of Library and Information Science at the University of Wisconsin-- Milwaukee.

JUDITH THOMPSON is a former high school English teacher, and chairman of the Education Committee, Human Relations Commission, Lawrence, Kansas.

OSWALD WHITE is the president of Buckingham Learning Corporation in New York.

GLORIA WOODARD has been an elementary school teacher in Texas and Kansas, and is now an elementary school librarian in Prince George's County, Maryland.

GEORGE A. WOODS is the children's book editor for the New York Times.

INDEX OF CHILDREN'S BOOKS MENTIONED*

1. TITLE INDEX

---

*Editors' Note: Adults' books have been included whenever they have been recommended for young readers in this anthology.

Bobbsey Twins in the Land of Cotton (by Laura L. Hope) p. 119-120.

Boy Scouts at the Panama-Pacific Exposition (by Lt. Howard Payson) p. 120.

Bronzeville Boys and Girls (by Gwendolyn Brooks) p. 177.

Bunny Brown and His Sister Sue in the Sunny South (by Laura L. Hope) p. 118, 119, 121.

Call Me Charley (by Jesse Jackson) p. 17, 22, 176.

Canalboat to Freedom (by Thomas Fall) p. 60.

Captain of the Planter (by Dorothy Sterling) p. 25, 177-178.

Cay (by Theodore Taylor) p. 41-42, 47, 108-111.

Charlie and the Chocolate Factory (by Roald Dahl) p. 112-115.

Child's Story of the Negro (by Jane D. Shackelford) p. 151.

Christmas Carol (by Charles Dickens) p. 19.

Chronicles of Negro Protest (by Bradford Chambers, ed.) p. 25, 46.

Colonial Twins in Virginia (by L. F. Perkins) p. 148.

Color Me Brown (by Lucille W. Giles) p. 55.

Coming of Age in Mississippi (by Anne Moody) p. 25.

Corrie and the Yankee (by Mimi Levy) p. 179.

Counting Rhymes (Mother Goose) p. 161-162.

Crispus Attucks, Boy of Valor (by Dharathula H. Millender) p. 124-133.

Dead End School (by Robert Coles) p. 48.

Denny's Story (by Eunice Smith) p. 162.

Diddie, Dumps, and Tot, or Plantation Child Life (by L. C. Pyrnelle) p. 148.

Doctor Dolittle: A Treasury (by Hugh Lofting) p. 87-88.

Doctor Dolittle's Post Office (by Hugh Lofting) p. 80-82.

Doctor Dolittle's Zoo (by Hugh Lofting) p. 82, 85-86.

Don Sturdy and the Port of Lost Ships (by V. Appleton) p. 119.

Don Sturdy in Lion Land (by V. Appleton) p. 120.

Dream Keeper (by Langston Hughes) p. 176.

Edgar Allan (by John Neufeld) p. 53, 173.

Empty School House (by Natalie Carlson) p. 18-19, 22.

Epaminondas (by Eve Merriam) p. 154.

Epaminondas and His Auntie (by Sara Cone Bryant) p. 6, 7, 153-154.

Evan's Corner (by Elizabeth Starr Hill) p. 19, 45.

Eyewitness: The Negro in American History (by William L. Katz) p. 25.

Famous American Negroes (by Langston Hughes) p. 177.

211

2. AUTHOR INDEX

Bontemps, Arna. Frederick Douglass: Slave, Fighter, Freeman (Knopf, 1959) p. 179.

Bontemps, Arna. Golden Slippers (Harper, 1941) p. 176.

Bontemps, Arna (with Langston Hughes). Popo and Fifina (Macmillan, 1932) p. 176.

Bontemps, Arna. The Lonesome Boy (Houghton, 1955) p. 176.

Bontemps, Arna. The Sad-Faced Boy (Houghton, 1937), p. 176.

Bontemps, Arna. The Story of the Negro (Knopf, 1969 rev. ed.) p. 166, 176.

Bontemps, Arna. We Have Tomorrow (Houghton, 1945) p. 176.

Bontemps, Arna. You Can't Pet a Possum (Houghton, 1934) p. 176.

Borton, Elizabeth. Our Little Ethiopian Cousin (L. C. Page & Co., 1935) p. 175-176, 182.

Boston, L. M. The Treasure of Green Knowe (Harcourt, 1958) p. 58.

Boyleston, Helen D. Sue Barton, Visiting Nurse (Little, 1938) p. 118-122.

Bragdon, Henry Wilkinson and S. P. Cutchen. History of a Free People (Macmillan, 1967, 6th ed.) p. 180.

Braune, Anne. Honey Chile (Doubleday, 1937) p. 148.

Brooks, Gwendolyn. Bronzeville Boys and Girls; illustrated by Ronni Solbert (Harper, 1956) p. 177.

Bryant, Sara Cone. Epaminondas and His Auntie. (Houghton, 1938) p. 6, 7, 153-154.

Buckmaster, Henrietta. Flight to Freedom: The Story of the Underground Railroad (Crowell, 1958) p. 179.

Bulla, Clyde Robert. Indian Hill (Crowell, 1963) p. 172.

Burch, Robert. Skinny (Viking, 1964) p. 164.

Burchard, Peter (author-illustrator). Bimby (Coward-McCann, 1968) p. 60.

Cain, Alfred E. (ed.). Negro Heritage Reader for Young People (Negro Heritage Library, Educational Heritage, Inc., 1965) p. 185.

Cain, Alfred E. The Winding Road to Freedom (Negro Heritage Library, Educational Heritage, Inc., 1965) p. 186.

Carlson, Natalie. The Empty School House; illustrated by John Kaufman (Harper, 1965) p. 18-19, 22.

Chambers, Bradford (ed.). Chronicles of Negro Protest (Parents, 1968) p. 25, 46.

Chandler, Ruth Forbes. Ladder to the Sky (Abelard, 1965) p. 166.

Chapman, Abraham (ed.). Black Voices: An Anthology of Afro-American Literature (St. Martin's, 1970) p. 25.

Christmas, Walter (ed.). Negroes in Public Affairs and
Government (Negro Heritage Library, Educational Heritage
Inc., 1966-) p. 186.
Coles, Robert. Dead End School; illustrated by Norman
Rockwell (Little, 1968) p. 48.
Conroy, Jack (with Arna Bontemps). The Fast Sooner Hound
(Houghton, 1942) p. 176.
Credle, Ellis. Across the Cotton Patch (Nelson, 1935) p.
148.
Cullen, Countee. The Lost Zoo; illustrated by Joseph Low
(Follett, 1969, rev. ed.) p. 55.
Cuthbert, Marion. We Sing America (Friendship Press,
1936) p. 150.

Dahl, Roald. Charlie and the Chocolate Factory (Knopf,
1964) p. 112-115.
Dannett, Sylvia G. L. Profiles of Negro Womanhood (Negro
Heritage Library, Educational Heritage Inc., 1964-) p.
186.
Dawson, Charles C. ABC's of Great Negroes (Dawson Pub-
lishers, 1933) p. 150.
De Leeuw, Adele. The Barred Road (Macmillan, 1964 rev.
ed.) p. 166.
Desbarats, Peter. Gabrielle and Selena; illustrated by Nancy
Grossman (Harcourt, 1968) p. 23.
Dickens, Charles. The Christmas Carol (G. Routledge &
Sons, 1843) p. 19.
Dixon, Franklin W. A Figure in Hiding (Grosset, 1937) p.
118.
Dixon, Franklin W. Hunting for Hidden Gold (Grosset, 1928)
p. 118-119, 121.
Dixon, Franklin W. The Sinister Sign Post (Grosset, 1936)
p. 118.
Dixon, Franklin W. The Twisted Claw (Grosset, 1939) p.
118-119.

Erwin, Betty K. Behind the Magic Line; illustrated by Julia
Iltis (Little, 1969) p. 23-24.
Ets, Marie Hall (with Ellen Tarry). My Dog Rinty; photo-
graphs by Alland (Viking, 1962 rev. ed.) p. 166, 176.
Evans, Eva Knox. Araminta (Putnam, 1935) p. 148.
Evans, Eva Knox. Araminta's Goat (Putnam, 1938) p. 117-
118, 148.
Evans, Eva Knox. Jerome Anthony (Putnam, 1936) p. 148.
Evans, Eva Knox. Key Corner (Putnam, 1938) p. 149.

Fall, Thomas. Canalboat to Freedom; illustrated by Joseph
Cellini (Dial, 1966) p. 60.

Fauset, A. H.   For Freedom (Franklin Press, 1927) p. 150.

Flower, Jessie Graham.   Grace Harlowe's Overland Riders Among the Kentucky Mountaineers (Altemus, 1921) p. 118, 120-121.

Fox, Paula.   How Many Miles to Babylon? illustrated by Paul Giovanopoulos (David White, 1967) p. 45.

Franklin, John Hope, John W. Caughey and Ernest R. May. Land of the Free (Benzier Bros., 1966 rev.) p. 180.

Friedman, Frieda.   A Sundae with Judy (Morrow, 1949) p. 58.

Frierwood, Elizabeth Hamilton.   Whispering Willows (Doubleday, 1964) p. 161.

Giles, Lucille W.   Color Me Brown (Johnson Publishing Co., n.d.) p. 55.

Goldston, Robert.   The Negro Revolution (Macmillan, 1968) p. 46.

Gould, Jean.   The Dunbar Boy; illustrated by Charles Walker (Dodd, 1958) p. 179.

Graham, Lorenz.   I, Momolu; illustrated by John Biggers (Crowell, 1966) p. 43-44.

Graham, Lorenz.   South Town (Follett, 1958) p. 53, 167.

Graham, Lorenz.   Whose Town? (Crowell, 1969) p. 43-44.

Graham, Shirley.   The Story of Phillis Wheatley (Messner, 1949) p. 176.

Graham, Shirley.   There Was Once a Slave: The Heroic Story of Frederick Douglass (Messner, 1947) p. 176.

Greenberg, Polly.   Oh Lord, I Wish I Was a Buzzard; illustrated by Aliki (Macmillan, 1968) p. 43.

Hamilton, Virginia.   The House of Dies Drear; illustrated by Eros Keith (Macmillan, 1969) p. 44.

Hamilton, Virginia.   Time-Ago Tales of Jahdu; illustrated by Nonny Hogrogian (Macmillan, 1969) p. 44.

Hamilton, Virginia.   Zeely; illustrated by Symeon Shimin (Macmillan, 1967) p. 44.

Harris, Janet (with Julius W. Hobson).   Black Pride (McGraw-Hill, 1969) p. 46.

Harris, Joel Chandler.   Uncle Remus, his Songs and Sayings (Appleton, 1881) p. 36, 68.

Hill, Elizabeth Starr.   Evan's Corner; illustrated by Nancy Grossman (Holt, 1967) p. 19, 45.

Hobson, Julius W. (with Janet Harris).   Black Pride (McGraw-Hill, 1969) p. 46.

Hogan, Inez.   Nicodemus books (12 titles) (Dutton, 1932-1945) p. 148, 171.

Holding, James.   The Lazy Little Zulu (Morrow, 1962) p. 159.

Holland, John. The Way It is (Harcourt, 1969) p. 55.

Hope, Laura L. The Bobbsey Twins at the Seashore (Grosset, 1950) p. 121.

Hope, Laura L. The Bobbsey Twins in the Country (Grosset, 1950 rev.) p. 118, 120, 121.

Hope, Laura L. The Bobbsey Twins in the Land of Cotton (Grosset, 1942) p. 119-120.

Hope, Laura L. Bunny Brown and His Sister Sue in the Sunny South (Grosset, 1921) p. 118, 119, 121.

Hope, Laura L. The Horseshoe Riddle (Grosset, 1953) p. 117.

Horvath, Betty. Hooray for Jasper; illustrated by Fermin Rocker (Watts, 1966) p. 23.

Hughes, Langston. The Dream Keeper (Knopf, 1932) p. 176.

Hughes, Langston. Famous American Negroes (Dodd, 1954) p. 177.

Hughes, Langston. Famous Negro Music Makers (Dodd, 1954) p. 177.

Hughes, Langston (with Milton Meltzer). A Pictorial History of the Negro in America (Crown, 1963) p. 166.

Hughes, Langston (with Arna Bontemps). Popo and Fifina (Macmillan, 1932) p. 176.

Hunter, Kristin. Soul Brothers and Sister Lou (Scribner, 1968) p. 23-24.

Hyde, Margaret O. Your Brain (McGraw-Hill, 1964) p. 165.

Jackson, Jesse. Anchor Man (Harper, 1947) p. 176.

Jackson, Jesse. Call Me Charley (Harper, 1945) p. 17, 22, 176.

Jackson, Jesse. Tessie; illustrated by Harold James (Harper, 1968) p. 18.

Justus, May. New Boy in School; illustrated by Joan Balfour Payne (Hastings, 1963) p. 163.

Katz, William L. Eyewitness: The Negro in American History (Pitman, 1967) p. 25.

Kay, Helen. A Summer to Share (Hastings, 1960) p. 162-163.

Keats, Ezra Jack (author-illustrator). A Letter to Amy (Harper, 1968) p. 23.

Keats, Ezra Jack (author-illustrator). Peter's Chair (Viking, 1967) p. 23.

Keats, Ezra Jack (author-illustrator). The Snowy Day (Viking, 1962) p. 23, 66, 158, 160.

Keats, Ezra Jack (author-illustrator). Whistle for Willie (Viking, 1964) p. 23, 158.

Keene, Carolyn. The Mystery of the Tolling Bell (Grosset, 1946) p. 118.

Keene, Carolyn. Nancy Drew and the Mystery Inn (Grosset, n. d.) p. 120.

Keyes, Leroy (with O. J. Simpson). Black Champions of the Gridiron (Harcourt, 1969) p. 28, 32.

King, Martin Luther. Martin Luther King Treasury (Negro Heritage Library, Educational Heritage Inc., 1964) p. 186.

Knox, Rose B. Miss Jimmy Deane (Doubleday, 1931) p. 148.

Lattimore, E. F. Junior, a Colored Boy of Charleston (Harcourt, 1938) p. 149.

Lawrence, Jacob (author-illustrator). Harriet and the Promised Land (Simon and Schuster, 1968) p. 44-45.

Lester, Julius. Black Folktales (Baron, 1969) p. 29-30, 32, 36-37, 40, 48.

Lester, Julius. To Be A Slave; illustrated by Tom Feelings (Dial, 1968) p. 15, 25, 29-30, 32, 36-37, 40, 49.

Levy, Harry. Not Over Ten Inches High; illustrated by Nancy Grossman (McGraw-Hill, 1968) p. 58.

Levy, Mimi. Corrie and the Yankee (Viking, 1959) p. 179.

Lexau, Jean M. Benjie; illustrated by Don Bolognese (Dial, 1964) p. 158.

Lindsay, Maud. Little Missy (Lothrop, 1922) p. 148.

Lofting, Hugh. Doctor Dolittle: A Treasury (Lippincott, 1967) p. 87-88.

Lofting, Hugh. Doctor Dolittle's Post Office (Lippincott, 1923) p. 80-82.

Lofting, Hugh. Doctor Dolittle's Zoo (Lippincott, 1925) p. 82, 85-86.

Lofting, Hugh. The Story of Dr. Dolittle (Lippincott, 1920) p. 5-6, 7, 37, 78, 80, 82-88, 154.

Lofting, Hugh. The Voyages of Doctor Dolittle (Lippincott, 1922) p. 78-80, 82, 84-88.

McGovern, Ann. Black is Beautiful; photographs by Hope Wurmfeld (Four Winds, 1969) p. 55.

Means, Florence. Tolliver (Houghton, 1963) p. 161.

Meltzer, Milton (ed.). In Their Own Words (3 Vols.) (Crowell, 1964-67) p. 46.

Meltzer, Milton. Langston Hughes (Crowell, 1968) p. 25.

Meltzer, Milton (with Langston Hughes). A Pictorial History of the Negro in America (Crown, 1963) p. 166.

Merriam, Eve. Epaminondas (Follett, 1968) p. 154.

Millender, Dharathula H. Crispus Attucks, Boy of Valor; illustrated by Gray Morrow (Bobbs, 1965) p. 124-133.

Mississippi Black Paper, with a foreword by Reinhold Niebuhr and an introduction by Holding Carter III (Random, 1965) p. 183.

Moody, Anne. Coming of Age in Mississippi (Dial, 1968)

219

p. 25.

Morais, Herbert M.   The History of the Negro in Medicine (Publishers Co. , 1968) p. 186.

Nelson, Truman.   The Torture of Mothers (Beacon Press, 1968) p. 183.

Neufeld, John.   Edgar Allan (S. G. Phillips, 1968) p. 53, 173.

Newcomb, Covelle.   Black Fire: A Story of Henri Christophe (McKay, 1940) p. 166.

Nolan, E. W.   Shipment for Susannah (Nelson, 1938) p. 149.

Norris, Gunilla.   The Good Morrow; illustrated by Charles Robinson (Atheneum, 1969) p. 45.

Ormsby, Virginia.   Long Lonesome Train Whistle (Lippincott, 1961) p. 164.

Patterson, Lindsay (comp.).   Anthology of the American Negro in the Theatre (Publishers Co. , 1968) p. 186.

Patterson, Lindsay (comp.).   The Negro in Music and Art (Publishers Co. , 1968) p. 186.

Payson, Howard Lt.   The Boy Scouts at the Panama-Pacific Exposition (Hurst and Co. , 1915) p. 120.

Pendleton, Louis.   King Tom and the Runaways (Appleton, 1890) p. 147-148.

Perkins, L. F.   Colonial Twins in Virginia (Houghton, 1924) p. 148.

Perkins, L. F.   The Pickaninny Twins (Houghton, 1931) p. 176.

Petersham, Maud and Miska.   The Rooster Crows: A Book of American Rhymes and Jingles (Macmillan, 1945) p. 160.

Petry, Ann.   Harriet Tubman: Conductor on the Underground Railroad (Crowell, 1955) p. 25, 177.

Petry, Ann.   Tituba of Salem Village (Crowell, 1964) p. 25.

Politi, Leo.   The Angel of Olvera Street (Scribner, 1946) p. 171-172.

Politi, Leo.   Moy Moy (Scribner, 1960) p. 171-172.

Pyrnelle, L. C.   Diddie, Dumps, and Tot, or Plantation Child Life (Harper, 1930) p. 148.

Quarles, Benjamin (with Dorothy Sterling).   Lift Every Voice; illustrated by Ernest Crichlow (Doubleday, 1965) p. 25.

Randall, Blossom.   Fun for Chris; illustrated by Eunice Young Smith (Whitman, 1956) p. 16, 162.

Ray, Bert.   We Live in the City (Children's Press, 1963) p. 165.

Rinkoff, Barbara.   Member of the Gang; illustrated by

Harold James (Crown, 1968) p. 61.

Robinson, Wilhelmena S.   Historical Negro Biographies (Publishers Co., 1968) p. 186.

Romero, Patricia W. (with Charles H. Wesley).   Negro Americans in the Civil War (Publishers Co., 1968) p. 186.

Schechter, Betty.   The Peaceable Revolution (Houghton, 1963) p. 158.

Scott, Ann Herbert.   Big Cowboy Western; illustrated by Richard W. Lewis (Lothrop, 1965) p. 23.

Scott, Ann Herbert.   Sam; illustrated by Symeon Shimin (McGraw-Hill, 1967) p. 23.

Selsam, Millicent E.   Tony's Birds; illustrated by Kurt Werth (Harper, 1961) p. 158.

Shackelford, Jane D.   Child's Story of the Negro (Associated Publishers, 1938) p. 151.

Shackelford, Jane D.   My Happy Days (Associated Publishers, n.d.) p. 151.

Sharpe, Stella.   Tobe; photographs by Charles Farrell (University of North Carolina Press, 1939) p. 151.

Shotwell, Louisa.   Roosevelt Grady; illustrated by Peter Burchard (World, 1963) p. 19-21, 22, 24, 158, 160-161.

Simpson, O. J. (with Leroy Keyes).   Black Champions of the Gridiron (Harcourt, 1969) p. 28-32.

Smith, Eunice.   Denny's Story (Whitman, 1952) p. 162.

Steptoe, John (author-illustrator).   Stevie (Harper, 1969) p. 23, 45.

Sterling, Dorothy.   Captain of the Planter; illustrated by Ernest Crichlow (Doubleday, 1958) p. 25, 177-178.

Sterling, Dorothy.   Forever Free: The Story of the Emancipation Proclamation (Doubleday, 1963) p. 158.

Sterling, Dorothy.   Freedom Train: The Story of Harriet Tubman (Doubleday, 1954) p. 177.

Sterling, Dorothy (with Benjamin Quarles).   Lift Every Voice; illustrated by Ernest Crichlow (Doubleday, 1965) p. 25.

Sterling, Dorothy.   Mary Jane; illustrated by Ernest Crichlow (Doubleday, 1959) p. 164, 172, 178-179, 183.

Sterling, Dorothy.   Tear Down the Walls! (Doubleday, 1968) p. 25, 46.

Sterling, Dorothy.   Tender Warriors (Hill, 1958) p. 178.

Sterne, Emma Gelders.   The Long Black Schooner; The Voyage of the Amistad; illustrated by Paul Giovanopoulos (Follett, 1968) p. 25, 177.

Sterne, Emma Gelders.   Mary McLeod Bethune (Knopf, 1957) p. 177.

Stowe, Harriet Beecher.   Uncle Tom's Cabin (John P. Jewett and Co., 1852) p. 154, 175.

Strachan, Margaret Pitcairin.   Where Were You That Year?

(Washburn, 1965) p. 67.

Stratemeyer, Edward. The Rover Boys in New York (Grosset, 1913) p. 119.

Stratemeyer, Edward. The Rover Boys in Southern Waters (Grosset, 1907) p. 117.

Stratemeyer, Edward. The Rover Boys in the Mountains (Mershon Co. , 1902) p. 117.

Stratemeyer, Edward. The Rover Boys Shipwrecked (Grosset, 1924) p. 117.

Swift, Hildegarde. Railroad to Freedom; illustrated by James Daugherty (Harcourt, 1932) p. 51-52.

Tarry, Ellen (with Marie Hall Ets). My Dog Rinty; photographs by Alland (Viking, 1962 rev. ed.) p. 166, 176.

Taylor, Theodore. The Cay (Doubleday, 1969) p. 41-42, 47, 108-111.

Travers, P. L. Mary Poppins (Harcourt, 1934) p. 154.

Treviño, Elizabeth Borton de. I, Juan de Pareja (Farrar, 1965) p. 101-106.

Turnbull, Colin M. The Peoples of Africa (World, 1962) p. 158.

Twain, Mark. The Adventures of Huckleberry Finn (C. L. Webster and Co. , 1885) p. 9, 136-141, 154.

Udry, Janice May. What Mary Jo Shared; illustrated by Eleanor Mill (Whitman, 1966) p. 23.

Udry, Janice May. What Mary Jo Wanted; illustrated by Eleanor Mill (Whitman, 1968) p. 23.

Ulrich, Homer. Famous Women Singers (Dodd, 1953) p. 166.

Walter, Mildred Pitts. Lillie of Watts; illustrated by Leonora E. Prince (Ward Ritchie, 1969) p. 45-46.

Weik, Mary Hays. The Jazz Man; illustrated by Ann Grifalconi (Atheneum, 1966) p. 31.

Weiner, Sandra. It's Wings that Makes Birds Fly (Pantheon, 1968) p. 55, 59.

Wesley, Charles H. (with Patricia W. Romero). Negro Americans in the Civil War (Publishers Co. , 1968) p. 186.

Williams, Edward. Not Like Niggers (St. Martins, 1969) p. 44, 45.

Williams, Garth (author-illustrator). The Rabbit's Wedding (Harper, 1958) p. 177.

Woodson, Carter G. Negro Makers of History (Associated Publishers, 1945) p. 150.

Yates, Elizabeth. Amos Fortune, Free Man; illustrated by Nora Unwin (Dutton, 1950) p. 94-101, 176-177.

Zagoren, Ruby.   Venture for Freedom; illustrated by Ann
    Grifalconi (World, 1969) p. 40-41, 47.